Food for Reversing Heart Disease

A FULL CIRCLE BOOK

Food *for* Reversing Heart Disease

Dr. Bimal Chhajer MD

Food For Reversing Heart Diseases

Copyright © Dr. Bimal Chhajer, 2006
All rights reserved.

First paperback Edition, January 2006

ISBN 81-7621-172-9

Published by arrangement with author.

Published by
FULL CIRCLE PUBLISHING
J-40, Jorbagh Lane, New Delhi-110003
Tel: 24620063, 24645057, 24641011 • Fax: 24645795
email: fullcircle@vsnl.com • website: www.atfullcircle.com

No part of this booklet may be reproduced or transmitted in any form or by any means electronic or mechanical including photocopying or recording or by any information storage and retrieval system without permission in writing from Osho International Foundation.

Typesetting: SCANSET

J-40, Jorbagh Lane, New Delhi-110003
Tel: 24620063, 24645057, 24641011 • Fax: 24645795

Printed at Nutech Photolithographer, Delhi-110095

PRINTED IN INDIA

06/06/01/01/11/SCANSET/NP/NP/NP

Contents

Preface 9

SECTION I 11
    Need for such a book 12
    Will the taste be there? 14
    Acknowledgment 16
    Who can make use of this book? 21
    What is special about this book? 23
    Vegetarian food *vs* non vegetarian food ... 25
    Food and enjoyment 27
    The heart and its Functions 29
    What is heart disease? 31
    How the blockages take place 32
    How to recognize heart disease 34
    What is a heart attack? 36
    Risk factors leading to heart disease 39
    Tests to confirm heart disease 41
    How to prevent and reverse heart disease 43
    Dr. Dean Ornish — the real proof 45
    What is SAAOL? 48
    Reversal — the most rational treatment ... 49
    In the treatment of CHD
       the importance of yoga 52
    SAAOL recommendations 53

Is diet alone sufficient for reversing heart disease? 55

SECITION II 57

SAAOL Heart Program 58
Zero Oil Concept 67
Preferred methods of cooking 69

SECTION III 71

Standard measures and explanations 72
What do I Eat Today? 73
A typical SAAOL meal for a day 74
Scientific information about
  components of food 75
Lipid Profile Report 97
Chart of Nutritive Value of different Foods 100
Height-Weight Charts 107
Oil Controversy 109
Dietary tips 111
Food for Diabetics with Heart Disease 115
Food for Overweight People 117
Changing concepts about Cardiologists 119

SECTION IV 123

Soups 124
Salads 133
Cereals 146
Dals 191
Vegetables 213
Zero Oil Raita 340
Zero Oil Chaat 368

Zero Oil Snacks 381

SECTION V 503

    Addresses of SAAOL Centers

    How to Register for SAAOL Heart Program?

Preface

I have named this book as the zero oil cookbook, and food for reversing heart disease. Let me explain these two terms to you.

The common belief is that without oil as a cooking media no good food can be created or cooked. Almost all households use oil (fat extract of many natural food items marketed by hundreds of oil companies) to prepare, cook and season spices when they prepare food for consumption. Some of the common names of these oils available in India are Saffola, Cornola, Dhara, Dalda, Sweekar, Sundrop, Gold winner, Sanola, Postman, Mastan, Palmoil, Sungold etc. Ghee is another Indian fat used popularly as a cooking medium derived from milk. The cooking methods described in this book do not use any kind of oil. That is why it is called zero oil. One must remember that use of these oils can be detrimental for our health as in the modern era we do not exercise or perform physical activities required to utilize these high calorie fatty items. We understand that some fat is necessary for our body and that can be obtained from the invisible or hidden fat inside all natural and so called non-fatty items. We also do not recommend any milk product or extracts like cheese, butter, cream or margarine as they also contain very high amounts of oil.

Most of us know and agree that it is the fat (in the form of cholesterol and triglycerides) that gets deposited inside the arteries of the heart (called coronary arteries) to cause one of the most common and dreadful diseases of mankind called Coronary Heart Disease. This disease can be called as the "disease of fat deposits" and the common man knows this disease as angina, ischaemia, heart attack, coronary thrombosis or heart stroke or MI (medical terms: coronary heart disease, coronary artery disease, ischaemic heart disease, myocardial infarction etc.). The food items described in this book will help not only in preventing further deposits of cholesterol and fat inside the heart tubes, but also removing or reversal of the deposits. The common belief that these blockage cannot be removed once formed, has been proved wrong by the scientific research carried out in the last one decade. The reversal of coronary blockages has been proved by using sophisticated techniques like quantitative angiography and PET scan (a test not yet available in India). The cardiologists and the latest textbooks of cardiology have now agreed that the blockages can be removed, as sufficient data is available to prove the same. This book is a step to guide people about the food part of total lifestyle changes required to reverse heart disease.

I will confess here that to reverse heart disease (the blocks that cause heart disease) requires a complete change in lifestyle including guided exercises, yoga, meditation, control of risk factors like overweight, high blood pressure, high blood sugar, abstinence from consumption of tobacco in any form and a complete guidance on stress management. However, food plays a major role and this modified food cooking system will be a major step towards reversal of heart disease.

Another fact that I would also like to highlight is that this book has been created for common people who do not have lot of knowledge about medical science or nutrition. To make them understand the book without difficulties and to make practical use of the methods I have tried purposefully to simplify (sometimes oversimplify) the hard-core medical information without sacrificing or distorting the scientific information as far as possible. The reader must understand that many times while calculating the calories an approximate estimation has to be carried out to avoid meticulous details, which may confuse the common people. If someone is interested in more accurate data for scientific purpose he or she should consult textbooks meant for dietitians and doctors.

> "Books and friends should be few but good,"
> "Eat to live and not live to eat."
>
> — **Proverb**

SECTION I

Need For Such A Book

If we consider the human body as a machine then the fuel is food. Like car, scooter, and train or airplane uses fuel in the form of petrol or diesel our body uses food as fuel for running the machine. Without this fuel the body cannot work. This fuel in the form of food is needed by everyone and thus eating forms a very important part of our life.

Some of us work hard to earn this fuel. Some of us just get more than adequate quantity. But the body needs fuel according to its use, in the form of physical activities or exercises. If you supply more then it gets stored.

There are three kinds of food fuel that the body can use — the carbohydrate, the protein and the fat. All the food items that we eat have different proportions of these three items. Some have more carbohydrates like rice and wheat; some have more proteins like mutton and pulses and some are loaded with fat like butter and oils. Each of them can act as a fuel for the body.

Though body can break any of these foods for fuel (energy or power) in the short run in an emergency but it is best to properly balance the three fuels for long term running of the body. When born, the body is made in such a way that it will run for about hundred years and for such a long-term running the balancing of these fuels is of utmost importance. Without this proper proportion there will be defects in the body and when they reach a significant magnitude it is called a disease.

Most of the people are unaware of this important aspect of food and eating; though it forms the most important aspect of our everyday life. Lack of knowledge in this respect sooner or later gets us into the problem of ill health.

The dieticians, who are supposed to be experts in these subjects, have been either taken in the mild way or taken as a doctor when the disease actually comes, or here also people follow their advice as a treatment course, for a short while till the disease is controlled. Dietitians on their part have been shortsighted by not supplying their patients with the basic information and concepts. They advise about what to eat and what not for a temporary period. These have led to non-education of the people, who become potential patients because without knowledge they have a more or less planned destiny.

The medical doctors, who are considered as the actual health keepers of the society, on their part have found it below their dignity to talk about food and nutrition. These physicians have generally understood their duty as only to intervene when a disease actually comes as an emergency. Once the emergency is tackled, they do not usually try to prevent the future possibility of another emergency because by that time they are trying to solve somebody else's emergency.

The brunt of these happenings have been thus borne by the patients and the apparently healthy people who are gradually going towards a full fledged disease.

The aim of writing this book is to make people aware of the actual fuel requirement of the body, increase their knowledge about the composition of various kinds of foods available, advise them what to do and what not to do (along with the reasons as well) and instruct them how to cook the same with excellent taste. Only this way they can put into practice what they have learnt in their practical life.

> *"If the doctors of today don't become dieticians, the dieticians of tomorrow will become doctors."*
>
> — **Proverb**

Will The Taste Be There?

In the last few years of conducting courses for heart patients, we at SAAOL, have found that most of the worries about taste in the zero oil food comes from the misbelief that without oil the food cannot taste good.

Years of practice of cooking food using oil or ghee has almost wiped off our ideas about cooking good food without oil. We can't even imagine it. From generations the Indian cooking has used one or the other kind of fat. The daughters have learnt the same from the mothers. The conditioning has been so deep rooted that whenever I talked about zero oil food, people have shown disbelief in their eyes. When I talk of good taste without oil, many of the ladies have questioned my experiences with food preparations.

One thing that I noticed during my practice was that whenever I told my patients to eat food without oil or ghee they would necessarily eat only boiled food. Then they would complain about the taste. They can't imagine eating boiled food for a long time.

Many of the housewives and experienced ladies have then started cooking food with a little oil, after a strong advice from me against oils for heart patients. When I argued they would say it is impossible to season the spices (called masalas, in India) without oil.

Questioned by so many experienced people, few years back I really started developing the food items without oil or ghee because I understood that I can't give my patients these two items because they will increase the fat in the blood and lead to further deposits. The beginning was difficult. I asked myself why can't I season the masalas without oil, may be using only water. The answer came handy, cook it with water and see. This gave me a break.

When I was conducting courses at the All India Institute of Medical

Sciences I could not really do lot of innovations in cooking. I used to advise people to take fruits, boiled vegetables, dal (cooked pulses), khichdi (a combination of rice and different kinds of pulses). I did not know what to do. People would complain, but would take the same food as they were afraid of getting a heart attack.

But after starting my private practice when I had a free hand, I started looking into possibilities. We experimented alongwith the cooks at the resorts where we were holding our camps and with the help of our gifted dieticians and the idea of cooking things with water for seasonings and the results were wonderful. We produced a number of items. Then there was no looking back. And now we have hundreds of recipes.

Talking about the taste, I must tell you the food items that SAAOL makes are as good as any other oil-cooked foods. Our patients know it. The hotels where I conducted the courses cooked food often much better than the usual. If you ask me why there is no difference in the taste, the answer will be that we use all the masalas which give the taste, the only difference being that we used water instead of oil to season those masalas.

So simple as that!

"One swears by wholemeal bread,
one by sour milk,
Vegetarianism is the only road to salvation of some,
Others insist not only on vegetables alone, but on eating those raw,
At one time only one thing that matters is calories;
At another time they are crazy about vitamins or about roughage.
The scientific truth may be put quite briefly;
eat moderately, having an ordinary mixed diet and don't worry."

— **Robert Hutchison** (1871-1960)
Newcastle Medical Journal Vol. 12, 1932

Acknowledgment

Tough the idea about creating zero oil foods for reversing coronary heart disease came in my mind very early but the credit of putting everything in the form of a book goes to a team of people who helped me to do the same. Over the last three years the hard work of my colleagues in the **SAAOL Heart Center** and the innumerable small helps from the vast members of **SAAOL Family.** (we describe SAAOL Family as a huge group of people who joined our program all over India & abroad and their relatives who helped them follow the SAAOL Heart Program) has culminated into this new kind of cooking method. **I am sure this will prove be one of the most popular ways of cooking, in times to come for people who really care for their health.**

Two persons who really worked very hard to compile the recipe parts of the book are our present dieticians of the program Mrs. Yamini Attri and Ms. Veenu Sindhwani. The are the first two to be congratulated. We had set a target to compile all the items that we cook for our patients in the current format and it took nearly one year to complete it. Both of them worked hard complete the job. The Hindi translations of these recipes were also done by these two wonderful ladies. I must thank them for their help and efforts. Veenu also wrote her M.Sc. (Nutrition) thesis on our program and really worked hard on scientific evaluation of the diet recommended by us un the SAAOL Heart Program.

These two ladies, who take most credit about the book after me, has been with us for more than two years and worked for hours together do discuss, write and rewrite the recipes. They had to learn computers to do the same. Sometimes they would cook the items at their homes for photography. I am highly thankful to them and acknowledge that without that this book would have been a distant possibility.

Two more dieticians also helped us during our program to create new recipes and deserve to be acknowledged are Ms. Ruchi Gupta and Ms. Subha Krishna. Ruchi worked with us in the beginning of the SAAOL Heart Program in Delhi and had to train our cooks in the Surajkund and Bhadhkal lake resorts about how to cook different wonderful items without use of ghee or oil. She needs to be acknowledged for her help and for the challenge she took up in the initial phase of the program. Subha belongs to Chennai and worked as our dietician only for a single course. She first attended the course with her father (who had already undergone a Bypass Surgery). She then worked as a dietician for us. But in the short time she created many South Indian recipes for us. I remain thankful for her help.

From time to time our participants in the SAAOL course took part in the zero oil cooking competitions during our Heart Club meetings and contributed wonderful recipes. Some of these also found place in the book. There are many ladies whose names I may not be able to recollect now (except some like Mrs. Vishnoi Mrs. Tuli, Mrs. Chandan, Mrs. Airi, Ms. Deepa, Mrs. Omlata Sharma and Mrs. Wasan). After learning the concept from us they tried many items at their homes and later shared with us the same. I am so thankful to all of them.

Another group of experts who indirectly helped me to cook the zero oil items were the chefs of different hotels and resorts where we used to conduct our programs. The cooked of the Haryana Tourism Corporation at Surajkund and Badhkal Lake resorts, where I helped maximum of our courses were very helpful to us in formulating all the menus we ordered form time to times. Then there were a number of hotels where we held our courses like Biji's Hill Retreat, Lonavala, Jade Garden at Worli Mumbai, (owned by one our participants, Mr. Gul Advani), Hotel Taj Coramandal, Hotel Park Sheraton, Hotel Quality Inn in Chennai, Hotel Atria and Quality Inn in Bangalore, Hotel Ramada Manohar ion Hyderabad, Hotel Kennilworth and Great Eastern Hotel in Culcutta, Hotel Batra in Ludhiana and Hotel Mount View in Chandigarh-all the chefs of these places cooked all the zero oil food items with great taste. I feel they also contributed to this book.

Mrs. Shobha Bijur (wife of one of our participants from Bombay and one of my best friends now, Mr. Sharad Bijur) also needs to be acknowledged for her idea about writing down all the recipes with zero oil after she prepared most of the items at her home for her husband. She also authored a cook book called "Hearty food for Heart Patients" which I Distributed to most of my patients during the last year. It was her idea and instance which prompted me to write this book with all the scientific ingredients and I would like to acknowledge her contribution Both of the Bijurs were instrumental in getting SAAOL from the close corridors of Delhi and begin the outside courses in different cities of India. To them I am indebted for all the time to come.

All our resident doctors have contributed to the development of the SAAOL Heart program over the years. Without their help and enthusiasm the program would not have been a popular one. I would thank all of them including Dr. Arijit Chakraborty, Dr. Sunil Sikand, Dr. Nehal Ahmed, Dr. Rajat Dhar, Dr. Vishal Sharma, Dr. Mukesh Yaday and Dr. Kapil Sharma. Their unquestioned support and help would be something I shall always recollect with pleasure. I remember, during the first one year of our program, when the food items created by us were not that tasty like today, our resident doctors would order separate oily food for themselves during the couses. Two of these doctors who had to do this (eat outside food) were our earlier residents especially Dr. Arijit and Dr. Sunil Sikand. They also helped me in the process because I could make out by this behavior that my food items were not that tasty and I need to improve the taste, which I did in the later stage, when this behaviour weaned. I would thank them for their contribution also.

Three residents had been exceptionally helpful to me. Dr. Nehal Ahmed is one wonderful doctors whom I fortunately employed to work with me. I was under the impression that he would leave for England for further studies within a short time of 4-5 months. But he liked us and stayed with us for more than a year, to my delight. He was a wonderful person and introduced the use of more and more computers in my office, as computers was his hobby. He helped me a lot in improving my program. Nehal is now in England and has promised to work for me when he returns from UK after his studies. Dr. Vishal sharma, who was also intorduced by Dr. Nehal, is one of the very good persons who works with me. A highly obedient doctors with an eye to work more and methodically, helped me in all aspects-typing, record maintenance of our patients, coordinating camps and much more. He jad been full ideas. I acknowledge him for all his contribution. Dr. Kapil Sharma, who is also our present resident doctor, has not only helped me in writing parts of the book but also helped correcting the defects. He has a habit of reading more and would always be ready to discuss the scientific aspects of Heart disease. His whole hearted support has also been unquestionable. I am personally thankful to him and all of them.

All the people in our Delhi office over the years, Ms. Soniya Narula (now Mrs. Wadhwa), Ms. Deepti Choudhary, uncle Meghraj Baid and others are also people whom I would like to thank as they were our support and gave us more time for writing the book. Mr. Ajit Nahata, now our administrative incharge (he is also my nephew) at Delhi office, recently took over lot of burden from my shoulder (jobs related to administration, coordination, printing and planning) and gave me more free time to write the very important aspects of the book. I am thankful to him for his efficiency and help.

Books when written have huge number of spelling mistakes and grammatical defects. To correct all these was Dr. Raghunath Airi (he is also a participant of our program) without whom the work would not have been so readable. Dr. Airi, a Sanskrit Scholar, previously worked as the principal in a college in Haryana took all the pains to correct and recorrect all the recipes of the book. The Hindi translations were also all corrected by him. I am grateful to him for sparing time for SAAOL.

Sudheermon, our Computer operator in the office typed all the pages of the book in Hindi as well as in English. In the Last leg we could add another gentleman, Bidyut to assist him. With the help of Both we could finish the book in record time.

There is always a women behind every man, successful or not, and I also accept that for whatever small I have achieved the credit goes to my wife, Madhu. For the last 9 years Madhu has always been there for me, giving me inner support in every step I have taken so far. She gave me confidence, spared me from family responsibilities, brought up our children upto my satisfaction and encouraged me whenever there was a crisis.

My Children, Gourav and Garvit, both sons had to miss me as I kept busy in the last 2-3 years. I would like to mention here that they also sacrificed for the book, Sorry sons! My parents have always been blessing (they stay with my elder brother) me and without them I would not have been where I am. Their satisfaction on whatever I did has always encouraged me to do more & more. This book is definitely a tribute to them.

Friends and seniors of mine who really contributed to my work and ideas have been Dr. Vijay Kumar, Cardiologist now in Vijaya Heart Foundation, Chennai, would hereby acknowledge them too.

From the Art of Living, point of view I owe a lo to my late Gurudev, the well known Acharya Shree Tulsiji and the present great Saint Acharya Mahaprajna. Without their guidance I could not have compiled my program. I use Preksha Meditation and kayotsarg in my program for reversing heart disease. Both have been developed by these two great saints, Sri Dharmananda, presently director of Adhyatma Sadhna Kendra at Delhi guided me in my first few years and I must thank him for all he did for me. Mr. L.K. Jha, Mr. V.K. Trehan, Mr. Arun Kumar, now give training on Yoga-Mediation in my program, I would also thank them for their contribution.

At the end I must thank all my patient-participants who allowed me to guide them-there are thousands of them. I am indebted to all of them indirectly for having followed my program & diet to show tremendous improvements. They were all there to help my from time to time, encourage me and this book has really come out because of them.

"Gratitude is born in hearts that take time to count up past mercies"

— **Chhajer E Jefferson**

Who Can Make Use Of This Book?

This book is an effort to help the common men and women, who may be experts in their respective fields, but have little or no knowledge about what they eat, their correct proportions, their calories and importance. Even if they have a reasonable theoretical knowledge they cannot apply it to their food habits because of lack of practical insights. This book is meant to help them.

It has been written specially for the heart patients, more specifically for people suffering from coronary heart disease. In this disease, as you know, fat and cholesterol accumulates and deposits inside the tubes supplying blood to the heart. The zero oil cooking that is being advocated in this book, will in a great way put a stop to the supply of these fats and cholesterol. Naturally any person who has a heart ailment must make use of this book. There are more than three crore families in India who have heart disease patients in their homes.

There is another much bigger group of people, consisting may be of about 20 crore people in India, who have more chances of developing heart disease in the near or distant future. This book will be mandatory for this group also. If we believe in the proverb: "Prevention is better than cure", it becomes more important for them, because this zero oil food will help in preventing the heart disease in future. Prominent in this group are people who have a family history of heart disease or diabetes or high blood pressure. People who are overweight, have high blood pressure or diabetes (high blood sugar problem), lack of exercise and have plenty of stresses in life also fall in this group.

The executives who have a stress-full life along with a sedentary lifestyle (lack of physical activities and exercises) can use this book. If their cooking can be modified at home according to SAAOL they will not only be able to prevent problems like heart attack but also gastritis, peptic ulcer, diabetes and overweight.

Cancer of the gastro-intestinal tract (food pipe) is also a very common problem in modern society. The healthy food habits of SAAOL, given in this book will also help in preventing gastro-intestinal cancer. Food rich in salads and vitamins are specially good for cancer prevention.

This book is also directed to educate people who do not only want to cook healthy vegetarian food but also want to know more about the scientific aspects of food. This group will also include the writers of cookbooks (there are hundreds of these in the market) and students. Those who cook in sophisticated hotels must also now make themselves conversant with the zero oil food cooking because there are now a growing number of people who would demand such food from them.

A word of caution for the use of zero oil cooking methods for children or young group who are below the age of 18 years. I agree that fats are probably the main supplier of calories for this particular group who are in the growing age, especially who are underweight also. They can be given supplements of oil or butter if you want to give them more calories.

"A disease known is half cured."

— **Proverb**

*"Look at your health; and if you have it
praise God and value it next to a good conscience;
for health is the second blessing that we mortals are
capable of; a blessings that money cannot buy."*

Izzak Walton (1593-1683)
English writer

What Is Special About This Book?

As a doctor when we talk to patients we often use very difficult, but medically common words. And when we write, our words are more medically oriented. The writing becomes difficult to understand by the common people. This is what will happen if you read a medical journal. Within a few minutes you will close the book without comprehending most of it. Many less popular writers fail to understand this particular aspect of reading. The catch is that you have to talk in the reader's language.

In this book I have tried to solve this problem as most of the expected readers would not have much exposure to medical vocabulary and many of them will be housewives. I have tried to make it as easy as possible. Try to read it like a story book or novel and you will love it.

The most important aspect of the book is the non use of any kind of fat or oils in any of the recipes. Not a drop of oil is to be used to prepare any of them. This has a lot to contribute to the reversal of heart disease. Oil is medically called the triglycerides. The cholesterol content (to see the difference of triglycerides and cholesterol please see the chapter on scientific informations) also has been kept at a bare minimum in most of the recipes. Creams, salad oils, butter, ice creams and fatty decorations have not been used.

This book is different from most of the cookbooks in the context of contents. In the recipes we have tried to give you the calorie values per standard estimation along with the contents of carbohydrates and proteins or fats. Knowledge about the calories will help people to control their weight or even to increase the weight (for underweight people).

This book also gives a very wide information on heart disease and medical aspects of heart ailments in simple language. Medical facts have been written in simple layman's language.

The most important aspect of the book is the index. Many people do not use the cookbooks as they cannot choose properly what to eat. I have tried to provide an index where you can easily decide what you should eat. If you want some choices from soups – just go through the list. The headings will help you to know what is available. I have given a different colour to these index pages. If you need to lose weight look for low calorie food index. If you want to keep a normal weight or increase weight you can choose which food recipe to consume.

While deciding the calories in the food – the serving size varies according to the culture, geographical distribution, size of utensils, individual taste and preferences, economic status and many other things. The design of each individual helping is according to the convenience of measurement of each ingredient required for a particular preparation.

Sometimes the total volume of one serving may just be sufficient for one individual or may not be enough for the whole family. The readers are therefore advised to consider the energy and micronutrient (carbohydrates, protein, fats) composition along with the total volume factors and the number of persons sharing it. If more than one person is consuming the item, it is needless to say, the total energy content will be divided in proportion to the volume consumed.

One of the very special features of the book is to allow you to enjoy your sweet dishes and desserts without being discouraged about the normal notion that "Sweet dishes and desserts are high in calories". This notion becomes true to some extent because normally in sweets and desserts lots of sugar (each gram contains 4 calories) fat in the form of butter or cream (each gram contains 9 calories) is used which makes it high in calories. And thus is bad for overweight, diabetics and hypertensives.

However, our preparations do not contain any fat and sugar and can be substituted with artificial sweetners like Sugarfree or Equal and thus making it relatively low in calories.

Vegetarian Food *vs* Non Vegetarian Food

Coming from a practising Jain family, right from my childhood, I was taught that vegetarianism is the only choice we have, because the Jains are forbidden from consuming any non-vegetarian food. Later on, I realized as a medical doctor that vegetarianism also has many scientific advantages.

When I was devising food for preventing or curing heart disease I minutely analyzed the advantages and disadvantages of both kinds of foods in great details. It is a well known and proven fact that one of the major contributors to coronary disease has been the consumption of red meat and eggs, particularly the yolks. All kinds of meat are rich sources of cholesterol (which deposits inside the arteries) and triglycerides (fats). They have very little fibre. Though chicken and fish are somewhat better in this respect, they too can lead to aggravation of heart disease. A lot of oil and ghee is also used, mostly, to cook these meat preparations, especially in India.

Another factor that aggravated my feelings against any kind of meat is probably the secretion of some chemicals called adrenaline and adrenalinelike substances inside these animals when they are slaughtered. Man basically is a vegetarian animal — consider the gut or the teeth or the health — vegetarianism is the hallmark of human beings. Most of the flesh-eaters are more prone to be short tempered and aggressive according to our Hindu beliefs. It may be that the chemicals secreted just before the death of the animal which yielded the meat, is responsible for this.

On the other hand vegetarian food has a variety of salads and cereals, and legumes which offer better health. Vitamins, minerals and antioxidants are found in plenty in vegetarian food. The fruits are rich in minerals, trace elements, carotenes and flavonoids which are always contributors to good health. The fibre present in vegetarian foods is plentiful and prevents the absorption of cholesterol and fat and extra calories, thereby preventing heart disease, overweight and even cancer.

The only non-vegetarian food item I allow is probably the whites of eggs. There is no fat in it and this can be scientifically allowed for consumption by heart patients, therefore.

Now, vegetarianism has made strides ahead of non-vegetarianism. People in the West have turned back to vegetarianism after centuries of meat-based eating. We, Indians, who have a tradition for vegetarianism, supported by our religion, are still moving, unfortunately, towards non-vegetarianism. I hope that soon better sense would prevail !

Food and Enjoyment

When we eat food whether it will lead to pleasure or unhappiness depends on our social upbringing and exposure to different food items in the past and other such influences. This behaviour I consider to be *Internal Conditioning*. This psychological factor determines whether one would like or dislike the food that is served.

When I stayed in the hostel in my student days I used to have food which always had no taste, the chapatis were hard and thick and looked quite awful, too — but I used to love it. Whenever any member of my family would visit us they would wonder how could I consume such frugal and tasteless food. It was impossible for them to imagine how I could eat my hostel food, leave alone enjoy it. It is all internal conditioning.

Someone who eats meat or fish, for him it is impossible to think of a good meal without non-vegetarian food as he is conditioned to it. But once he becomes a vegetarian he hates non-vegetarian food and wonders how he relished it in the past. It's a matter of internal conditioning, once again.

When I moved to Delhi I did not like *chowmein* — the popular Chinese food or even *pasta* or *macaroni*. But the culture of visiting Chinese restaurants changed me. I enjoy the food now. Apply this to yourself now and you'll find you have done similar things in your past and developed a taste for new and varied dishes.

After starting the SAAOL programme a non-vegetarian patient visited me, and asked: "Doctor you don't eat non-vegetarian food?" I said "no." He said, "50% of your enjoyment in life is gone." I asked, "next." He said, "Alcohol?" I said, "No." He replied, "75% of your life's enjoyment is gone." I then asked, "What else?" He enquired whether I smoked or drank tea or coffee and I replied in the negative. His ultimate opinion was that I should commit suicide because he found that my life had no pleasures left.

But I must assure you I enjoy my food better than many other people around me. It is a matter of understanding and internal conditioning, and having no guilt about eating things that could be potentially harmful.

Enjoyment of food depends on your habits and how you have conditioned yourself. Once I asked a person to write down all the things he loved or things that gave happiness to him. There were more than one hundred items in the list. I just deleted non-vegetarian food and two more food items which were fried. He was still left with so many items. It included his walks, his wife and children, his car, his work, his office, his friends, TV, movies and music!

> *"What is food to one man is bitter poison to others."*
>
> — **Lucretius**
> Roman poet philosopher — 99-55 BC

The Heart And Its Functions

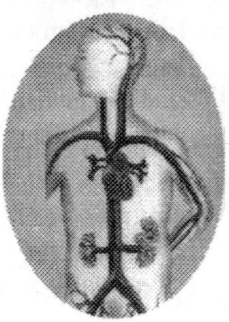

The human heart is a small muscular organ situated in the center of the chest, tilted to the left side. In size, it is roughly that of a clenched fist and weighs about 350 gms. As it is such an important and delicate organ, it is protected by the chest bone or sternum and the ribs in front.

How the Heart Works

The heart is mostly made up of a strong muscle tissue called the myocardium, and it works continuously like a tireless pump, quietly day and night, throughout a man's lifetime. It beats at the rate of about 72 times a minute, and if we calculate the number of minutes in our lifetime, it amounts to about 2,500,000,000 beats in a life-span of 70 years. It circulates about 5 litres of blood every minute, amounting to about 700 million litres of blood in a lifetime. During physical exercise and mental stress, this function can increase up to 6-fold or even more, thus making heart the most efficient pump known to mankind. In spite of all the advances made in the fields of science and medical technology, nobody has been able to artificially replicate such a pump.

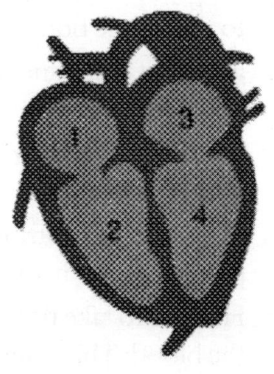

    Internally, the heart is divided into 4 chambers, and has four major valves. The upper two chambers are called the atria and the lower two, the ventricles. The right atrium receives the impure or deoxygenated blood (which has been deprived of its oxygen content by the tissues for their various functions) via the veins from the whole body, this blood goes to the right ventricle which contracts and pumps it through the pulmonary arteries (blood vessels connecting the heart to the lungs) to the lungs where it is oxygenated. The oxygenated or purified blood from the lungs goes to the left atrium via the pulmonary veins (the only veins in the human body to carry oxygenated blood) and into the left ventricle which contracts and pumps it with tremendous force throughout the entire body and supplies it to the billions of tissues which make up the human body. In this manner, the blood circulates through the human body.

Functions

The primary function of the heart is to supply blood and essential nutrients to the whole body. The body uses oxygen to stay alive. Besides supplying blood, oxygen and nutrition to all parts of the body, the circulatory system also regulates the body's internal temperature, distributes hormones and removes the harmful by-products of metabolism, in addition to a host of other functions.

The main functions of the heart are:

- supplying blood to the entire body.
- supplying oxygen and nutrients (digested food particles that we eat) to the whole body and to billions of cells in the body
- giving vitamins and minerals to the cells of the body, without which they cannot survive.
- carrying or drawing the blood back to the heart, and sending to the lungs for a refill of oxygen.
- helping in the distribution of hormones, neuro chemicals from one part of the body to another.
- Helping to take the waste materials to the kidney for purification of the blood. The kidneys extract wastes from the blood.

What Is Heart Disease?

Coronary heart disease (a blanket term which covers more than 95% of heart patients) can truly be called as the *disease of ignorance,* as it develops due to the lack of knowledge. The human body is one of the best machines in the world and if maintained properly it cannot develop a snag. Heart disease is actually a result of long period of mis-management of the heart usually by a wrong lifestyle. With the wrong food, excess fats and cholesterol, lack of control of diabetes and high blood pressure, less exercise, smoking and consumption of tobacco and excessive stress, people start developing blockages in the heart tubes. At the start of life this is always from zero. Year after year, the blockages grow until the blockages reach the range of about 70%. And that is when the heart disease is diagnosed.

The term heart disease mostly refers to the disease which is caused by accumulation of fat and cholesterol in the arteries (blood-carrying tubes in the walls of the heart). It is because this particular disease accounts for more than 95% of heart ailments. This means that out of 10 patients with heart ailments more than 9 will have obstruction in the blood flow to the muscles of the heart.

This disease of blockage of the heart arteries is medically called Coronary Heart Disease (CHD). Over the years, the same disease has been referred to by various names by different people in different regions. The most common of these names is "angina". Angina means a pain on the left side of the chest often radiating to the left arm. Since this pain is commonly found in 80 % of the people having coronary heart disease, angina also became the most common name for it.

A somewhat less known name of the same disease is Ischaemia (shortage of oxygen). All the problems of the CHD occur due to shortage of oxygen (of course due to the blockage in the tubes supplying blood to the heart muscles). Ischaemia is a more scientific term. CHD is also referred to as Ischaemic Heart Disease or IHD.

How The Blockages Take Place

When the heart supplies the blood to the aorta (the main artery for the body) it retains two branches for its own supply. The muscles of the heart which have to contract continuously obviously need a continuous supply of blood. This blood brings nutrients and oxygen, which gives it power in the form of calories.

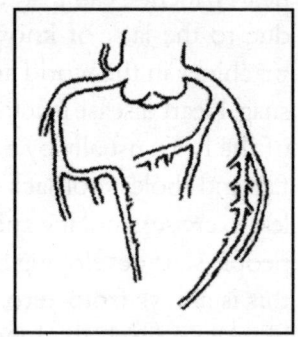

These tubes are called coronary tubes, because when they divide and re-divide, they look like a crown on the head of a king. There are two main tubes that form this crown or corona.

Out of the two, one is on the right side, called the Right Coronary Artery or RCA which has a diameter of 5 mm. It gives off a series of branches as it goes down and circles around the right side of the heart and proceeds as the PDA. The tube can be divided into three parts — the proximal third, the middle third and the distal third.

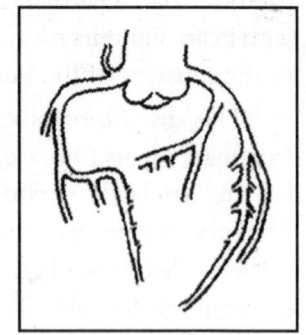

The branch to the heart on the left is called the Left Main (LM) which immediately divides into two branches.

The first branch, the Left Anterior Descending (LAD), is so named as it supplies to the front (called anterior in medical language) of the heart, and goes down (called descending in medical language). It supplies the blood through numerous branches to the heart muscles. It gives off some branches towards the right called the septal branches (named as S_1, S_2, S_3 and so on) and some on the left direction called the diagonal branches (D_1, D_2, D_3 and so on). For the purpose of easy description, this artery (LAD) can also be divided into three parts — the proximal third, the middle third and the distal third. The LAD is bigger than the RCA in size and is more important as it supplies the main part of the Chamber four or Left Ventricle.

The second branch on the left side of the heart is called the Left Circumflex (LCx) as it circles down the circumference of the heart on the left side. This is little smaller than the RCA in size.

The circumflex artery gives off branches to supply all the areas in the back of the left side of the heart. Some of the branches of this tube are called Obtuse Marginal and are referred to as OM_1, OM_2, OM_3 and so on.

How To Recognize Heart Disease

Angina is the sensation of heaviness or pain in left side of the chest which typically radiates to the left arm. It may be associated with sweating, choking sensation and breathlessness.

Angina pain usually occurs on sudden excitement, anxiety, climbing stairs, walking, bathing or during any stressful activity. Angina is specially felt on minimal exertion after heavy meals. The symptoms are relieved on taking rest or by putting a sorbitrate (nitro-glycerine) tablet to dissolve below the tongue. This pain is never an excruciating pain in nature and does not stay for a long time. If these latter two symptoms occur then it indicates a heart attack, medically known as Myocardial Infarction.

Recognition of angina depends on the patient's knowledge about the disease and on the physical activity performed. If one performs heavy physical activity from time to time (where the heart rate is raised beyond 120-130/minute) one can identify angina early. People who do not physically exert themselves feel and recognize angina quite late, because they never reach a higher heart rate. Many such physically inactive persons sometimes get fatal heart attacks which may even result in death simply because they could not identify angina in time and take the proper medication and care.

Angina does not occur at blockages of 40 to 50% which are widely prevalent in most people. If it occurs, it is more likely to be precipitated by a sudden episode of a coronary artery spasm which is the most frequently seen manifestation of stress.

The most common symptoms of angina are:

1. **Chest pain**: The pain of angina may have its severity from mild to severe, whereas the pain of a heart attack is very severe. It usually

occurs in the centre of the chest and radiates to the left arm but at times may even radiate to the right arm, shoulders or the lower jaws. The pain usually lasts for 5 to 10 minutes.

2. **Breathlessness** or **shortness of breath.**
3. **Sweating.**
4. **Nausea** (sensation of vomiting) and **vomiting**
5. **Dizziness** and **fainting.**
6. **Pain** or **heaviness** in the chest especially after heavy meals.
7. **Choking** sensation in the throat.
8. **Heaviness** or **tightness** in the chest or upper abdomen.
9. **Weakness** and easy **fatigability.**

What Is A Heart Attack?

Angina appears when the blockage becomes 70% or more. These blockages always develop under a membrane called internal membrane (Intima), which gets stretched gradually with the increase in blockage.

Finally, one day this membrane ruptures (breaks off) which is followed by clotting of blood, changing the block now to 100%. This cuts off the blood supply entirely, leading to a heart attack.

This 100% block leads to severe pain, sweating and ultimately some area of the heart muscle dies, leading to permanent damage of the heart.

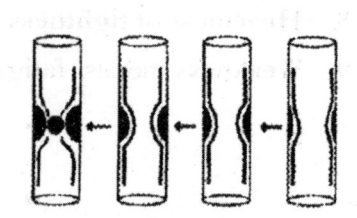

Degrees of blockage

A heart attack or *myocardial infarction* (medically called MI or *coronary thrombosis*) is the consequence of the complete obstruction of blood supply to a part of the heart muscles. This occurs due to a 100% blockage in any of the coronary arteries or their branches. The heart muscles are completely deprived of their blood and oxygen supply which leads to the death of the patient.

The severity of the heart attack would depend on how much area of the heart muscle is actually involved. It is mild, if only 5 to 10 % area is involved and most such patients survive. But if the dead area is more than 30 to 40 % of the heart muscles, the attack is considered severe, and if not managed properly and immediately, can even lead to death.

Almost all the heart attacks are sudden in onset and the cause is a rupture of the growing blockages. The blockages are usually covered by a thin membrane called the *Intimal* membrane, which also keeps the deposits intact. This elastic membrane gets more and more stretched as more and more fatty deposits occur. But if the fatty deposits continue below this permeable membrane, one day the time will come when the membrane cannot stretch further and breaks off. This leads to the formation of a clot or *thrombus* inside the tube, closing the *lumen* completely. This completes the process of a heart attack. The area of the *myocardium* (heart muscles) which gets the blood through the closed artery dies, in the event of no blood supply.

A heart attack often occurs after a heavy meal full of fat, or after sudden anger or excessive sorrow or grief or excessive stress. Heart attacks occur more frequently in the early mornings. Heart attacks also occur during the process of *Angiography* and *Angioplasty* when the catheter or balloon is inflated and completely blocks the lumen of the coronary artery or breaks off the blockage by mechanical means.

The diagram and few paragraphs above, give some clues to prevention of heart attacks. The simple message is *"Do not create more blockages. If you can reduce them, a heart attack would never occur."*

A suitable comparison would be to a bundle of currency notes being guarded by a rubber band. If you keep on putting more and more notes inside the rubber band, one day the rubber band has to snap due to excessive stretching. This is the situation of a heart attack where the membrane also breaks off. Now if you stop putting more notes, the rubber band will not break. Further, if you start taking out one or two notes from the bundle everyday, the rubber band will never break.

The same principle applies to the prevention of heart attacks. Control of all the risk factors of heart disease by adequate change in the lifestyle can prevent heart attacks. The expected parameters to prevent heart attacks are:

1. Cholesterol 130 to 160 mg/dl
2. Triglycerides 60 to 120 mg/dl
3. HDL Cholesterol 40 to 60 mg/dl
4. Blood Glucose (Fasting) 70 to 100 mg/dl
5. Blood Glucose (PP) below 140 mg/dl

6. Blood Pressure 120/80 mmHg
7. Maximum permissible exercise
8. Body weight in proportion to height

What you can do, in a nutshell, to ensure these parameters:

9. Stop smoking completely
10. Control stress
11. Oil/ghee in food is banned completely
12. Consume salads and fruits in plenty
13. Restrict consumption of milk and milk products
14. Avoid meat of any kind.

Risk Factors Leading to Heart Disease

Coronary Heart Disease (CHD) or Coronary Artery Disease (CAD) or Ischaemic Heart Disease (IHD) is one of the leading causes of morbidity and mortality throughout the world. It is on a constant rise now in India too. The main cause of this disease is deposit of cholesterol and fat in the inner smooth lining of the blood vessels (coronary arteries, which supply blood to the heart), resulting in blockages and obstruction in blood flow.

Certain conditions and lifestyle habits are now recognized and documented as being responsible for the deposit of cholesterol and fat in blood vessels as well as the increased rate at which they are being deposited. These are referred to as Risk Factors.

The risk factors are the reasons which lead to or aggravate the deposit of cholesterol or fat in the coronary arteries. All the factors which are important in the development of coronary heart disease have been classified into 2 categories:

1. Modifiable Risk Factors:
In this group come those risk factors which can be altered and prevented so that the further progress of heart disease can be arrested.

2. Non-modifiable Risk Factors:
There are three risk factors which cannot be altered such as age, sex and heredity.

The modifiable risk factors are:
1. Stress
2. High levels of blood cholesterol

3. High blood triglyceride level
4. Low blood HDL level
5. Lack of antioxidants in the diet
6. High blood pressure
7. Diabetes mellitus
8. Obesity or overweight
9. Sedentary lifestyle or lack of physical activity
10. Smoking or tobacco consumption

The non-modifiable risk factors are:
1. Age
2. Sex
3. Heredity

Tests to Confirm Heart Disease

There are various tests available for the confirmation of coronary heart disease.

1. **Physical Checkup** — Before any other tests are ordered, a complete physical examination of the patient is performed that involves measuring blood pressure and pulse rate. A fresh lipid profile as well as blood sugar tests are also ordered.
2. **ECG (Electrocardiogram)** — It is one of the safest tests available. The cardiologists use it most widely. Changes in the ECG are confirmatory of heart disease.
3. **TMT (Treadmill Test)** — It is done only when the Electrocardiogram does not provide any conclusive evidence of Coronary Artery Disease or gives equivocal findings. This is one of the highly reliable non-invasive tests for the confirmation of Coronary Artery Disease.
4. **ECHO Cardiogram** — It is usually done to find out the pumping power of the heart. It also gives good information about the walls of the heart.
5. **Angiography** — In this test a long wire is used to fill up the blocked tubes of the heart with a radio opaque dye, and thereafter, approximate percentages of the blockages are reported. This is a test which carries a definite risk in itself, in spite of being costly and imprecise. Only those who need to go in for an angioplasty or bypass surgery should go ahead with this test.
6. **CT. Angiography** — This is a recent development in the field of diagnostic cardiology which is going to revolutionise the way in which coronary artery blockages are viewed. In this procedure the

blockage can be viewed by taking help of the conventional CT scan procedure. Advanced CT scanners have now been developed which can specifically define these blockages. The most important feature of this process is that this form of angiography is *non invasive* unlike the conventional angiography which is invasive. The process does not require any admission in hospital and can be performed very quickly as an outdoor process.

How To Prevent And Reverse Heart Disease

The most rational solution to coronary heart disease lies in a permanent process which not only arrests the progress of the blockage but also reverses it. The blockage has gradually occurred over a period of time consisting of several years, as the excess cholesterol from the blood flows through the coronary arteries and gets deposited (due to the risk factors enumerated earlier) in the arterial wall. These deposits are mostly soft mass of fat with connective tissues and are in a reversible phase. It has now been proved that cholesterol and fat are easily soluble in the blood, and can be picked up from the blockages if we can create an ideal situation for this process to occur.

It is essential to create this ideal situation. SAAOL Heart Program helps and trains people to create these, the ideal situations. It is based on cutting down of all the risk factors at a time with a carefully selected set of yogasanas, meditation; a perfect practically possible stress management program; complete education and understanding of coronary heart disease; the cessation of tobacco intake, smoking and food awareness including training in cooking. It directs one to a perfect lifestyle which can reverse the blockages. All of these have to be done under the guidance of cardiologists, doctors, dieticians, and yoga instructors in order to avoid complications, which are easy to develop in the case of heart patients.

All heart patients know a little bit about some preventive measures, and they try doing these without much accuracy and consistency, making unsuccessful efforts and finally submitting to the surgical treatment. Had it not been happening, none of these patients would go to a hospital in cases of emergency.

The SAAOL Heart Program has developed this expertise over the last decade after a lot of experimentation and effort. Each and every patient joining the program in the initial phase has helped the program to improve gradually. Heart attacks and other complications have been extremely low.

The SAAOL Heart Program is not magic — it cannot perform like a magician or god who would remove the blockage in a moment. It takes at least two weeks to see the first signs of improvement. The improvement will also depend on the efforts put in by patients, his/her age, the stage of blockage, the co-operation of the family members and so on. We have on record some Angiographies of our patients, carried out after attending the SAAOL Heart Program which proves that blockages can be reversed.

Reading books is a good way of learning but cannot substitute for practical training. Otherwise, the bookshops would have been chockfull of books selling treatment programs only. Books contain hundreds of pages — some of them very important — but most of them are not relevant to patients and difficult to understand. It is much more difficult to translate and put the written word into practice. If this were not so, then every patient could have become a doctor by buying medical books and learning whatever doctors know.

Nevertheless, what helps definitely is the fact that you have someone who can give you the information you need, not so voluminous that you don't comprehend it at all and definitely not less so that you do not learn at all.

Dr. Dean Ornish — The Real Proof

It was little thought that this particular second-year medical student of the Baylor College of Medicine, Houston, would one day be one of the greatest pioneers in the most effective and logical treatments developed for the cure and reversal of heart disease, America's No. 1 killer. This American killer disease is rapidly growing to considerable proportions in our own country, too.

Dr. Dean Ornish, born and bred in Dallas, received his preliminary education from a public school. His father, being a dentist by profession, was quite content with the thought that some day his son would follow in his footsteps. Dr. Ornish joined the Rice University at Houston and discovered that he was no longer the brightest student. So depressed was he that he even contemplated suicide, but as fate would have it, an episode of glandular fever gave him the chance to reconsider, and thus rendering us a pioneer in the reversal of Coronary Heart Disease and salvation from it.

Like many others of his generation in 1972, he too sought the enlightenment of the Orient and under the wings of his Guru, the honorable Swami Sachidanand he succeeded in touching his inner self and realized that the less he needed success, the less strained he felt. This led him to suspect the connection between depression and heart disease. And in 1977 he started researching the causes of heart disease and factors that could possibly bring about its reversal.

His explorations began while he was still a second year medical student, and for a very long time no one could see the potential in his work. His seniors and critics dismissed him as young, inexperienced and foolishly idealistic. While he was still in his third year at medical school he received his first big breakthrough. He was introduced to Henry Groppe, an oil business consultant, who had a firm interest in preventive medicine.

Dr. Dean Ornish formulated a plan of lifestyle changes which had 4 major disciplines, all aiming at an integrated attack on heart disease and its reversal:

1. Stress management which would comprise yoga, meditation, imagery and breathing exercises all together for the duration of not more than an hour a day.
2. Light aerobic exercise which would usually be quite convenient and usually just half an hour's walk.
3. He would ask his patients to stop smoking.
4. A strictly vegetarian diet extremely low in fat content was adhered to.

Dr. Ornish's lifestyle plan is simple and easy to understand and follow. His approach to combating heart disease and its reversal produced remarkable results. Truly we can say that "the greatest truths are the simplest ones". And in 1989 he started publishing data showing that his *"Firehouse Gang"* as he preferred to call them, who were at one time all very seriously ill were in fact improving.

The attention of the world was soon focussed on his work and invitations to medical conferences began pouring in. Currently he is also receiving grants from many international organisations including the U.S. National Institute of Health (NIH). *Dr. Dean Ornish's program recently got fresh support from a very reputed insurance company "Medicare" of U.S.A.* They have agreed to send 1,800 patients in the next 3 years to Dean Ornish's Program at the cost of $7200 per patient. With this, the company will save a huge amount of money in the medical claims for treatment of heart disease. The acknowledgment of the tremendous potential of this humble man's work will one day lead us to the development of a far better and more advanced medical therapeutic approach to the cure and reversal of heart disease from which everyone can benefit.

Dr. Ornish published his first report as early as 1979. In 1983, in a report published in JAMA (the Journal of the American Medical Association) he showed that a lowering of all risk factors of heart disease in patients occurred who followed the lifestyle advised by him. He also showed that the pumping power of the heart also increased in his patients. In 1990, Dr. Ornish gained wide recognition to his work after he showed angiographically that a reversal of arterial blockages did occur in patients enlisted in his program. This scientific report featured in the most prestigious medical journal — the Lancet. He was then frequently quoted in *Newsweek, USA News, Reader's Digest, Span* etc. — some of the most widely recognized magazines in the world. He showed all the proof of reversal when he used the latest medical gadget "the PET Scan" to prove his reversal theory. This scientific report was again published in the year 1995 by JAMA (Journal of the American Medical Association). The whole scientific world had to at last stop and listen. The theory became widely accepted in the USA and the world. Today, Dr. Ornish offers his reversal programs in eight major hospitals in USA including Harvard Medical School, Boston and Beth Israel Hospital, New York City.

Dr. Dean Ornish's results are now widely accepted. The latest textbooks of cardiology have also begun to include a separate chapter on Reversal of Heart Disease. The latest edition (1997) of the most reputed textbook of cardiology, one of the most popular and voluminous books in the medical sciences — Braunwald's textbook writes elaborately about how Dr. Dean Ornish proved that blockages can be reversed.

What Is SAAOL?

The SAAOL — Science And Art Of Living program was established in 1995 and is the most comprehensive cardiac rehabilitation and Heart Disease Reversal Program in India. Till now 3200 patients have benefited from the SAAOL Heart Program with a success rate of 98%.

Purpose: To reduce the risk of heart disease through complete change in lifestyle that includes diet modification, stress management, exercise, yoga, meditation, health education and counselling. Our primary goal is to foster independence: enabling individuals to self-monitor their activities and to take primary responsibility for healthier lifestyle behaviors and risk factor reduction. In practical terms, the SAAOL offers the following:

1. Lifestyle modification
2. Medical evaluation/drug treatment
3. Risk factor evaluation/stratification
4. Exercise prescription based on individual functional capacity
5. Personalized exercise program
6. Education and support for risk factor modification
7. Dietary counselling
8. Smoking cessation
9. Stress management
10. Yoga
11. Meditation.

Reversal — The Most Rational Treatment

A blockage occurs due to the slow but steady deposits of fatty material – cholesterol and triglycerides — inside the arteries of the heart which our modern lifestyle has allowed to grow. The most rational solution to coronary heart disease lies in adopting a permanent process, which not only arrests the progress of the blockages but also reverses the same. In order to slowly reverse the blockages an ideal body environment is required in which cholesterol and fat can be picked up from the blockages. The SAAOL Heart Program helps people to create that ideal body environment by training them on how to cut down all the risk factors simultaneously, which includes complete education and understanding of coronary heart disease, carefully practicing a selected set of yogasanas, meditation, a perfect and practically possible stress management program, cessation of tobacco intake or smoking and food awareness that includes training in zero oil cooking. Thus, it directs one into a perfect lifestyle, which can reverse the blockages.

All these have to be done under the guidance of cardiologists, dieticians, yoga experts in order to avoid complications — which are easy to develop for heart patients. The ideal and the most scientific treatment of CHD would naturally be controlling or modifying risk factors for the development of heart disease. These are:

Physical

1. Developing a regular physical activity and exercise regimen.
2. Maintaining a normal bodyweight.

Behavioral

1. Properly managing stress, anxiety, worry and anger.

2. Saying no to smoking and tobacco-related products.
3. Avoiding faulty food habits, e.g. excess of milk and milk products, non-vegetarian food etc.
4. Avoiding intake of visible oil in food.

Medical

1. Maintaining normal blood pressure
2. Maintaining normal serum cholesterol
3. Maintaining normal serum triglycerides
4. Maintaining normal HDL cholesterol
5. Maintaining normal blood sugar

If heart disease has to be prevented, these factors should be properly controlled. The development of CHD is closely linked to three factors:

First of all, the level of increasing stress in daily life.

Secondly, the level of decreasing physical activity and

Lastly, faulty dietary patterns pursued.

All are equally important.

Stress Management

Stress being the most important cause of CHD, properly managing one's life is very important. The impact of stress can be reduced to a great extent if we can identify the cause of stress and find a remedy for it. We can at least modify our reactions towards those causes, if it is not absolutely possible to eradicate them.

Physical Activity

Patients with a varying severity of disease and belonging to different age groups have different levels of physical fitness. Thus, the amount of exercise performed by the heart patient should be according to his or her requirement. The exercise regimen is constructed in such a manner so as to open up the collaterals (small tubes which are closed and take over the functions once the normal arteries of the heart get clogged) through appropriate cardiovascular conditioning. Yoga, meditation, kayotsarg and health rejuvenating exercises (HRE) form an integral component of such a regimen.

Dietary Habits

CAD occurs because of the development of blockages (deposits of cholesterol and triglycerides) present in the three major tubes. Unless and until we stop the supply of these fats and oils from outside, we can never get rid of the disease. Hence the food that is to be consumed by the heart patients should be absolutely free from oil and fat. Also the amount of milk, which is an animal product contains cholesterol, should be restricted. Thus, an absolute vegetarian diet should be consumed, which is also full of fibre and antioxidants.

SAAOL enables each patient to identify the risk factors and accordingly modify them. This not only prevents heart attacks and heart disease but also reverses already existing heart disease.

In the Treatment of CHD The Importance Of Yoga

Introduction

Yoga and relaxation techniques/methods have been successfully used for the amelioration of high blood pressure and coronary heart disease over the past few decades. Recent researches have proved that this form of treatment not only reduces high blood pressure but also reduces the serum cholesterol levels, serum triglyceride levels, serum free fatty acid, blood glucose, body weight and coronary artery disease. No form of medicine is as effective as yoga in the treatment of coronary heart disease. Unlike medical drugs, this form of therapy has no side effects. Yogic practice also improves physical fitness and helps to improve an individual's efficiency. Here, we are using a particular lifestyle enhancement intervention based on *Preksha Yoga*.

Definition

Yoga is the philosophical doctrine developed in India at about 500 BC. Based on moral principles, meditational techniques and a special type of physical training called *Hatha Yoga* which involves control of posture and respiration. It is said to bring about the right interaction, and co-ordination of the mind and body, in proper combination.

SAAOL Recommendations

Five Different Groups Of Practices

1. Health Rejuvenating Exercises (HRE)
2. *Asanas* or Relaxing Postures
3. *Pranayama* or Breathing Exercises
4. *Kayotsarg* or Relaxation
5. Meditation: *Preksha Dhyaan*
6. Moral Teaching and *Anupreksha*

Training and Timings

Total duration of the daily practice of yoga should be about 40 to 60 minutes. However, meditation can be practiced for longer periods, if one desires. The best time to practice yoga and relaxation is early in the morning which is also very convenient for a regular practitioner or a professional who has to go to work everyday. Ideally, the stomach should be empty during the practice. Some of the optimum requirements other than these are loose and comfortably fitting clothes, quiet surroundings and an adequately ventilated room.

The training should consist of four separate sessions, each of 2 hours duration, where the patients along with their spouses are taught all these procedures. They can, however, consult the manual from time to time while they practise at home to verify any procedure.

Rules and Regulations

1. Regularity and punctuality in practice is essential.
2. The time fixed for practice should be maintained. Early morning

hours are best suited for such types of practices because the bowels are clean and the stomach is empty. For some people evening hours are also suitable. At least a 2-hour gap must be allowed between meals and practice.

3. If one needs a cup of coffee or tea or milk, it can be taken half an hour before the practice of asanas. The ideal goal of its practitioner is to stop tea and coffee completely.
4. *Place:* A clean and airy place without noise or disturbance is ideal for doing exercises and asanas.
5. *Dress:* Comfortable, loose and light clothing is good for such practices.
6. *Sleep:* About 6 to 8 hours sleep is required daily for an adult. If one goes to bed early, it will be possible to have sound sleep and to get up early in the morning. Then and only then does it become possible to maintain the proper timing for yoga practice.
7. *Rest:* While doing asanas, if one feels tired, he/she should take rest. Never cross the limits of your capacity. Your capacity will increase slowly. After completion of the asanas five minutes of Kayotsarg (muscular relaxation) is necessary. After that, meditation can be practiced.

Is Diet Alone Sufficient for Reversing Heart Disease?

A big "No" again! Though diet forms an integral part of our lifestyle prescription for reversal, changing the diet only is not enough for causing a reversal of heart disease. Suppose the best marks for reversal are 100 then following the prescribed diet will give you 30 only. The rest will include a combination of exercises, yogasanas, meditation and the practice of stress management techniques.

SAAOL Heart Program has been devised to help the heart patients to reverse heart disease. It advocates a new outlook towards life, a guided lifestyle for cutting down the stresses, living a life where exercise forms an important component, loving people around you, doing meditation, quitting smoking or tobacco, controlling anger and working adequately to dispense your responsibilities in life. All components are necessary.

To talk of reversal we have to write another book with 500 pages (I intend to do it in future). But let me make the understanding very clear at this point.

Heart disease is caused due to a number of reasons, that is, in medical science what is described as a multifactorial disease. Even if all of these reasons are present in one's lifestyle it will take a minimum of ten years to develop a blockage severe enough to cause a heart disease. In the reversal process the theory is to withdraw all these reasons as far as possible. So, by changing only the diet you will be able to change about 30 percent of the causes (this may vary from person to person, depending on how dependent they were on an oily diet initially). But for reversal we need more changes than just in food habits alone.

To be more precise, let us first count — the reasons that lead to the occurrence of heart disease. These are:

1. Stress in the form of anger, worry, anxiety and fear.
2. High cholesterol levels in blood due to incorrect food in-take.
3. High triglycerides (or fat/oil) in food and blood.
4. Low HDL cholesterol (also called good cholesterol).
5. Lack of exercise and physical activity.
6. Diabetes or high blood sugar.
7. High blood pressure or hypertension.
8. Overweight or obesity.
9. Smoking and consumption of tobacco.
10. Consumption of alcohol.
11. Lack of fibre in the diet.
12. Lack of antioxidants in the diet.

Naturally, reversal will call for control over almost all the above factors. The last years of experience have shown us hundreds of people doing this and achieving the reversal of heart disease. A complete training program can help along with a good follow-up.

"Whatever is worth doing at all is worth doing well."

— **Earl of Chesterfield** (1694-1773)
English statesman and man of letters

SECTION II

SAAOL Heart Program

What is SAAOL?

SAAOL is a medically integrated system to cure and prevent coronary heart disease. Developed by Dr. Bimal Chhajer, MD, a cardiologist who has pioneard the concept and "Reversal of Heart Disease". Saaol is a very popular program all over India for treating heart patients by non invasive methods.

Originating in Rajasthan, the word SAAOL (pronounced "Saaol") is frequently used in the Marwari language by people in Rajasthan. The literal meaning of this word is "best possible". Anything that is to be done has to be done with Saaol, the "best possible" way. If you walk, do it with Saaol ; if you eat, do it with Saaol; if you talk, do speak with Saaol and if you perform, do everything with Saaol. That's what Saaol means.

In English SAAOL stands for S-A-A-O-L, " Science And Art Of Living". The name itself is self explanatory. It combines the hard-core medical science, the science of cardiology with the philosophical wisdom, the art of living. Going with proven practice of cardiology, SAAOL also adopts the art of yoga, stress management, cooking and communication. It is the best combination of both — science and art.

Medical science — a powerful tool with basic faults.

Medical science has made tremendous progress in the last few decades. It has now become the cornerstone of treatment. Combined with reasoning, proof and research , the application of this science has spread all over the world. With the implementation of modern technology medical science has improved its efficacy and the use of computers has made it even more advanced. The regular use by an increasing number of patients, has helped medical science to gradually build a huge infrastructure. People then, in large numbers, wanted to become experts of medical science — the medical doctors. Soon medical colleges came up and with the number of medical doctors growing up with time, medical science has emerged more powerful and a completely accepted system of health care.

But there was a problem. *Medical science tried to repair the human machine but faulted in the maintenance. Instead of informing the people about what to eat, what not to eat, how to exercise or maintain a healthy body, medical doctors concentrated more on repairing the body only when things actually went wrong.* Without proper knowledge, as more and more people got ill, medical science tried to solve the problems by using medicines and surgery. This artificial creation of crisis and then a solution at the time of crisis made the medical doctors more important. They enjoyed the importance and conveniently forgot the maintenance part. This went on. *People suffered because of lack of knowledge and got the disease; the doctors and surgeons prospered.*

They used more and more medicines and opened more and more operation theatres, hospitals. Medicines helped some diseases like infections and controlled them to a good extent. But most of the diseases like coronary heart disease, diabetes, arthritis, cancer and high blood pressure which were not due to infections kept on increasing. Medical companies took over the medical science. Now medical research would mostly mean how to develop new drugs which will make more profits for the company. *The basic research and dissemination of information on maintenance of the human body took a back seat.*

This is what is the fault with medical science. They are knowingly allowing the human machine to get ill. The maintenance is gradually forgotten.

The patients gradually realized the discrepancy of the medical science. When health care budgets of governments went up, they also did a retrospective analysis and found that the preventive aspect has to be given more importance. The federal government of USA took a lead in this aspect. The non governmental organizations also projected the same faults of medical science.

Public awareness suddenly grew all over the world, almost exponentially. More and more people started looking at medical science and the proponents a little suspiciously. They started searching for an alternative system which is oriented in solving the problems permanently, without invasion or side effects of drugs.

The theory of SAAOL

SAAOL believes that the body is a unique machine which can run for hundred years if we provide it with proper environment. Though it can adapt to little changes in its maintenance, fuel and stress or strain, *on prolonged misuse the machine gets damaged. But this machine is also unique in the sense that it can also self repair its damages. This is unlike most of the manmade machines like cars and computers, which cannot repair themselves. Once damaged the manmade machines either need replacement or repair from outside. The human body is much superior to these machines.*

SAAOL utilizes this unique feature of the body. It only provides the body with the best environment to help in the repair process. The blockages of the heart arteries had developed because we were eating wrong food, excessive fats, not exercising our body and giving the mind more burden than it could handle. SAAOL *attempts to undo these factors by a combination of providing correct knowledge, and training the human body to correct these mishappenings.*

SAAOL does not consider the body as a simple combination of different organs which can be separately treated as is done by medical science. It believes that the whole human body is a single unit and each of the organs are interactive and interdependent. To treat such a body we can not take an individual organ approach. SAAOL subscribes to the theory that if you disturb one organ it will also have an impact on the others. Emotional disturbances of mind will also affect the stomach and damage the heart; the chemical (medicine for example) given to help one organ would damage the other. It wants to dissociate itself from unnecessary medications. SAAOL takes a holistic view of the body.

What SAAOL does?

SAAOL provides information and training to keep the body healthy and remove the diseases, especially the heart disease. A team of people, experts in cardiology, medicine, nutrition, yoga-meditation and process of stress control, work under the same roof with a similar frame of mind. Patients and people who want to prevent disease are admitted for a few days along with their spouses in a small group and trained in the theory and practice of "Science and Art of Living".

The training deals with a detailed theoretical explanation about the wrong lifestyle practices and their remedy; physiology of the human body and the pathology of the diseases and how in our practical life it is possible to implement this theoretical understanding. It also provides a complete practical training on health rejuvenating exercises and yogic practices destined to help the heart in its repair. The SAAOL Heart Program training gives equal importance to stress control in our practical life. The training gives a complete model for stopping the production of stress, release of Stress and lastly the management of stress. Nutrition and diet form another most important component of SAAOL's training for heart patients. Besides providing all practical ways to calculate the calories of food, balancing the different types of nutrients, SAAOL also provides practical training how to cook all kinds of tasty food without the use of any kind of fat.

Inception of SAAOL

SAAOL word was probably chosen while I was in New York discussing about starting this new system of treatment process with my cousin Sanjay Jain in December, 1994. He too is a philosopher. We wanted to give the name which was most appropriate. I was at that time working at the famous All India Institute of Medical Sciences (AIIMS). We both agreed that since it has both the ingredients of science and art, it should have a name which will represent both. Hailing originally from Rajasthan in India, both of us knew the Marwari language well. Further discussions led to the name "SAAOL".

The inception of the idea, (of using something like Saaol) , in a medical doctor like me, in whom there were no other ideas except for the modern medical science goes back to about twelve years back. I had passed my MBBS then and was working in the department of cardiology in a Delhi hospital. Death of one dear patient whom I was treating (now I realize it was maintenance and not treatment) for angina led to a sea change in my attitude as a doctor. He came to me for a treatment of angina and I prescribed some medicines. After taking the medicines he improved immediately. Both the patient and doctor (myself) felt good about the improvement because the complaint had vanished. Within a few months I had to increase his medicines few times because the pain was back. Every time I increased the number of tablets he reported a tremendous relief. Then one day he suffered a massive heart attack and expired in front of my eyes.

While analyzing the cause of death of this patient, which gave a severe blow to my conviction as a doctor, after a spell of successful treatment with medicines I looked for the reason. As a believer in the theory that " everything that happens must have a reason".

I started analyzing. "Why did he die, if I was doing the correct treatment?" I asked myself.

When the answer came I was shattered. The patient was actually increasing his blockages during the short spell of successful treatment with drugs which I gave him. He was eating meat and chicken, ghee and butter. Leading a high stress lifestyle he was also overweight. Thus the deposits of cholesterol and fat went on and I kept on prescribing more tablets to maintain the relief. Suddenly I realized that I was not treating the disease but was busy in giving relief from angina pain. He was dead because I did not tell him that if he did not change his food habits and stress, the blockages will grow and grow. I should have done that. I almost felt that I was a part of his death. It was me who killed him. I should have given him advice to change his lifestyle!

That blow was severe enough to make me question the wisdom of the powerful and established medical science and the proponents of the science of cardiology. I found myself against everybody in the field because I explained that what is being done by most of the cardiologists is not treatment but maintenance. This maintenance, I found was destined to lead to a heart attack — it's a matter of time only — as the blockages kept growing. It's a failing maintenance.

I asked too many questions, I was told, I was not practical, because

I was questioning the popular system of writing prescriptions for heart patients. How can anybody who has almost graduated recently, challenge the ongoing system of the mighty science of medicine and surgery!

I started analyzing further. I understood that the departments of medical science which take care of infections with antibiotics are probably doing treatment. They were killing the bacteria and leading to a cure. This can be called a treatment. If the disease is over after administration of medical drugs, it can be called a treatment. Most of the diseases like diarrhoea, bronchitis, pneumonia, malaria get a treatment because the disease is over after successful administration of medications.

But what about the heart disease ? The tablets had to be taken throughout life and still the disease would grow. It could not be called a treatment. Rather it was only maintenance. I realized that both maintenance and treatment should go on simultaneously. Thus the Saaol concept was born. In the next twelve years the concept grew. More and more items and ideas were added while I actually started developing a complete systematic program. Two years at the King Georges' Medical College, Lucknow (while I was doing my MD) and the next six years in AIIMS, New Delhi saw a lot of items add up. The food cooking concepts were developed. What I had in mind in September-October, 1995 took the shape of the present SAAOL Heart Program .

After resigning from the All India Institute of Medical Sciences I formed the SAAOL Heart Centre in 1995 to run the program independently.

SAAOL in the last ten years

This book is being released to commemorate the successful completion of ten most fruitful, progressive and colourful years of SAAOL Heart Program. Starting from a scratch, just in this small period, SAAOL has become a name to reckon with. Its success and uniqueness has made it almost an alternative to the age old practice of bypass surgery and angioplasty.

These years have been very adventurous and successful for SAAOL as it was a completely new concept. More so because it works diagonally opposite to whatever the common practice has been in the last few decades. Initially it was very difficult to convince people that it will work and I had to explain and convince for hours. Doing it in government hospitals was easy compared to private setups.

But as time passed by, things gradually became easier. By word of mouth the news spread since our exparticipants were so convinced and improved that they started recommending their near and dear ones. The media also supported us. Lots of people who got reblockages after angioplasty and bypass surgery joined SAAOL because they were left with no other alternative. SAAOL path lead them to a stage of improvement.

The word spread like fire and people from distant places came to join the SAAOL Heart Program. There were people from many states (Punjab, Haryana, UP, MP, Himachal Pradesh, Rajasthan, Bihar, West Bengal, Maharashtra and many more). A few of them also came from USA, U.K., Middle East, Nepal, Sri Lanka, Bangladesh and even from South Africa and Kenya.

As Delhi program started doing well we were requested by a lot of people to hold the SAAOL Heart Program training in different parts of the country. One of my patients Mr. Bijur, from Mumbai was very keen and promised to help in organizing everything for us in Mumbai. He surveyed all the nearby resorts for us in Mumbai which ultimately resulted in the first SAAOL camp outside Delhi.

Mumbai: The first course started on 28th Feb, 1997. The response was very encouraging. Mumbai, which has the maximum number of heart surgeries and angioplasties was full of people who were keen to join us. Mr. Bijur, Mr. Babbar, Mr. Damani, Mr. N. Gir — all our patients in the Delhi camp helped us a lot. Mr. Babbar lent us his posh office in New Marine lines, Mr. Damani gave us his guest house and Mr. Bijur received all the calls from prospective patients. The SAAOL family (we call all our participants a part of the family — The SAAOL Family) helped organize the Mumbai camps. We had to hold another course after 3 weeks again seeing the good response. Now we have hundreds of patients there. The courses were held in Lonavala / Khandala area in the Biji's Hotels. Presently the courses at Mumbai are held every three months at Indian Merchants Chamber near Churchgate.

Chennai: After a splendid success in Mumbai SAAOL soon spread its wings to Chennai. The first course was held there on 25th April, 1997. This course was special because this was the first non-residential course of SAAOL. The response again was encouraging. The course was inaugurated by the Honorable Mayor of Chennai, Shri. M. K. Stalin (son of the Chief Minister of Tamil Nadu Shri. Karunanidhi). The course was held in a 5-Star Hotel, Park Sheraton. Gradually more courses were organized in Chennai. Many of our participants had come there from neighbouring states and cities to join us. Our course had people from Karnataka, Tamil Nadu, Andhra Pradesh and Kerala. The subsequent visits showed that those who joined the earlier camps had also improved. Soon after we decided that the SAAOL Heart Program would have to be continued in the south. We started holding regular courses in Chennai, Hyderabad, Bangalore. We are now holding this course every three months at Bangalore.

Calcutta: When the SAAOL Heart Program went smoothly in Mumbai and Chennai, we planned a course in Calcutta also. We kept Calcutta courses also as non-residential. The first course was inaugurated on the 18th July, 1997 by the well known Member of Parliament Shri. Somnath Chatterjee at the Great Eastern Hotel in the heart of Calcutta. After the first successful camp, another was held with greater zeal. Now we hold regular courses in Calcutta at short intervals. I have a special attraction to Calcutta as this is the city where I grew up.

Chandigarh: The beautiful capital of Punjab and Haryana was our next target. Since many from this city had already attended our Delhi courses we had no problems there. One of our participants, Mr. Kulwant Singh and his family were kind enough to extend their help in organizing the camp. The first course was held in Hotel Mount View (a non-residential one) from 1st to 3rd August, 1997. The response was very encouraging. The second course was held in the year 2001 at Hotel Sunbeam in the sector 17th.

Bangalore : After a series of courses in Mumbai, Calcutta and Chennai, success brought us to Bangalore, the most expanding cosmopolitan. I went for a lecture to Bangalore in Sept. 1997, and even with the sitting capacity of four hundred, people had to stand outside the hall and listen this lecture. Then and there we decided to hold our camp and one of our patients, Mr. S.S. Prasad volunteered to help us in Bangalore. The first course at Bangalore was a running success. We went completely full. Now the course is regularly held at Hotel Rama on Lavelle Road.

Hyderabad: The city of Nawabs was the other metro to come under the shelter of SAAOL. The first camp was successfully launched on 25th of June, 1998. The camp was conducted at Hotel Ramada Manohar, one of the beautiful hotels of Hyderabad. The attendance in the camp was beyond our expectations. The credit for such a move goes to our patient Mr. Adi Narayana Rao who helped us in all possible aspects.

While we were in different metropolitan cities we observed a contrast in the risk factor profile of people who consulted us with heart diseases. Thus, we carried out a survey and we found that the risk factors were different in different parts of the country. In Delhi it was non-vegetarian food, obesity and stress. Mumbai had more heart patients whose main problem was stressful living. In Chennai the stress problem was not as bad, but the people there consumed a lot of coconut oil and oil products. We found that in Calcutta more heart patients smoked heavily and they had a sedentary lifestyle. In Bangalore the distribution was not very marked because it was mixture of all the risk factors being a cosmopolitan.

SAAOL in Overseas

Gradually the SAAOL's way of life is gaining popularity overseas also. Many of our overseas participants who have done camps in India spread the good words when they go back. Recently I was invited for lectures on heart care awareness in the Middle East countries of Oman & Dubai. I was also invited for lectures at the Bangladesh capital Dhaka. The responses at both the places have been overwhelming.

Zero Oil Concept

The most common form of lifestyle, which people have in this modern era, is sedentary lifestyle. Very few are involved in regular physical activities. Most of us have a lifestyle which has minimal of physical work, no exercise and bad dietary habits i.e. sedentary lifestyle.

Now, it is known to all that fat forms blockages in the arteries (tubes which carry blood) like coronary arteries. These fats are called cholesterol and triglycerides. They get deposited in layers over a period of years. When these blockages become significant the tubes (arteries) get choked leading to a disease called coronary artery disease (angina, heart attack).

In the past 50 years cholesterol (an animal fat) was considered as the only constituent of the blockages. It was only in the last one decade or so that triglycerides (a plant fat) has been found to be equally responsible for creating blockages. Triglycerides is the chemical name, known to the common man as "Cooking Oil". The oil manufacturing companies exploited the naivety of the people, misled them to believe that oils are harmless by promoting their sales with captions like "Cholesterol Free" or "Zero cholesterol Oil". Well, it is true that oil does not have cholesterol because it is made from plant seeds whereas cholesterol comes from animal products (meat, milk & their products). The layman started buying these oils. What they failed to realize was that these oils are also hundred percent fats because they are triglycerides and triglycerides are equally harmful. Oils also have high calories content (each gram gives nine calories) that can lead to obesity, diabetes and high blood pressure. It is best to minimize the fat content in our food (optimum requirement of fat by the body is 10% of the total calories).

This can be easily obtained from all the food items, as every food contains oil known as invisible fat or hidden fat. This means that all the visible sources of fat (i.e. cooking oil) should be completely cut down. Now, this would raise a query: How to prepare delicious food without oil?

What if the food is prepared without oil? Will the taste be there? If you think rationally the answer would be yes. The taste comes from the spices (masalas). Oil itself does not add taste. It is our mindset, which was trained to believe all these years, which says that taste comes from oil. But when we ask to remove the oil, the masalas get removed automatically. This happens because the housewife does not know how to put the spices, when no oil appears in the frying pan. This prompted SAAOL to develop the concept of "Zero Oil". By "Zero Oil" we mean cooking without using a single drop of oil. SAAOL cooks the spices and food in water and since the spices are there the color, taste and flavor remain intact.

SAAOL also realizes that the mindset of people finds it difficult to accept water as the cooking media. So we have named water, when used as cooking media — "SAAOL oil". By introducing the zero oil concept in your cooking there will be no risk of taking in cholesterol and triglycerides. This can also be helpful in reducing weight, since the high calorie gain from fat is removed.

We can now aptly say that SAAOL oil contains no fat, no cholesterol, is 100% mineral and good for health.

Preferred Methods Of Cooking

In India there is a tradition of cooking foods with lot of oil which is to be avoided by heart patients. So, our methods of cooking are:-

Roasting: Roasting and baking are essentially the same. They are carried out in an oven between temperatures of 120^0C and 260^0C. Generally, the term roasting is applied to papad while baking is used for breads, cakes and biscuits. The food is cooked partially by dry heat and partially by moist heat, if the food is high in moisture content. In baking, the oven atmosphere should be moist initially so that the moisture condenses on the cold dough. This helps in heat transfer and plays a part in the formation of crust. Roasting and baking involve heat transfer from the heat source in the oven by radiation, conduction and convection. Heat is transferred directly onto the container of the food through which it is conducted to the food. Convection currents of air help keep the temperature of the oven fairly uniform. This process has an advantage that it does not involve oil and the most important thing is that the food is cooked properly with plenty of taste.

Boiling: Boiling involves cooking in water. In this the medium transferring heat is water. Water receives heat by conduction through the sides of the utensils in which the food is cooked and passes on the heat by convection currents, which equalize the temperature and become very vigorous when boiling commences. Water is a poor conductor of heat and its heat capacity is high i.e. it requires more heat than any other liquid of the same weight to raise the temperature. The boiling point of water is 100^0 C and it is altered at high altitudes and in presence of electrolytes.

Steaming: Steam is the medium of cooking in steam, "waterless" cooking and pressure-cooking. Cooking by these methods involves moist heat. In steaming, food is cooked by steam from added water, whilst in waterless cooking the steam originates from the food itself. Pressure cooking is a device to reduce the cooking time by increasing the pressure so that the boiling point of water is automatically raised. While water boils at 100°C at normal atmospheric pressure, it boils at 121°C at a pressure of 1.07 kg/cm² which is the pressure at which food is cooked in a kitchen pressure cooker. In cooking by steam, the food is heated as a result of steam condensing on the food, and the release of the large quantity of heat contained in the steam. This continues until the heated food reaches the same temperature as steam.

Zero Oil Way Of Frying

1. Heat a karhai (preferably a non-stick pan).
2. Dry roast the cumin seeds (jeera) until they crackle and turn brown.
3. Add ground onion in the karhai (non-stick pan) and keep roasting it. When it starts sticking upon the hot surface, add small amount of water and keep stirring.
4. Add ginger and garlic paste (according to your taste/wish).
5. Roast the onion, ginger and garlic till it turns to brown. (Note: Do not add more water at a time as it gives the food a boiled taste.)
6. Then add tomato paste in the karhai and roast it with little amount of water.
7. Roast till the water bubbles start forming.
8. Add turmeric powder and cook for sometime (as turmeric takes time in cooking).
9. Finally add all the masalas/spices like salt, red chilli powder, coriander powder according to taste.
10. Now, zero oil masala is ready.
11. If you want to make vegetables — add vegetables, if you wish to cook dal — add boiled dal or soaked dal. Cook as required.
12. Add garam masala (A combination of cloves, mace, nutmeg, black cardamoms, red chillis).
13. Garnish it with finely chopped coriander leaves.

SECTION III

Standard Measures and Explanations

Correct weighing or measuring of foodstuff is essential to get good results in cookery. However sometimes foodstuffs have to be taken in very small quantities, which may not be practical to weigh. Also, this requires the use of a kitchen weighing scale which may not be available in each home. Therefore, standard measurement of foodstuffs becomes more handy and can be used everytime.

Standard Measures

1 full plate	250 gm
1 quarter plate	150 gm
1 bowl	200 ml
1 cup	200 ml
1 glass	250 ml
1 teaspoon (tsp)	5 gm
1 tablespoon (tbsp)	15 gm
1 small katori	100 gm
1 medium katori	150 gm

Note: gm stands for gram and ml stands for millilitre

What Do I Eat Today?

Whenever you want to eat something delicious or try out a new recipe you might be confused about it. However it becomes easier if you have a readymade chart available with you. You can immediately glance through the various lists and decide what you wish to eat. We have presented here a user friendly index with different categories for e.g.. if you wish to have a soup look through the main index and go to soup index which will gave a list of different soups. Choose the soup you want from the list and go to that page for the recipe.

Further I have seen that many hospitals give a diet chart but it becomes very monotonous at times when you have a limited number of food items listed in the chart. So, if it's breakfast time and you want to have something different from the normal routine menu — go to the breakfast index, see through the various choices available and select from them. There are so many items listed that you can have different variety on each day of the week.

I will advise you to take planned meal according to the calories so that you will not have problem in taking normal calories.

A housewife can plan the meals according to her family's requirements for her husband, children or any member of the family.

So, go ahead and choose what you want!

"Any colour, so long as it's black."

— **Henry Ford** (1963-1947)
US car manufacturer

"Any tasty food, so long as it's oil free."

— **SAAOL**

A Typical SAAOL Meal for a Day

Breakfast
8:30 am

Bread/Dalia/Roti/Cornflakes
Salad/Cooked Vegetable/Chutney/Fruits
Sprouts/Dal/Egg White
Tea

Mid-morning
11:00 am

Fruits/Snacks

Lunch
1:30 pm

Salad
Chapati
Rice
Subzi
Dal
Curd

Evening Tea
4:30 pm

Tea
Snacks

Dinner
8:00 pm

Soup
Salad
Chapati
Rice
Subzi
Dal/Curd

Scientific Information About Components Of Food

All the food items that we consume can be divided into seven scientifically named groups. These nutrients are called carbohydrates, proteins, fats, vitamins, minerals, fibres and water. No other items are available in any food, other than these seven. The body requires these for growth, maintenance and development. Without any of these the body will not be able to survive but in excess these can also cause damage. Therefore we must know how much of each of these foods is to be consumed for good health. We should also be aware of the functions of each of these different types of food. This is what this chapter deals with.

Of course I do not want you to become doctors and dietitians, but I would like to provide adequate information so that you can consciously decide about what you want to eat and what would be the best combination that you can choose.

Carbohydrates are the foods, which give you energy that you require for your daily activities. They sustain you throughout the day.

Proteins are the building blocks of the body. It is proteins that form the bulk of the muscles of the body. They are the main constituents of the wall of each cell of the body. They are also the major components of the nerves.

Fats — the so-called oils and cholesterol — are also components of the cell wall, the nerve cells and the brain. Fats also form the energy store of the body. Whenever there is excess energy supplied to the body (in the form of foods eaten throughout the day) they will get converted into fats and get stored inside the body. This is what leads to overweight problem and heart disease.

Vitamins are the protective food items. They protect the skin, eyes, bones, nerves and the heart. Without adequate vitamins we will contact many diseases like blindness, bleeding gums, weak bones and a degenerated brain. Vitamins are required in very small quantities.

Minerals (like calcium, potassium, and sodium) form the bones, give strength to the structure of the body, form major part in haemoglobin and form the digestive enzymes, and help in breaking the foodstuff (metabolism). Without them life would not have been possible. We get minerals in all common food items and juices that we consume..

Fibres are food items that cannot be utilised by the body but are essential in the metabolism of life. They serve by removing constipation, stopping the absorption of cholesterol and preventing cancer. Fibres are very important for reduction of weight and control of diabetes. Fruits, vegetables and sprouts are very rich in fibres.

Water does not provide any energy (or calories) but is probably the most important part of our food. There is no function of the body — starting from chewing, digestion, absorption that can be carried out without water. Water forms more than 50 % of blood, helps in excretion of toxins from the body through the kidneys, regulates temperature of the body and most importantly helps in carrying oxygen to all parts of the body.

In this chapter we are going to discuss a lot more scientific information about food and for those who want more scientific data the next pages will be very important.

Information given in plenty can also confuse many common readers. I have not tried to give much information on chemical structure, reactions that lead to production of energy, how they are aborbed and so on. I have made efforts to simplify scientific informations and sorted out the unwanted information.

At a glance

Foods that provide vitality	Foods that provide energy	Helpful foods
Carbohydrates Proteins Water	Vitamins Minerals	Fibres Fats

"Reason, observation and experience — the holy Trinity of Science."

— **Robert G. Ingersoll ZZ**(1933-99)
US Lawyer

A. What Is Calorie? How Much Calories Do We Need Or Spend?

What is Calorie?

As we measure money in rupees, weight in kilograms, energy is measured in calories. If I talk for a minute I will need about two calories. If I run I shall be requiring about 10 calories per minute. For any work we need calories. Even when we sleep the heart keeps on beating for which it requires half a calorie every minute.

How much is your calorie expenditure?

In a normal day activities for most of the common people (those not engaged in physical labour like porters or labourers) require about 1600 calories in a day. A labourer may require may be 3000 calories. If you don't do any work and only sleep throughout the day and night you will probably require about 800 calories per day. I am giving you a chart which gives how many calories we usually require for the usual activities.

Activity	Approximate calories per minute
Sleep	0.5 calories
Reading	1.4 calories
Eating	1.8 calories
Converse	1.8 calories
Writing	1.9 calories
Standing	2.0 calories
Driving a car	2.1 calories
Slow walking	3 to 4 calories
Casual walking	4 to 5 calories
Fast walking	6 to 8 calories
Jogging	7 to 9 calories
Running	10 to 12 calories

If you apply your mind a little more you will be able to estimate how many calories you spend while sewing, gossiping or playing badminton.

Someone who is spending 1600 calories in a day should take food in such a quantity, which will provide 1600 calories in a day and he will have no excess or deficiency. It is like a bank account.

B. What Are Calorie Foods — Carbohydrates, Proteins And Fats

CARBOHYDRATES (CHO)

Carbohydrate supply energy and allow proteins to be used for tissue building and repair. In the reversal diet almost 70% of energy required by the body is provided by carbohydrates. The energy value of 1 g of carbohydrate is 4 Kcal.

Composition

Carbohydrate contains carbon, hydrogen and oxygen. Some

carbohydrates are relatively small molecules. Others are larger and more complex and consist of molecules linked in chains. The members of simplest class having single unit is monosaccharide. Glucose is an example of this class. The disaccharide contains two sugars cane/beet sugar (sucrose), milk (lactose) are members of this class. Carbohydrates made of long chains of sugars are polysaccharide e.g. starch, glycogen, cellulose, plant gums and mucilages.

Functions

The main function of carbohydrate is to provide energy. It is a quick source of energy. It also aids in the utilization of body fats and exerts a sparing effect on proteins.

Food Sources

Carbohydrate are synthesized by plants. Sugar, cereal grains, legumes and dried fruits are rich sources of carbohydrates found in foods. White sugar is the richest. Cereals, grains, legumes and dried fruits vary in their carbohydrate content. Some processed foods like noodles, dried nonfat milk solids, jams, jellies, breads and candies contain appreciable quantities.

Fresh fruits and vegetables are considered low in carbohydrates but bananas, dates, white potatoes and sweet potatoes are rich sources.

Deficiency

If less than the requirement is consumed the body first burns its own fat and then its tissue proteins for energy. To prevent this, daily requirement should be regularly met.

PROTEINS

Protein is the most abundant component of the body next to water. 1 g of the nutrient provides 4 kcal of energy. The major portion of proteins is located in muscle tissues, the remainder is widely distributed in blood, other soft tissues, bones and teeth. Proteins are present in all living tissues in both plants and animals.

Proteins are built from simpler compounds called 'amino acids', often called "building stones" of proteins. Out of 23 or more amino acids present in plant and animals, some can be synthesized in sufficient quantities in the body. 8 Amino acids are essential for maintenance and can't be synthesized in the body. These have to be supplied by the food and are called "essential amino acids".

The protein quality depends on the kinds and amounts of essential amino acids present in that food, e.g., cereals are low in lysine and pulses contain a small amount of methionine. But cereals and pulses are normally consumed together with other foods as vegetable, curd, etc. so lack of one is supplemented by the other food.

Functions of Proteins

1. Building new tissues in growth stages of life, from conception upto adulthood and after injury.
2. Maintenance of tissues already present and replacement of regular losses.
3. As regulatory substances for maintenance water and acid - base balance.
4. As precursors for enzymes, antibodies, some hormones and B-vitamins.
5. For milk formation.
6. For energy.

Food Sources

Plants are the primary source of proteins because they can synthesize protein by combining nitrogen & water from soil, CO_2 from air.

Although protein is widely distributed in nature, few foods provide highly concentrated amounts. Non-veg and milk products. (not recommended for reversal diet) are primary sources. Cereals, grains, dals and legumes rank second and fruits and vegetables are low protein foods. Those containing no proteins are sugars and syrups and pure fats and oils.

Deficiency

Insufficiency of protein in diet results in stunted growth. If limitation is severe and prolonged, the protein content of blood may be reduced below normal.

FATS

Fats are concentrated source of energy in our diet. The reversal diet allows 10% of the total energy from fats. 1 gm of fat provides 9 kcal. The chemical term of fat is "triglyceride".

Composition

Fats are composed of carbon, hydrogen and oxygen. If the substance is a liquid at room temperature it is oil and if solid at room temperature it is called fat. There are four parts of every fat molecule. The core of molecule is glycerol. The fatty acid is attached to each of the 3 carbon units of glycerol molecule.

The types of fat depends on saturation/unsaturation of fatty acid.

Certain fatty acids contain as many hydrogen atoms as the carbon chain can hold, these are called "saturated". There are others that have only one "double bond and is referred as monounsaturated. A third group may have 2,3,4 or more double bonds and is called "polyunsaturated".

Sources

The richest sources of fats in the diet are vegetable oils like corn oil, peanut oil, olive oil, til oil, mustard oil, sunflower oil, coconut oil and animal fats like butter and ghee. Nuts are highest contributors of fat. Meat, poultry & fish vary in their fat contents. All cheese except cottage cheese (depends on the milk) contain appreciable amounts of fats. The fat in egg is only concentrated in the yolk. Products like potato chips, cakes, pastries, cookies and candy bars also contain appreciable amounts. Most fruits and vegetables contain least fat but avocado and coconut contain 20% fat.

Functions

1. Richest and concentrated source of energy.
2. They carry fat soluble vitamins (A,D,E, K) in the body and help in absorption of these vitamins which is necessary for growth and maintenance of a healthy skin.
3. Since it is a bad conductor of heat, a layer beneath the skin helps to conserve body heat.
4. Acts as a cushion for the vital organs.
5. Increases palatability and satiety value of foods.

Deficiency or Excess

When diet is deficient in fats or carbohydrates, the body tends to burn its own fat for energy. Continued deprivation of energy due to insufficiency of fat and carbohydrates in diet may lead to proteins being used up for energy. Therefore adequate amounts should be regularly supplied.

But in case there is an excess of fats it may result in.
1. Retardation in digestion and creation of bodily discomfort.
2. Excess fat storage and extra burden on the heart and other organs.

C. What are Nutrient Food — Vitamins and Minerals

VITAMINS

The discovery of Vitamin has brought in a new era in nutrition. The percentage of body weight attributed to vitamin is minute. But the amount, even though small, is indispensable for normal functioning.

Earlier it was thought that diet containing proteins, carbohydrate, fats, minerals and water was enough to maintain life. But later researches showed that some vital factor was missing. This was later named as "vitamins". Vitamins are organic compounds required for normal growth and maintenance of all animal life. They are important for their regulatory and protective functions. They are carried with the bloodstream to all parts of the body.

Unlike other nutrients, they are required in very small amounts. But they are necessary for the body as they cannot be synthesized by the body. The lack of vitamins results in definite deficiency disorders, which are specific for each particular vitamin.

Vitamin-A

Sources: It is found in animal foods mainly as 'retinol'. Plants provide a source of Vitamin A in the form of orange - yellow pigments called 'carotenoids'. Vitamin-A present in animal foods like butter, ghee, milk, curd and egg yolks have to be avoided or allowed in restricted amounts for reversing heart disease.

Plant sources are spinach, coriander and other green leafy vegetables and fruits like mango, papaya, yellow pumpkin.

Vitamin-D

Also called ' sunshine vitamin', Vitamin-D is essential for the proper absorption of calcium and phosphorus from the digestive tract and their deposition in the bones.

Sources: Main source of Vitamin-D is sunlight. It is also found in small quantities in egg yolk, milk and milk products. The richest source known are fish liver oils.

Vitamin E & K

Vitamin E has antioxidant properties and prevents the oxidation of Vitamin-A and carotene in digestive tract and to regulate the rate of oxidation of food inside the body.

Vitamin-K is essential for the formation of prothrombin by liver. Prothrombin helps in clotting of blood when in contact with air.

Sources: Vitamin-E is widely distributed in foods. Even the cheapest kind of cereal diet contains Vitamin-E. Richest sources are vegetable oil, green leafy vegetables. Little amount is also present in milk. The principal dietary sources of Vitamin-K are green leafy vegetables, cauliflower, cabbage and soyabeans.

Vitamin-C

Vitamins-C is a part of cementing material which holds the body cells in place. It helps the body to build resistance to infection. It also helps in absorption of calcium and iron.

Sources: Fruits and vegetables are the main source of vitamin-C. Citrus fruits like oranges, grapefruit, lemons and lime, berries, melons, pineapple, guava, green leafy vegetables, cabbage and tomato are all good sources of Vitamin-C.

Vitamin-B Complex

B-Complex vitamin are a group of related nutrients, that are important for the well-being of every cell in the body. Since these are a part of human enzyme system, they are essential for the normal metabolism of food.

Thiamine (Vitamin B1)

Beriberi, a nervous system deficiency is caused by lack of thiamine in diet. Thiamine is necessary for catalyzing the oxidation of carbohydrates in the body. It also helps in normal functioning of nervous system and heart. It is essential for proper growth.

Sources: Nearly all foods, except sugar, fats and oils contain thiamine. Plant sources include pulses, nuts, oilseeds and whole grain cereals. Parboiled rice and fresh peas are good sources of thiamine. Leafy vegetables, milk, eggs, fish are fair sources.

Under most ordinary cooking, thiamine losses occur. If cooking water is not discarded, a minimal quantity is lost.

Riboflavin (Vitamin B2)

It is a water soluble yellow pigment. It serves as a coenzyme in several of the enzyme system of body involved in metabolism of energy nutrients.

Sources: Milk is the rich source of riboflavin so are products such as curd, buttermilk. Green leafy vegetables and pulses are also good sources of the vitamin. Brewer's yeast is considered as the best source.

Niacin

Niacin is a component of two important coenzymes involved in respiration and breakdown of glucose to produce energy.

Sources: Cereals are major source of niacin in Indian diet and they are supplemented by pulses and meat. Unrefined and parboiled cereals retain more niacin than refined ones. Milk, eggs, vegetables and fruits contain very small amounts. Brewer's yeast is very concentrated source of niacin.

MINERALS

The minerals are referred to as inorganic or ash constituents. About 4-6% of body weight is made of mineral elements. The largest concentration of minerals is found in bones and teeth. Minerals are also found in soft tissues and in blood and other body fluids.

Some of the functions of minerals are:

1. Maintenance of acid-base balance
2. Control of water balance
3. Contraction of muscles
4. Normal response of nerves to physiological stimulation.
5. Clotting of blood.

Minerals don't act singly but work with the help of other minerals and organic compounds.

Calcium and Phosphorus

Both are found together in bones, teeth, soft tissues and body fluids. They are also involved in normal muscle contraction, nervous stimuli, clotting of blood and maintenance of permeability of cell membranes.

Sources: The best source is milk and milk products like curd, cottage cheese (paneer). The millets, ragi and sesame seeds have a high concentration of calcium. Green leafy vegetables are also good sources.

Iron

Iron is particularly important because it is essential for the process of oxidation in the body.

It combines with proteins for the development of haemoglobin of blood. Its main function is to carry oxygen from the lungs to the cells and to carry carbon dioxide from the cells to the lungs for exhalation.

Sources: Liver and yolk of egg are good sources of iron. Dried fruits as apricots and prunes, green leafy vegetable like spinach are good sources of iron. Fresh and canned fruits and other vegetables supply minerals but in a low quantity. Enriched and whole grain cereals furnish iron in significant amounts.

Iodine

Iodine is an important dietary nutrient which helps in normal functioning of thyroid glands. A very small amount is required to keep the body healthy.

Marine or sea fishes have high contents of iodine. The leaves and flowers of plants (spinach, turnip greens and broccoli) also have high concentration of iodine than roots. Iodized salt is an effective means of providing supplements.

Sodium

Sodium is largely found in blood plasma and in the fluids outside the cells.

Sources: Sodium is widely distributed in foods as meat, fish, poultry, eggs and milk. But major sources are common salt, bread and all food items with added salt. Water also provides about 7.5 mg of sodium.

Potassium

Potassium is mainly concentrated within the cells rather than in the extracellular or interstitial fluids. It contributes to the capacity of the body to conserve the mineral.

Sources: Potassium is found almost in all foods, both plant and animals and in drinking water. The foods like dried yeast, cocoa, dried legumes (peas, soyabeans and white beans), molasses, potato, spices, banana also contain potassium more than a gram per 100 gram.

D. Water

Water is an essential nutrient, yet it is overlooked when talking of nutrient needs of body. Approximately 55-70% of total body weight is made up of water. Actually it is possible to survive a longer time without food than without water. The requirement depends on factors like environmental temperature, humidity, occupation and diet. In general around 1.5-2 litres of water per day is enough (apart from water obtained through food which an individual may eat).

Function

Water is used in the body in a variety of ways.

i) as a building material in the construction of every cell.

ii) as a solvent for normal functioning of the body cells i.e. the nutrients are carried to the cells and waste products of metabolism are removed.

iii) as a lubricant in the joints and between internal organs.

iv) as a body temperature regulator it aids in the removal of heat from the body.

Sources

Water for the body comes from the fluids of the diet, the solid foods of the diet and the water produced by the metabolism of energy nutrients within the tissues. Water contents of food varies widely, with most foods in the average diet containing more than 70% moisture. e.g. green beans, contains 92% water while milk contains 87%.

Effect of Deficiency

Body normally maintains a water balance i.e. the amount of water ingested is equal to water excreted or lost.

Water is lost from the body through kidneys (urine), skin (perspiration) lungs (expired air), intestinal canal (faeces) and eyes (tears). The loss of water is influenced by individuals's physical activity, environmental temperature, due to diarrhoea, vomitting protracted fevers, etc. The severity may result in dehydration when the output of water exceeds the intake. Dehydration can be severe and call for medical attention too. So this can be easily overcome by use of water, salt or special attention to water plus minerals.

E. FIBRES

Fibre is an important component of a healthy diet. This basically comes from plant based foods. Cellulose, hemicellulose and pectins which are components of the skin of fruits, covering of seeds and structural part of plants are referred to as fibres. There are two types of dietary fibres — soluble and insoluble. Fibrous foods are filling, with fewer calories than many other choices. They also add roughage to the diet which in turn aids in digestion and elimination. These are parts of plants that can't be broken down in the intestine by human enzymes, so they can't be absorbed.

Soluble fibre can lower total blood cholesterol and LDL cholesterol. The mechanism is yet unconfirmed but it is believed that people who eat more soluble fibre may eat fewer foods high in saturated fats. Soluble fibres also slow down the movement of food through the small intestines.

Insoluble fibre themselves don't lower total blood cholesterol but they do fill up and contribute to proper bowel function. They also speed up the movement of food through the intestines and promote regularity. Cellulose, hemicellulose and lignins are insoluble fibres.

Dietary fibre is also considered important for preventing constipation. The benefits of fibre in lowering blood cholesterol explains why heart disease is less frequently caused in people on high fibre diets. Dietary fibre also helps in regulating blood sugar and also have a favourable effect on blood pressure. Studies are also done where fibres show protection against cancer especially colon and rectum cancers.

Switching over to a high fibre diet from a low one should be done gradually so as to avoid diarrhoea, gas and other types of stomach and intestinal disorders.

The exact amount of fibre required by the human body cannot be exactly stated. This amount varies from 100 mg/ to 5-6 gm per day. But an average mixed diet consisting of raw vegetable, fresh fruits with skin, cooked vegetables and fruits will usually provide sufficient fibre. This quantity can be increased by use of whole grains like whole wheat bread and whole pulses. The more the fibre content of food the better it is for heart patients. High fibres also help in reducing weight.

SOURCES OF DIETARY FIBRE

Soluble	Insoluble
Oat bran, rolled oats, broccoli, brussel sprouts, grapefruit, apples	Whole wheat breads, cereals, cabbage, carrots, turnips, cauliflowers, asparagus, peas, kidney beans, wheat bran

F. Antioxidants

Ever since the medical science has propagated the immense benefits of vitamins, the scientists have been striving hard to prove the authencity of these magic substances. The concept of antioxidants is relatively new.

In fact, oxidation stands for the process of utilisation of oxygen by cells of the body through the bloodstream. When oxygen is being used by the body, it burns toxic substances such as ozone, and carbon monoxide. However in this process, free radicals are produced, which if in excess, cause problems. These free radicals damage the membranes of the cell, disturb chromosomes and genetic material and destroy valuable enzymes, causing a chain reaction of damage throughout the body and are also implicated in the process of ageing. There are two ways in which we can substantially reduce the damage caused by free-radicals. Firstly, to avoid substances and activities that encourage the production of free radicals e.g. cigarette smoking, pollution and ultraviolet radiation from the sun. Second step is to consume plenty of antioxidants in our daily diet.

Antioxidants are a powerful group of nutrients that protect the body from many diseases and also delay the ageing process. They comprise

B-carotene (Vitamin-A), Vitamin-C and Vitamin- E. These antioxidants help in combating the effects of free radical damage.

Antioxidant unravels a whole new avenue of treating a wide variety of pathological conditions such as:

i) Cardiovascular disease — CHD, high blood pressure
ii) Cerebrovascular disease — Stroke
iii) Metabolic disease — Diabetes Mellitus
iv) Neurological disease — Alzheimer's disease, epilepsy
v) Degenerative disease — Cataract, arthritis, ageing
vi) Cancer

These vitamins are present in many types of food and occur naturally in fruits and vegetables which we can consume in plenty, especially when they are in season, whereas taking drugs in comparison is full of side effects and they are no match for natural nutrients.

We stand an increasing risk from free radicals in our food. The main source is fats (such as cooking oil when they are heated to high temperatures). As fats are heated, their chemical structure breaks down to form peroxides. These, then, further break down to form the free radicals. Polyunsaturated fats such as sunflower and safflower oils are least stable at high temperatures. These become oxidized more quickly than mono unsaturated fats such as olive oil, groundnut oil etc. Let us analyse the components of antioxidants individually.

Vitamin-A

There are two types of Vitamin-A. One found in animal products such as meat and milk which is called retinol and the other present in fruits and vegetables called β-carotene and it is the B-carotene which acts as antioxidant.

Vitamin-A is needed for growth and for keeping the body tissues healthy. Its deficiency causes abnormality in the skin and eyes and also causes retardation of healthy bone formation and good teeth condition. The deficiency may lead to complete blindness if not treated on time.

One of the most common causes of blindness in India is Vitamin A deficiency. β-carotene is present in various coloured fruits and vegetables like spinach, coriander, amaranth, drumstick, cabbage, carrot, mangoes, peaches, tomatoes etc. This carotene is converted to Vitamin-A in the body. β-carotene is not destroyed by cooking or by ultraviolet light, however only 30% – 50% of β-carotene is absorbed.

Daily requirement for an adult is 600 mg of retinol or 2400 mg of β-carotene. Requirement for growing children, pregnant women and sick patients is higher. 1 mg Bcarotene = 0.25 mg retinol.

However, prolonged intake of vitamin A in excess may cause toxic symptoms like headache, nausea, vomiting, drowsiness, anorexia, dry itchy skin, alopecia, cracking of lips etc.

Vitamin-C (Ascorbic Acid)

Besides acting as an antioxidant Vitamin-C possesses many extraordinary properties. It helps in the growth and repair of body tissues, gums, blood vessels, bones and teeth. It is involved in the manual system and helps the body to fight off bacteria and viral infections. Deficiency of vitamin-C is related to haemorrhage, slow healing of wounds, scurvy, gum bleeding, reduced formation of bones. Vitamin-C is present in amla, the richest source of Vitamin-C, citrus fruits — lemon, sweetlime (musambi) orange — guava and green leafy vegetables like spinach.

Cooking and canning destroys it. Daily requirement for an adult is 40 mg/day. It is not stored in the body; excess amount is lost through urine.

Vitamin-E

Vitamin-E also acts as an antioxidant and is concentrated in the membranes and protects them from the action of peroxidases. Vitamin-E also protects Vitamin-A from oxidation and inhibits oxygen toxicity, thus being a scavenger of free radical oxygen. It strengthens the immune system by strengthening the white blood cells and helps in preventing heart diseases.

Vitamin-E is present in vegetable oils, wheat germ, sprouts, whole grains, lettuce etc. Overdoses may cause blurred vision.

There are some trace elements which also work as antioxidants in our body e.g. Selenium, Molybdenum etc. However, we are not discussing them here.

G. Scientific Data from SAAOL

Ms. Veenu Sindhwani, our past dietician, worked on her MSc thesis for two years and studied the food composition advised and supplied by SAAOL Heart Program. She analysed all the items that our patients consumed after going back home by using food frequency charts and 24 hour dietary recall tests. Her study on 50 patients in 1996-97 concluded that SAAOL Heart Program provides one of the best food composition that can be advised to the heart patients. The gist of results are given here in form of scientific abstract and analytical tables.

Scientific Abstract

The present investigation was undertaken to study the effectiveness of a lifestyle modification programme in the control of coronary heart disease (CHD). 50 patients, 40-70 years old with an established history of CHD, who had enrolled for a lifestyle modification programme were selected. Various cardiac related parameters were investigated before and after exposure to the programme. Anthropometric profile, blood pressure, pulse rate, presence of CHD symptoms and blood lipid profile were studied before and 8-9 weeks after the programme. Dietary pattern and nutrient intake were adjudged by the 24 hour dietary recall and food frequency questionnaire. Knowledge and awareness of the subjects regarding heart health and heart healthy nutrition was assessed by a close ended questionnaire before and after the 3 day training programme. A significant improvement in the frequency and duration of angina, effort tolerance and fatigue along with reduction in the dosage of CHD medications was observed. Significant reductions were also reported in mean weight, BMI, WHR and MUAC. No significant decrease in blood pressure and pulse rate was observed. The patients' cardiovascular risk status improved as evident by a significant reduction in the level of total serum cholesterol (9.31%), TG (10.4%) and LDL (13.46%) with a simultaneous increase in HDL (12.2%). Highly significant improvement in total/HDL cholesterol and LDL/HDL ratios was also reported. A highly significant reduction was indicated in energy (19%) and fat intake (81.3%), thus contributing to weight loss. The contribution of dietary fat to the total energy intake was reduced from 33.6% to 7.7% at post intervention level. While significant increases in carbohydrate, dietary fibre, iron, β-carotene and Vitamin-C intakes were found, the protein and calcium intakes were significantly decreased. The impact of the training on knowledge and awareness was also marked, as reflected by a four fold increase in the number of desired responses to the heart health and heart healthy nutrition questionnaire, after the intervention. These findings suggest that comprehensive changes in lifestyle can prove beneficial in the control of coronary heart disease.

H. CHANGES AFTER SAAOL PROGRAM

Parameters measured	Before joining SAAOL	After 3 months of joining SAAOL	Change %
Anthropometric measurements			
Weight (kg)	72.5 ± 9.89	68.19 ± 8.69	5.94
MUAC (cm)	27.96 ± 3.08	26.93 ± 2.66	3.68
BMI (kg/m^2)	25.96 ± 3.35	24.41 ± 2.84	5.97
WHR	0.98 ± 0.07	0.94 ± 0.06	3.95
Pulse rate (beats/min.)	70 ± 9	70 ± 6	–
Blood pressure			
Systolic (mm of Hg)	126 ± 19	123 ± 10	2.38
Diastolic (mm of Hg)	77 ± 8	76 ± 5	1.29
Total cholesterol (mg/dl)	215.08 ± 28.63	195.03 ± 26.15	9.31
HDL cholesterol (mg/dl)	37.49 ± 7.98	42.08 ± 6.62	12.2
LDL cholesterol (mg/dl)	140.15 ± 26.90	121.28 ± 23.1	13.4
VLDL cholesterol (mg/dl)	35.77 ± 12.58	32.07 ± 13.15	10.31
TG (mg/dl)	178.0 ± 62.77	159.33 ± 66.43	10.4
Total/HDL cholesterol	5.88 ± 1.30	4.71 ± 0.93	19.9
LDL/HDL cholesterol	3.81 ± 1.07	2.83 ± 0.77	25.6
Energy intake (kcal)	2362 ± 373.3	1911 ± 104.5	19.0
Protein intake (g)	77.53 ± 18.76	70.92 ± 5.37	8.5
Fat intake (g)	88.32 ± 18.26	16.42 ± 1.44	81.3

contd...2

Parameters measured	Before joining SAAOL	After 3 months of joining SAAOL	Change %
Carbohydrate intake (g)	316.08 ± 57.02	370.1 ± 22.02	17.09
Dietary fibre intake (g)	9.10 ± 3.14	19.33 ± 2.96	112.0
Calcium intake (mg)	1261.9 ± 334.23	1015.1 ± 197.20	19.56
Iron intake (mg)	15.36 ± 3.85	24.10 ± 3.11	56.8
β- carotene intake (ug)	3435.6 ± 2775	8151.2 ± 2720	137.0
Vitamin C (mg)	136.7 ± 170.5	35.0 ±112.5	123.0

Percent Contribution Of Different Nutrients to Energy Intake

Nutrient	Before SAAOL	After SAAOL
Carbohydrate	53.52%	77.46%
Protein	13.12%	14.84%
Fat	33.6%	7.7%

Changes in the Angina Symptoms and Medications after the Program

Characteristic	Percentage
Angina Symptoms	
(Chest pain and breathlessness)	
1. Frequency	
Increased	2
Decreased	86
No change	12
2. Duration	
Increased	–
Decreased	74
No change	26
3. Effort tolerance	
Increased	84
Decreased	–
No change	16
4. Fatigue	
Increased	2
Decreased	84
No change	14
Medications	
Increased	–
Decreased	64
No change	36

Lipid Profile Report

Testing a patient for fats in the blood forms an integral part of clinical assessment of any patient suffering from coronary heart disease. Test known as Lipid Profile requires at least 12 hours of fasting, and no alcohol previous night. Lipid profile consists of 5 components.

(a) **Cholesterol:** Cholesterol is a white fat-like substance that is a basic ingredient of the human body. It is one of a group of substances known as lipids (fats), which do not dissolve in water.

Cholesterol is also found in many foods, although you cannot taste it or see it on your plate. All animals have the ability to produce cholesterol and all foods from animal sources like milk, egg yolk, cheese, butter, milk, poultry and fish contain cholesterol.

There has been consistent change towards the attitude of ideal cholesterol range ever since it was found out that higher values of cholesterol is a major risk factor for coronary heart disease. The large number of animal products we eat also contribute to about 400-500 mg of dietary cholesterol daily.

We recommend that cholesterol should be kept in the range of 125-175 mg per 100 ml of blood. According to the latest publication, for the reversal process to set in, we recommend that the cholesterol should be kept at around 140 mg per 100 ml of blood with or without drugs.

(b) **Triglycerides:** Fat is nature's storehouse of energy yielding fuel. Most of the fats are made up primarily of triglycerides — three fatty acid chains attached to a glycerol molecule.

All living things including plants have the ability to manufacture fatty acids and assemble them into molecules of fat to store energy. As a general rule animals manufacture fat composed mainly of saturated fatty acids and plants manufacture fats that are rich in polyunsaturated fatty acids. Some plants also manufacture monounsaturated fatty acids. The term saturated and unsaturated refers to the number of hydrogen atoms found in the fatty acids that make up the dietary fat. Saturated fats have maximum number of hydrogen atoms, polyunsaturated have the fewest. The degree of saturation determines which form (solid or liquid) the fat takes at room temperature.

Fats that consist primarily of saturated fatty acids are called saturated fats. They are typically solid at room temperature. Butter, lard, margarine and visible fat in meats are saturated fats. Much of the fat in milk (butter fat) is also saturated and solid at room temperature, but the process of homogenation breaks the fat into fine particles and scatters it throughout the liquid portion of milk.

Polyunsaturated fats on the other hand are usually liquid at room temperature. These liquid oils are found mostly in the seeds of plants. The oils from Safflower, Sunflower, Corn and Soya beans are unsaturated fats and made up primarily of unsaturated fatty acids.

Monounsaturated fats are also liquid at room temperature. Examples of fat rich in monounsaturated fatty acids are Olive oil, Rapeseed or Canola oil.

On an average we consume 50-60 mg of triglycerides per day in the form of so called safe-oils for heart patients (Saffola, Sunflower, etc.,). The recommended level of triglycerides is 125 mg per 100 gm of blood.

(c) **VLDL (Very Low Density Lipoprotein):** Some fat is normally found in the blood. It travels through the blood, from its food sources and body stores to the cells that use it. Fats also need Lipoproteins (carriers) to carry it through the bloodstream. The fat and the water repel each other. When fat is encased in a lipoprotein that prevents it from mixing it with blood, it can move effortlessly through the bloodstream. Although all lipoproteins carry some tryglycerides (fat molecules), the chylomicrons and very low density lipoproteins are the primary movers of triglycerides.

VLDL can easily be calculated by dividing TG by five. The recommended level of VLDL is 25 mg per 100ml blood.

(d) **LDL (Low Density Lipoproteins):** VLDL carry the fat that is made in the lever, along with cholesterol, to the cells, where the fat is stored. Once the VLDL has dropped off their triglycerides they contain mostly cholesterol and evolve into LDL molecules. The recommended level of LDL is 120 mg per 100 ml.

(e) **HDL (High Density Lipoprotein):** This is the only cholesterol, which we would like you to increase. HDL the good cholesterol picks up excess cholesterol circulating in the blood and blockages and carries it back to the lever, to be expelled from the body. The normal recommended level of HDL for the body is 40 mg per 100 ml.

It has been proven that when the blood HDL level is high, the incidence of coronary heart disease is low, but when the HDL is low, there is substantial increase in coronary heart disease. We can increase HDL by properly managing daily stresses in the life, increasing the intake of green leafy vegetables and fruits and increasing the level of our physical activity in our daily routine.

Chart Of Nutritive Value Of Different Foods

(All the values are per 100 gm of edible portion)

Foodstuff	Moisture (g)	Protein (g)	Fat (g)	CHO (g)	Fibre (g)	Energy (Kcal)
CEREALS						
1. Bajra	12.4	11.6	5.0	67.5	1.2	361
2. Barley (jau)	12.5	11.5	1.3	69.6	3.9	336
3. Jowar	11.9	10.4	1.9	72.6	1.6	349
4. Maize (makkai)	14.9	11.1	3.6	66.2	2.7	342
5. Rice	13.7	6.8	0.5	78.2	0.2	345
6. Rice flakes	12.2	6.6	1.2	77.3	0.7	346
7. Rice, puffed	14.7	7.5	0.1	73.6	0.3	325
8. Wheat, whole	12.8	12.1	1.7	69.4	1.9	341
9. Wheat flour	12.2	12.1	1.7	69.4	1.9	341
10. Refined flour	13.3	11.0	0.9	73.9	0.3	348
11. Semolina (suji)	–	10.4	0.8	74.8	0.2	348
12. Vermicelli	11.7	8.7	0.4	78.3	0.2	352
13. Brown bread	39.0	8.8	1.4	49.0	1.2	244
14. White bread	39.0	7.8	0.7	51.9	0.2	245
PULSES						
15. Bengal gram (whole)	9.8	17.1	5.3	60.9	3.9	360
16. Bengal gram dal	9.9	20.8	5.6	59.8	1.2	372
17. Roasted Bengal gram	10.7	22.5	5.2	58.1	1.0	369
18. Black gram dal	10.9	24.0	1.4	59.6	0.9	347

contd...2

Foodstuff	Moisture (g)	Protein (g)	Fat (g)	CHO (g)	Fibre (g)	Energy (Kcal)
19. Cowpea (Lobia)	13.4	24.1	1.0	54.5	3.8	323
20. Green gram (whole)	10.4	24.0	1.3	56.7	4.1	334
21. Green gram (dal)	10.1	24.5	1.2	59.9	0.8	348
22. Lentil	12.4	25.1	0.7	59.0	0.7	343
23. Moth beans	10.8	23.6	1.1	56.6	4.5	330
24. Peas (dry)	16.0	19.7	1.1	56.5	4.5	315
25. Rajmah	12.0	22.9	1.3	60.6	4.8	346
26. Red gram dhal	13.4	22.3	1.7	57.6	1.5	335
27. Soyabean	8.1	43.2	19.5	20.9	3.7	432

LEAFY VEGETABLES

Foodstuff	Moisture (g)	Protein (g)	Fat (g)	CHO (g)	Fibre (g)	Energy (Kcal)
28. Bathua	89.6	3.7	0.4	2.9	0.8	30
29. Beet greens	86.4	3.4	0.8	6.5	0.7	46
30. Brussel sprouts	85.5	4.7	0.5	7.1	1.2	52
31. Cabbage	91.9	1.8	0.1	4.6	1.0	27
32. Carrot leaves	76.6	5.1	0.5	13.1	1.9	77
33. Colocasia leaves	82.7	3.9	1.5	6.8	2.9	36
34. Coriander leaves	86.3	3.3	0.6	6.3	1.2	44
35. Curry leaves	63.8	6.1	1.0	18.7	6.4	108
36. Fenugreek leaves	86.1	4.4	0.9	6.0	1.1	49
37. Lettuce	93.4	2.1	0.3	2.5	0.5	21
38. Mint	84.9	4.8	0.6	5.8	2.0	48
39. Mustard leaves	89.8	4.0	0.6	3.2	0.8	34
40. Radish leaves	90.8	3.8	0.4	2.4	1.0	28
41. Spinach	92.1	2.0	0.7	2.9	0.6	26

ROOTS & TUBERS

Foodstuff	Moisture (g)	Protein (g)	Fat (g)	CHO (g)	Fibre (g)	Energy (Kcal)
42. Beetroot	87.1	1.7	0.1	8.8	0.9	43

contd...3

Foodstuff	Moisture (g)	Protein (g)	Fat (g)	CHO (g)	Fibre (g)	Energy (Kcal)
43. Carrot	86.0	0.9	0.2	10.6	1.2	48
44. Colocasia	73.1	3.0	0.1	21.1	1.0	97
45. Onion	84.3	1.8	0.1	12.6	0.6	59
46. Potato	74.7	1.6	0.1	22.6	0.4	97
47. Radish	94.4	0.7	0.1	3.4	0.8	17
48. Sweet potato	68.5	1.2	0.3	28.2	0.8	120
49. Tapioca	59.4	0.7	0.2	38.1	0.6	157
50. Turnip	91.6	0.5	0.2	6.2	0.9	29

OTHER VEGETABLES

Foodstuff	Moisture (g)	Protein (g)	Fat (g)	CHO (g)	Fibre (g)	Energy (Kcal)
51. Bitter gourd	92.4	1.6	0.2	4.2	0.8	25
52. Bottle gourd	96.1	0.2	0.1	2.5	0.6	12
53. Brinjal	92.7	1.4	0.3	4.0	1.3	24
54. Broad beans	85.4	4.5	0.1	7.2	2.0	48
55. Cauliflower	90.8	2.6	0.4	4.0	1.2	30
56. Cucumber	96.3	0.4	0.1	2.5	0.4	13
57. Drumstick	86.9	2.5	0.1	3.7	4.8	26
58. French beans	91.4	1.7	0.1	4.5	1.8	26
59. Capsicum	92.4	1.3	0.3	4.3	1.0	24
60. Jackfruit tender	84.0	2.6	0.3	9.4	2.8	51
61. Lady's fingers	89.6	1.9	0.2	6.4	1.2	35
62. Lotus stem (dry)	9.5	4.1	1.3	51.4	25.0	234
63. Mango (green)	87.5	0.7	0.1	10.1	1.2	44
64. Onion stalks	87.6	0.1	0.2	8.9	1.6	41
65. Parwal	92.0	2.0	0.3	2.2	3.0	20
66. Plantain (green)	83.2	1.4	0.2	14.0	0.7	64
67. Pumpkin	92.6	1.4	0.1	4.6	0.7	25
68. Ridge gourd	95.2	0.5	0.1	3.4	0.5	17
69. Tinda	93.5	1.4	0.2	3.4	1.0	21
70. Tomato (green)	93.1	1.9	0.1	3.6	0.7	23
71. Water chestnut	70.0	4.7	0.3	23.3	0.6	115

contd...4

Foodstuff	Moisture (g)	Protein (g)	Fat (g)	CHO (g)	Fibre (g)	Energy (Kcal)
NUTS & OILSEEDS						
72. Almond	5.2	20.8	58.9	10.5	1.7	655
73. Arecanut (supari)	31.3	4.9	4.4	47.2	11.2	249
74. Cashewnut	5.9	21.2	46.9	22.3	1.3	596
75. Chilgoza	4.0	13.9	49.3	29.0	1.0	615
76. Coconut (dry)	4.3	6.8	62.3	18.4	66.6	662
77. Coconut (fresh)	36.3	4.5	41.6	13.0	3.6	444
78. Coconut (tender)	90.8	0.9	1.4	6.3	-	41
79. Coconut (milk)	42.8	3.4	41.0	11.9	-	430
80. Coconut (water)	93.8	1.4	0.1	4.4	-	24
81. Gingelly seeds (til)	5.3	18.3	43.3	25.0	2.9	563
82. Groundnut	3.0	25.3	40.1	26.1	3.1	567
83. Groundnut (roasted)	1.7	26.2	39.8	26.7	3.1	570
84. Mustard seeds	8.5	20.0	39.7	23.8	1.8	541
85. Pistachio nut	5.6	19.8	53.5	16.2	2.1	626
86. Piyal seeds (chironji)	3.0	19.0	59.1	12.1	3.8	656
87. Walnut	4.5	15.6	64.5	11.0	2.6	687
SPICES						
88. Asafoetida (Hing)	16.0	4.0	1.1	67.8	4.1	297
89. Cardamom	20.0	10.2	2.2	42.1	20.1	229
90. Chillies (dry)	10.0	15.9	6.2	31.6	30.2	246
91. Chillies (green)	85.7	2.9	0.6	3.0	6.8	29
92. Cloves	25.2	5.2	8.9	46.0	9.5	286
93. Coriander	11.2	14.1	16.1	21.6	32.6	288

contd...5

Foodstuff	Moisture (g)	Protein (g)	Fat (g)	CHO (g)	Fibre (g)	Energy (Kcal)
94. Cumin seeds	11.9	18.7	15.0	36.6	12.0	356
95. Fenugreek seeds	13.7	26.2	5.8	44.1	7.2	333
96. Garlic	62.0	6.3	0.1	29.8	0.8	145
97. Ginger	80.9	2.3	0.9	12.3	2.4	67
98. Mango powder (amchoor)	6.8	2.8	7.8	64.0	13.7	337
99. Black pepper	18.2	11.5	6.8	49.2	14.9	304
100. Poppy seeds (postdana)	4.3	21.7	19.3	36.8	8.0	408
101. Tamarind pulp	20.9	3.1	0.1	67.4	5.6	283
102. Turmeric	1331	6.3	5.1	69.4	2.6	349

FRUITS

Foodstuff	Moisture (g)	Protein (g)	Fat (g)	CHO (g)	Fibre (g)	Energy (Kcal)
103. Amla	81.8	0.5	0.1	13.7	3.4	58
104. Apple	84.6	0.2	0.5	13.4	1.0	59
105. Apricot, fresh	85.3	1.0	0.3	11.6	1.1	53
106. Apricot, dry	19.4	1.6	0.7	73.4	2.1	306
107. Bael fruit	61.5	1.8	0.3	31.8	2.9	137
108. Banana	70.1	1.2	0.3	21.2	0.4	116
109. Cape gooseberry (Rasbari)	82.9	1.8	0.2	11.1	3.2	53
110. Red cherries	83.4	1.1	0.5	13.8	0.4	64
111. Black currants (Munakka)	18.4	2.7	0.5	75.2	1.0	316
112. Dates, fresh	59.2	1.2	0.4	33.8	3.7	144
113. Figs (Anjeer)	88.1	1.3	0.2	7.6	2.2	37
114. Grapes	79.2	0.5	0.3	16.5	2.9	751
115. Guava	81.7	0.9	0.3	11.2	5.2	51
116. Jackfruit (Kathal)	76.2	1.9	0.1	19.8	1.1	88
117. Jamun	83.7	0.7	0.3	14.0	0.9	62

contd....6

Foodstuff	Moisture (g)	Protein (g)	Fat (g)	CHO (g)	Fibre (g)	Energy (Kcal)
118. Lemon	85.0	1.0	0.9	11.1	1.7	57
119. Lichi	84.1	1.1	0.2	13.6	0.5	61
120. Malta	90.3	0.7	0.2	7.8	0.6	36
121. Musambi	88.4	0.8	0.3	9.3	0.5	43
122. Mango	81.0	0.6	0.4	16.9	0.7	74
123. Muskmelon	95.2	0.3	0.2	3.5	0.4	17
124. Watermelon	95.8	0.2	0.2	3.3	0.2	16
125. Orange	87.6	0.7	0.2	10.9	0.3	48
126. Papaya	90.8	0.6	0.1	7.2	0.8	32
127. Peaches (Aarhoo)	86.0	1.2	0.3	10.5	1.2	50
128. Pears (Nashpati)	86.0	0.6	0.2	11.9	1.0	52
129. Phalsa	80.8	1.3	0.9	14.7	1.2	72
130. Pineapple	87.8	0.	0.1	10.8	0.5	46
131. Plum (Alu bokhara)	86.9	0.7	0.5	11.1	0.4	52
132. Pomegranate	78.0	1.6	0.1	14.5	5.1	65
133. Raisins	20.2	1.8	0.3	74.6	1.1	3048
134. Sapota (chiku)	73.7	0.7	1.1	21.4	2.6	98
135. Seetaphal (sharifa)	70.5	1.6	0.4	23.5	3.1	104
136. Strawberry	87.8	0.7	0.2	9.8	1.1	44
137. Tomato	94.0	0.9	0.2	3.6	0.8	20
138. Zizyphus (ber)	81.6	0.8	0.3	17.0	–	74
MILK & MILK PRODUCTS						
139. Milk, Buffalo's	81.0	4.3	6.5	5.0	–	117
140. Milk, Cow's	87.5	3.2	4.1	4.4	–	67
141. Milk, Goat's	86.8	3.3	4.5	4.6	–	72
142. Curd (Cow's milk)	89.1	3.1	4.0	3.0	–	60

contd....7

Foodstuff	Moisture (g)	Protein (g)	Fat (g)	CHO (g)	Fibre (g)	Energy (Kcal)
143. Buttermilk	97.5	0.8	1.1	0.5	–	15
144. Sk. milk, Liquid	92.1	2.5	0.1	4.6	–	29
145. Chhenna, Cow's milk	57.1	18.3	20.8	1.2	–	265
146. Chhenna, Buffalo's milk	54.1	13.4	23.0	7.9	–	292
147. Khoa (Buffalo's milk)	30.6	14.6	31.2	20.5	–	421
148. Khoa (Cow's milk)	25.2	20.0	25.9	24.9	–	413
149. Skimmed milk powder (cow's milk)	4.1	38.0	0.1	51.0	–	357
150. Whole milk powder (cow's milk)	3.5	25.8	26.7	38.0	–	497
FATS AND OILS						
151. Butter	19.0	–	–	81.0	–	729
152. Ghee/Oils	–	–	100.0	–	–	900
SUGARS						
153. Sugar	0.4	0.1	–	99.4	–	398
154. Honey	20.6	0.3	–	79.5	–	319
155. Jaggery	3.9	0.4	0.1	95.0	–	383
156. Sago	12.2	0.2	0.2	87.1	–	351

Source: Nutritive value of Indian Foods, NIN, Indian Council of Medical Research.

Height-Weight Charts

The weight of a person is calculated not according to the age but according to the height. Some ideal body weight charts have been calculated by the scientists depending on the best weight (which will give the best possible health and longevity). Overweight is detrimental for heart patients and it is advisable to keep the weight at the ideal range.

Lot of people, who are overweight, do not consider themselves so. That's why we are putting here an ideal body weight/height chart. Please check up where you are. If you are in the higher side please work to reduce and if you are underweight please increase the weight. The best for heart patient or to prevent heart disease would be to keep a normal weight (if not low).

The latest scientific way to find out whether one is overweight or not is to calculate Body Mass Index (BMI). It is a weight/height ratio used to measure weight corrected for height.

BMI is calculated using the formula:

$$BMI = \frac{Weight\ (kg)}{Height^2\ (m)}$$

BMI can be graded as follows :
BMI
less than 25 kg/m^2	=	Normal
25 - 29.9 kg/m^2	=	Grade I obesity
30 - 40 kg/m^2	=	Grade II obesity
More than 40 kg/m^2	=	Grade III obesity

The Height-Weight chart is given on the next page.

ASSESSMENT OR DIAGNOSIS OF OBESITY
Ideal Height-Weight for Adults

Ht. (cm)	Ht. (inches)	Average wt. (men)	Average wt. (women)
145	4'9"		46
148	4'10"		46.5
150	4'11"		47.0
152	5'		48.5
156	5'1.5"		49.5
58	5'2.2"	55.8	50.4
160	5'3"	57.6	51.3
162	5'3.8"	58.6	52.6
164	5'4.6"	59.6	54.0
166	5'5.4"	60.6	55.4
168	5'6.1"	61.7	56.8
170	5'6.9"	63.5	58.1
172	5'7.7"	65.0	60.0
174	5'8.5"	66.5	61.3
176	5'10"	69.4	64.0
178	5'10.8"	71.0	65.3
182	5'11.6"	72.6	
184	6'4"	74.2	

(Adapted from the Life Insurance Corporation)

Oil Controversy

Let me mention in this chapter details about oils and clear out some of the wrong information for many of you.

The way the oil companies advertise it appears to some that some oil is really good for the blockages. The scientific name of oil is Triglycerides. If you take any standard oil it is almost 100% fat i.e. triglycerides. The oil companies use different ways and impress the consumers about the different fatty acids that make triglycerides.

Let me explain, Tri of Triglyceride means three; glyceride comes from glycerol. Triglyceride is composed of one molecule (small unit) of glycerol and 3 fatty chains (called fatty acid). These fatty acids present in the triglycerides can be of three kinds — polyunsaturated, monounsaturated and saturated fatty acids; if one hydrogen is absent it is called mono-unsaturated and if more than one Hydrogen is absent it is poly unsaturated. The difference between these three, in terms of composition or side effects is almost same. For example if saturated fatty acid is 92% harmful, mono will do 90% and poly will do 88% harm. Public does not understand this and the oil companies take advantage of it.

Take one example, one oil which has 70% poly unsaturated, 25% monounsaturated and 5% saturated has in all 100% triglyceride content. To advertise it writes "95% saturated FAT FREE", the last two words in bold and so is 95%. For people who do not understand saturated or monounsaturated — this advertisement appears as if the oil has only 5% fat — and they consume that particular oil in huge quantities without understanding that it has 100% fat out of which 95% are mono and poly type fat. Legally the oil company cannot be punished. The heart patients fall into the trap more easily as companies also write "CHOLESTEROL" Free. This is what is going on and the cardiologists have accepted these and the oil companies afterwards sponsor the doctors meet.

You would probably ask, "Doctor, what about your recommended oil?" I have none. I offer water for cooking food. That is what is zero oil. You may also ask, "Doctor, what about our body's oil requirement." According to National Institute of Nutrition (NIN) a minimum of 10% of calories required in our body should come from fat. If we take this figure at 1600 calories per day then 160 calories should come from fat. This will make about 18 to 20 gms per day of minimal fat requirement. SAAOL recommends this quantity only to the heart patient who wants to reverse his ailment, but in a normal person's diet this fat comes automatically from hidden fats in cereals and pulses. So, we do not require any further addition of raw oil in our food.

Dietary Tips

- Garlic is found to lower blood pressure, prevent coronary thrombosis, heart attacks and strokes. It has also been found to be beneficial in inhibiting growth of cancerous tumors and treating diabetes, yeast infections, allergies and stress.
- For suppressing strong odour of garlic, parsley can be chewed along with it.
- Honey is a good substitute for sugar. It is sweeter than sugar and is absorbed more quickly. Unlike sugar it contains Vit B, some minerals and enzymes in addition to its sugar content.
- To prepare Tofu: Soak dried soyabeans in water till soft, then crush and boil. Strain and separate the pulp and soyamilk. To this milk add lemon or citric or tartaric acid. The milk separates into curd and whey. Put the curd into a mould for setting. Within 2-3 hours, tofu is ready.
- Lemon is an excellent source of Vit C and also contains some amount of calcium, phosphorus, potassium and carotene. It is also found to be an antiseptic. It can be easily used as a low calorie salad dressing.
- Cardamom is mainly used as a cooking spice or for flavouring drinks. It is known as a carminative, relieving flatulence, stimulating the stomach and aiding digestion.
- Cut vegetables into small pieces as the flavour will be extracted easily in 20 minutes. If you cut them larger you will need to cook them longer to extract its flavour.
- It is not difficult to make delicious food without adding fat. Make judicious use of spices and herbs which can help in making dishes tastier and varied. Their intense flavour can compensate for the lack of fat.

- Cut down on salt.
- Add salt while eating rather than in cooking- you'll taste it more and thus use less.
- Use other flavourings in food like garlic, lemon juice, vinegar, tomatoes, herbs and spices.
- Avoid foods with high salt content, such as pickles and papads.
- Fresh herbs should be added at the last minute for maximum impact and save a sprig or two for garnishing.
- Dried herbs need to be stewed for a few minutes before they impart their flavour.
- Read food labels for calorie and avoid fat contents and avoid products with added sugar.
- Avoid tasting dishes too often. 3-4 spoonfuls of a sauce or gravy can contain a surprising number of calories. If you must taste, use a teaspoon.
- Never add acid foods to beans like tomatoes, lemon juice until the beans are soft. The acid can keep the beans from softening.
- Garlic is a classic example of a combination of food and folk medicine. It boosts immune response and increases resistance against various diseases. It also has antibacterial, antifungal and antithrombic effects.
- Mushrooms are fungi rich in potassium, phosphorus, copper and iron. They are also a good source of Vit-B1 & B2. They are known to be beneficial in reducing blood fat levels, have antibiotic properties, antitumour activity and boost immune system action against disease producing micro-organisms.
- Mustard is a popular culinary herb that stimulates the appetite and helps digestion.
- Onions, along with their culinary properties, help prevent blood clot and heart attacks. It has also shown to lower high blood pressure and cholesterol levels.
- Papaya is known for its ability to aid digestion. It contains enzymes

that help to digest proteins. Papaya is a rich source of beta-carotene, Vit-B and Vit-C.

- Potato is a good source of vegetable protein, potassium, Vit C, iron, phosphorus and enzymes. It relieves water retention & can sometimes be used to reduce hypertension and promote intestinal flora.
- Pumpkin is a good source of beta-carotene, calcium, iron and some Vit B. It helps to regulate blood sugar levels and is thus beneficial to hypoglycemics.
- Spinach is an excellent source of iron, calcium, chlorophyll, beta-carotene, Vit-C, riboflavin, sodium and potassium. It is also a diuretic and laxative.
- Sprouts are rich in chlorophyll, Vit-A, C, D, E, K & B complex and in minerals such as calcium, phosphorus, potassium, magnesium and iron.
- Sprouts are diuretics, appetizers and detoxify the body.
- Turmeric is not used as seasoning but also as a food preservative and colouring agent. It also has unique antioxidant and anti-inflammatory properties. It retards age related diseases by preventing free radical damage, inhibit the growth of cancer cells, protect the liver from cholesterol levels, alleviate joint swellings, reduce menstrual pain and has a beneficial effect in the treatment of AIDS.
- As with any other nutrient the body requires water in balanced amounts. Too much water particularly after meals will dilute digestive juices, weaken digestion and cause a sensation of coldness. On the other hand, insufficient water intake will promote constipation, accumulation of toxins, kidney damage, fatigue, apathy and dryness.
- Grains and legumes when cooked contain about 80% water, many fruits and vegetables contain over 90% water, while the content of soups and juices is almost 100% water.
- Nutritional benefits of yoghurt is to reinforce intestines with additional friendly bacteria promoting the growth of intestinal flora. It is a good source of quality proteins, vitamin and an excellent source of easily absorbed calcium. It is easily digestible.

➤ Like all tastes, salt is also an acquired taste.
➤ Start your meals with a bowl of low-fat, high-protein soup. It will reduce your appetite. But be aware of cream-based soups — they're more fattening than most other soups.
➤ Take time to eat your meals slowly. Gulping down your food is bad for digestion. If you put down your eating utensils between each bite, you will chew your food more thoroughly and enjoy it more.

"Anger is one step short of danger."

Food for Diabetics with Heart Disease

Diabetes is another very common disease of the modern society. Blood sugar, when it is high in blood than normal, the condition is called diabetes. For a normal person the fasting blood sugar (glucose, to be more scientific) should not be more than 110 mg per 100 ml. Ideally it should be 80 mg per 100ml to be called exact normal. It can be called high normal if the fasting blood sugar is about 100 mg plus. Borderline diabetes is a stage when the fasting blood sugar level is mostly above or near 110mg/100ml. Fasting blood level above this definitely indicates diabetes. Similarly, blood sugar tested after 2 hours of meal or good breakfast (called post prandial or simply PP blood sugar) should be below 130 for a normal person. Borderline is 150mg or so; while the frank diabetes will have a blood sugar (PP) of more than 160mg/100 ml.

Diabetes is a major lifestyle disease, one of the most common of the present time. To talk about the causes — lack of physical activity or exercise, overweight and excessive stress are the most important reasons of developing diabetes. Chances of developing diabetes are more if there is a history of the same disease in the family.

Now it is very common to have diabetic patients who also have coronary heart disease, as increased blood sugar in the blood helps more cholesterol to deposit inside the heart arteries. The clinical experience at SAAOL has shown that about 20 to 25 % of heart patients have diabetes throughout India. In Chennai and Tamil Nadu , in my statistics in SAAOL, almost 50 % of the heart patients have diabetes.

There is a wrong notion that taking more sugar can create diabetes . In a normal person (without diabetes) even taking sugar in good quantity will not create any problem but a person who has diabetes must not consume raw glucose or sugar.

There is another wrong notion in many people's mind, that diabetic patients should not take potato or rice. This is now scientifically accepted that rice and potato have complex carbohydrates and can be taken in normal quantity. Anything sweet to taste, would be having raw sugar or simple sugar. These are the items to be avoided by diabetic patients. The more sweet fruit is, the more damaging it is for diabetic patients.

Another item I usually permit, to the sweet loving diabetes patient, is artificial sweeteners. Aspertance (available in the medical shop as Equal or Sugar free) can be consumed freely as it neither raises blood sugar nor provides high calories. I allow the patients sweets with these sweeteners.

Food For Overweight People

Overweight is a problem for many people. As it aggravates heart disease I always want my patients to bring down the weight towards normal. Diet plays a definite role in the same. Food plays a major role as it supplies the calories.

One must remember that most of the overweight is basically due to storage of fat in the body. Each gram of this store can generate about 9 calories when burnt. If you can supply, in your food, 9 calories less than body's requirement you will reduce 1 gram of weight as body will burn that one gram fat to generate the calories.

Similarly if you plan to reduce 100 gm of weight, make the body deficient of $100 \times 9 = 900$ calories. Body to meet this deficiency, will break 100 grams of fat from its store and you loose 100 gms. It's like a bank account if you put less money than you spend daily, the account becomes smaller. On the other hand, put more money and the account will increase. The currency in the body weight is calorie. Your body weight is the balance of your calorie intake (food eaten) and output (regular expenditure).

Some people exercise a lot (this increases calorie expenditure) but are still not able to lose weight basically because they eat more calories.

At this moment let me explain that "eating less" and "eating less calories" are two completely different things. You would be amazed to know that it is possible to eat to your full stomach, fill it with the food of your choice and yet eat less calories! The concept behind this is called, "Eat more and weigh less. Yes, you can keep losing weight at a steady state if you eat low calorie food items and do not use oil (high calorie) in your cooking. The low calorie food items like salads, fruits and vegetables will give a sense of full stomach, satisfying the satiety. I have observed, many of my patients constantly losing their weight and yet having the food of their choice and satisfaction."

To lose weight I would like my patients to make a target of 2 - 3 kg per month. I want them to do the calculations themselves. I train them about how to count calories in a plate full of different food items. Once they know this by heart, the weight loss is in their hand. It's only a matter of getting educated.

Zero oil food is probably the best way to lose weight. Along with that if you can walk daily and do physical activity weight loss becomes much easier.

Changing Concepts About Cardiologists

The growing numbers of cardiac centres, heart institutes and hospitals with facilities of bypass surgery and angioplasty give a false impression that the science of cardiology is one of the most developing areas of medical science. But if you consider the growth in number of patients who have heart attacks and get admitted because of heart ailments and their sufferings — the cardiology science has become the most ineffective in terms of having a control over the disease. The growing number of patients is not a positive trend in the success chart of the department of cardiology but a negative one. Cardiologists have progressed, not the patients.

The worst has been translated as the best. It may be best for the profession of cardiologist and his increasing importance but bad for the patients. Seeing from the top it's the failure of cardiologists that they are not able to understand and tackle heart disease.

Someone asked me what would I mean by a cardiologist. My simple answer was, "One who takes real care of heart patients." Taking care has now become synonymous with writing prescriptions till the emergency comes; taking care of emergency after it actually happens; prescribing medicines till another emergency comes and so on. Some more cardiologists announced themselves experts in solving the problem of blockage by performing dangerous surgeries like bypass surgery, which are more of a temporary postponement of heart problem without solving the real cause of the disease. The prohibitory cost of such a process and the immediate (but short time) benefits made people think that it is a permanent solution. These cardiac surgeries often give a guarantee of 10-15 years but their experience and mine mostly find patients coming back after an average of 5 years, if not less.

The angioplasty cardiologists, also called intervention cardiologists, do very little to help the heart patients. Their balloons do some more damage to the already damaged inner wall of the heart arteries so that instead of 5-7 years, reblockages occur by six months or so.

It would have been desirable that every patient, before they consider any surgery should compulsorily be given a complete lifestyle training and advice. In such cases almost only 5% of patients reporting to these surgeons and angioplasty doctors would require surgery or ballooning. The science of cardiology has to orient itself in the future.

United States of America (USA) also got into the trap of these kind of cardiologists (surgeons and angioplasty doctors) a decade back. When the problem kept on increasing they found that a great percentage of their health budget is going towards paying for the cost of bypass surgery and angioplasty. Recently they have taken plenty of new and harsh measures to discourage these procedures which give temporary relief only.

Another important observation of mine is that only less than 0.01% of heart patients of India undertake bypass surgery or angioplasty in one year. (Total population of heart patients and the number of such interventions done in one year are roughly 1 crore : 30,000). But if you watch the activities of the cardiologists prime body called the Cardiological Society of India (CSI), they are all controlled by these small but powerful group of doctors who perform bypass surgery and angioplasty. Their conferences held every year and attended by thousands of cardiologists, hardly focus on the real treatment of heart disease — the removal of the process of deposit. Half of the items discussed in their conferences, ironically, revolve around bypass and angioplasty (performed on only 0.01% of patients who have heart disease). It seems, they have hijacked the conference with their money and power.

Rest half of these annual conferences actually deal with medicines (again promoted by medical companies) and instruments (promoted by the manufacturers). The real science of cardiology is almost not a part of the discussion. I fail to understand why people like these should be called cardiologists.

If modifying diet, teaching stress management or yoga and giving education on how to exercise along with medication is not the job of a cardiologist then I refuse to call myself a cardiologist.

Recently there has been a change in the patients' minds. They also look at these so called cardiologists (surgeons and angioplasty doctors) with suspicion. They have understood that these people have also become businessmen setting their services to market their unethical (unlawful) practices.

"The remedy is worse than the disease."

— **Francis Bacon**

"The art of medicine consists of amusing the patient while nature cures the disease."

— **Voltaire** (1694-1788)
French writer

SECTION IV

Soups

1 Colocasia Stem Soup

Ingredients

Colocasia stems rounds)	8-10 (peeled and cut into
Jaggery	3 tsp
Red chilli powder	½ tsp
Tamarind pulp (imli)	1 tsp
Salt	1 tsp
Water	4 cups
Garlic and crushed)	6 cloves (peeled

Method

1. Boil colocasia stems in water till soft.
2. Now add jaggery, red chilli powder, tamarind pulp and salt and bring to boil.
3. Dry roast garlic cloves till brown and add to the soup.
4. Serve hot.

Garlic : *Garlic is a wonderful plant useful in asthma, T.B., heart problems, paralysis, high blood pressure, bronchitis, cough and cold etc. But large doses can produce flatulance, headache, nausea and vomiting.*

Nutritive Information

CALORIES: **94.3 Cal**   PROTEIN: **3.9 gm**   FAT: **1.5 gm**
CARBOHYDRATE: **16.3 gm**   FIBRE: **2.9 gm**

2 Hot and Sour Soup

Ingredients

Carrots (chopped into thin strips)	250 gms
Capsicum (chopped into thin strips)	100 gms
Spring onions (chopped into strips)	250 gms
Pepper	½ tsp
Salt	to taste
Soya sauce	½ tsp
Chilli powder	½ tsp
Vinegar	1 tsp
Cornflour	1 tbsp (made into paste with ½ cup water)
Water	3 ½ cups

Method

1. Boil carrots, capsicum and spring onions in 3 ½ cups of water till tender.
2. Now add pepper, salt, soya sauce, chilli powder and vinegar.
3. Add cornflour paste to the soup.
4. Keep stirring as it comes to a boil.
5. Let it boil for another 2-3 minutes. Serve hot.

Carrot: *Carrot is sweet in taste, a tonic and is a boon for anemic people. The carotene present in them is provitamin A. Regular eating of raw carrots prevent ulcers, stones in the urinary tract, constipation and cancer.*

Nutritive Information

CALORIES: **64.5 Cal**   PROTEIN: **1.9 gm**   FAT: **0.30 gm**
CARBOHYDRATE: **8.78 gm**   FIBRE: **6 gm**

3 Spinach Soup with Macaroni

Ingredients

Spinach (palak)	500 gms (chopped)
Onion	1 small (chopped)
Cornflour	2 tbsp (made into paste with little water)
Salt	to taste
Pepper	½ tsp
Sugar	½ tsp
Macaroni	2 tsp

Method

1. Boil macaroni in ½ cup of water for 5 to 6 minutes. Keep aside.
2. Boil spinach with ½ cup of water till soft. Blend it in a mixer.
3. Add 3 cups of water, salt, pepper and sugar and bring to a boil.
4. Reduce heat and add cornflour paste and cooked macaroni. Keep stirring continuously until thick. Let it boil for a minute. Remove from heat.
5. Dry roast the onions till light brown and add to the soup. Serve hot.

Spinach : *Spinach is a good source of iron and beta carotene which is a provitamin A. Spinach has sufficient amount of fibre.*

Nutritive Information

CALORIES: **57.7 Cal**   PROTEIN: **10.4 gm**   FAT: **2.9 gm**
CARBOHYDRATE: **49.05 gm**   FIBRE: **1.85 gm**

4 Rasam Soup

Ingredients

Red gram dal (arhar dal)	250 gms (cooked in 3-4 cups of water)
Tomato	1 (chopped)
Peppercorns	2 tsp
Coriander seeds	2 tbsp
Cumin seeds	1 tsp
Garlic	2 cloves (crushed)
Coriander leaves	1 tbsp (chopped)
Mustard seeds	1 tsp
Asafoetida	a pinch
Dry red chilli	1
Curry leaves	few

Method

1. Roast peppercorns, coriander and cumin seeds and powder them together. Keep aside.
2. After cooking dal pour out only the liquid. Reserve the cooked dal for making any other curry.
3. To the liquid add roasted powders, crushed garlic, tomato and coriander leaves. Boil for 5 minutes.
4. Now dry roast mustard seeds till they pop, add dry red chilli, asafoetida and curry leaves. Stir for a while. Add to the rasam soup and serve hot.

Curry leaves: *The south Indian curry or sambar is not complete without these aromatic leaves. Regular eating of curry leaves, preferably raw, purifies the blood, cures morning sickness, diarrhoea, nervous disorder and premature greying*

Nutritive Information

CALORIES: **105 Cal**   PROTEIN: **6.28 gm**   FAT: **74 gm**
CARBOHYDRATE: **15.2 gm**   FIBRE: **1.4 gm**

5 Cold Soup

Ingredients

Tomatoes	6-7 (medium, chopped)
Cucumber	1 (finely chopped)
Onion	1 (chopped)
Garlic	1 flake
Capsicum	1 (finely chopped, seeds and core removed)
Chaat masala	½ tsp
Sugar	2 tsp
Pepper	½ tsp
Salt	to taste

Method

1. Grind chopped tomatoes, cucumber, onion and garlic in the mixer with a little water.
2. Then add enough cold water to give flowing consistency.
3. Add chaat masala, sugar, pepper and salt.
4. Serve chilled garnished with sliced capsicum.

Cucumbers: *Cucumbers are very good in summer as they quench the thirst immediately. Cucumber when taken raw acts as diuretic and is used in high blood pressure, toxemia of pregnancy, scanty urination. It can be used in juice, salads, raita and sandwiches.*

Nutritive Information

CALORIES: **196 Cal**   PROTEIN: **8 gm**   FAT: **1.5 gm**
CARBOHYDRATE: **37.4 gm**   FIBRE: **6 gm**

6 Spinach Soup

Ingredients

Spinach	1 kg
Water	2 cups
Ginger	1 tsp (peeled and chopped)
White sauce skimmed milk and flour)	8 tbsp (made using
Salt	to taste

Method

1. Cook spinach in 2 cups of water until soft and then cool.
2. Blend cooled spinach and ginger.
3. Again heat spinach-ginger mixture, white sauce and salt. Add water for desired thickness.
4. Simmer the soup for another 10-12 minutes. Serve hot.

Ginger: It is used in fresh, raw or dried form. Even if its taste is unpalatable, it is an essential ingredient for the spices and has pungency, flavour, aroma and above all, various medicinal values.

Nutritive Information

CALORIES: **289 Cal**   PROTEIN: **4.5 gm**   FAT: **7.1 gm**
CARBOHYDRATE: **33.6 gm**   FIBRE: **6 gm**

7 Black Beans and Rice Soup

Ingredients

Brown rice	100 gms (uncooked)
French beans	50 gms
Water	4 ltrs
Garlic	10 cloves (minced)
Red pepper	½ tsp (crushed)
Fennel seeds	½ tsp
Bay leaf	1
Parsley	100 gms (chopped)
Tomatoes	2
Pepper	1 tsp
Salt	to taste

Method

1. Bring water to boil in a large covered pot. Add beans, garlic, red pepper, fennel seeds, bay leaf and parsley. Cook over medium heat for $1^{1}/_{2}$ hour, stirring frequently.
2. Add rice, salt and pepper. Lower heat and simmer for 1 hour. Stir in tomatoes and cook for 30 minutes. Season to taste.

Brown Rice: *Rice is the staple food for around half the world's population. Nutritionally, brown rice is a good source of B complex vitamins. It also contains calcium and phosphorus. Although it contains iron, the phytic acid in the rice bran inhibits the absorption.*

Nutritive Information

CALORIES: **57.7 Cal**   PROTEIN: **10.4 gm**   FAT: **2.9 gm**
CARBOHYDRATE: **49.05 gm**   FIBRE: **1.85 gm**

8 Wheat Flour Soup

Ingredients

Wheat flour	2 tbsp
Water	2 cups
Salt	to taste
Hot milk (sweetened or plain skimmed milk)	

Method

1. Roast the flour to an aromatic golden brown on low flame in a heavy saucepan.
2. Stir continuously or the flour will burn.
3. When the flour is done, add water stirring continuously so that no lumps are formed.
4. Add more water if required. Bring to a boil.
5. Add salt.
6. Simmer on low for 2-3 minutes. Stir frequently.
7. Pour into porridge bowl.
8. Serve piping hot with plain or sweetened hot milk to be mixed as desired.
9. Stir in some cornflakes or any other cereal as desired.

Wheat flour soup is a good source of carbohydrates and is a nourishing recipe for the underweight.

Nutritive Information

CALORIES: **89 Cal**   PROTEIN: **7.75 gm**   FAT: **.4 gm**
CARBOHYDRATE: **16.55 gm**   FIBRE: **.24 gm**

Salads

9 Corn and Bean Salad

Ingredients

Corn on the cob	3
Tomato	1 (diced)
Celery	1 (diced)
Parsley	1 sprig
Spring onions	50 gms (chopped)
Honey	1 tsp
Alfalfa sprouts	1-2 cups
Vinegar	3 tbsp
Cooked beans	100 gms
Soya sauce	1 tbsp

Method

1. Scrape the corn from the cobs and mix with sprouts and beans.
2. Now mix the remaining ingredients in a blender to make the dressing.
3. Then pour this dressing over the corn salad mixture.
4. Chill and serve.

Celery: Celery is a popular green leafy vegetable. As a flavouring agent celery is particularly valuable in soups and stews. It is low in calories, helps to lower cholesterol levels and blood pressure. It helps to relieve joint pain and is a good source of potassium.

Nutritive Information

CALORIES: **100.7 Cal**   PROTEIN: **5.56 gm**   FAT: **0.45 gm**
CARBOHYDRATE: **43.85 gm**   FIBRE: **3.25 gm**

10 Tofu Tit Bits

Ingredients

Tofu	½ kg
Honey	1 tsp
Soya sauce	3 tbsp
Oregano herb	1 tsp
Onion paste	½ tsp
Garlic paste	½ tsp

Method

1. Cut tofu into small ½ inch cubes.
2. Mix garlic, onion and honey in soya sauce and coat tofu cubes.
3. Keep marinated tofu in refrigerator for 1 hour.
3. Marinate well and drain.
4. Mix in oregano until cubes are nicely coated.
5. Brown tofu in an oven and serve hot.

Tofu: It is a soft-cheese like food made by curdling fresh hot soya milk with a coagulant. It is rich in high quality protein and is also a good source of B-vitamins and iron. Herbs in the diet and herbal remedies are making a comeback as people rediscover the value of natural ingredients and natural cures and question the side effects of pharmaceutical drugs.

Nutritive Information

CALORIES: **230 Cal**   PROTEIN: **50.8 gm**   FAT: **30.5 gm**
CARBOHYDRATE: **40.8 gm**   FIBRE: **3.6 gm**

11 Sprout, Corn and Vegetable Salad

Ingredients

Bean sprouts (moong dal)	50 gms
Channa sprouts (kala channa)	50 gms
Corn (tender)	50 gms
Carrot	1
Cucumber	1
Broccoli florets	few
Lettuce	few leaves
Green chilli paste	1 tsp
Green coriander paste	2 tsp
Cumin seeds (jeera)	$1/2$ tsp
Mustard seeds	$1/2$ tsp
Asafoetida (hing)	a pinch
Lemon juice	2 tsp
Curry leaves	few
Chaat masala	$1/2$ tsp
Coriander leaves	few (chopped fine)
Salt	to taste

Method

1. Cut all the vegetables fine and set aside.
2. Heat a pan and add mustard and cumin seeds and asafoetida. Add curry leaves and sprouted channa. Cover with a lid.
3. After 2 minutes add bean sprouts and corn. Add a little salt and sauté for some time. Cover, remove and cool.

4. Mix this mixture with the vegetables in a salad bowl.
5. Add chaat masala, lemon juice and some salt.
6. Mix well and garnish with chopped coriander leaves.
7. Put it in the refrigerator till ready to serve.

Vegetarian food leaves a deep impression on our nature. If the whole world adopts vegetarianism, it can change the destiny of human beings.

Nutritive Information

CALORIES: **231 Cal**   PROTEIN: **13.37 gm** FAT: **2.65 gm**
CARBOHYDRATE: **39.03 gm**   FIBRE: **4.66 gm**

12 Tomato Salad

Ingredients

Tomatoes	5
Soya bean granules	100 gms
Chaat masala	2 tsp
Salt	to taste

Method

1. Cut tomatoes into small pieces.
2. Put some soya bean granules in water and strain them.
3. Combine both of them and put some chaat masala and salt and mix well.

Tomatoes *raw are a storehouse of vitamins and minerals. They are used in the treatment of anemia, nervous disorder and constipation. It is also used as a blood purifier. The juice of the tomato is a good drink during summer.*

Nutritive Information

CALORIES: **236 Cal** PROTEIN: **27.5 gm** FAT: **9.7 gm**
CARBOHYDRATE: **14.05 gm** FIBRE: **2.65 gm**

13 Cauliflower Salad

Ingredients

Whole cauliflower	1
Green chillis	3 (slit)
Lemon juice	1 tbsp
Turmeric (haldi)	$1/2$ tsp
Salt	to taste

Method

1. Wash the cauliflower florets and allow to dry. Make sure they are not wet.
2. Squeeze the lemon juice in a bowl.
3. To it add the turmeric, green chillis, salt and mix well.
4. Add the cauliflower florets and mix well.
5. Allow it to stay for a few hours and keep tossing the salad in between.
6. Then serve it.

Cauliflower: *Cauliflower may be taken raw or used in curries, or in mixed vegetable preparations. Fresh, raw or lightly cooked cauliflower is a good source of folic acid and vitamin-C. Leaves of cauliflower should be used along with the florets as it is a rich source of vitamin-A.*

Nutritive Information

CALORIES: **66 Cal**   PROTEIN: **5.9 gm**   FAT: **1.3 gm**
CARBOHYDRATE: **7.6 gm**   FIBRE: **2.0 gm**

14 Rajma Salad

Ingredients

Rajma (kidney beans)	250 gms (soaked overnight and pressure cooked)
Onion	1 small (finely chopped)
Garlic	2 cloves (crushed)
Tomato	1 small (chopped fine)
Salt	to taste
Green chilli	1 (chopped fine)
Vinegar	3-4 tsp
Lemon juice	2 tsp

Method

1. In a glass bowl add all the ingredients except the vinegar and lemon juice.
2. Pour vinegar and lemon juice over the salad and let it marinate for 30 minutes.
3. Toss just before serving.

Garlic: *The humble garlic clove is increasingly being shown to have existing potential as a safe prophylactic measure for everyday use against cardiovascular risk factors.*

Nutritive Information

CALORIES: **115 Cal** PROTEIN: **6.19 gm** FAT: **.47 gm**
CARBOHYDRATE: **18.72 gm** FIBRE: **1.62 gmn**

15 Italian Salad

Ingredients

Pasta, any shape	10-15 pieces
Cucumbers	2
Carrot	1
Large tomatoes	2
Large onion	1
Lettuce leaves	6-8
Corn kernels, preferably frozen	100 gms
Rajma (kidney beans)	50 gms
Cottage cheese (paneer)	50 gms

For the Dressing

Vinegar (white)	4 tbsp
Freshly ground black pepper	1/2 tsp
Garlic (crushed)	1/2 tsp
Salt	to taste

Method

1. Soak kidney beans overnight. Next day, pressure cook with a little salt.
2. Boil pasta in water with little salt. Drain and keep aside.
3. Peel and cut cucumbers into slices, grate the carrot, dice the tomatoes, slice onion into rings and tear lettuce leaves into pieces.
4. Wash frozen corn kernels and keep aside. If using fresh kernels, steam for 2-3 minutes before using.
5. Cut the cottage cheese into cubes.

6. Place all the ingredients for the dressing in a small jar and shake vigorously to mix.
7. Combine all the ingredients for the salad, pour dressing on top, toss well to mix and serve.

Italian salad is a recipe in which a wide variety of pastas can be used to make it more appealing.

Nutritive Information

CALORIES: **200.25 Cal**   PROTEIN: **11.1 gm**   FAT: **1.14 gm**
CARBOHYDRATE: **68.36 gm**   FIBRE: **2.09 gm**

16 Hot Salad

Ingredients

Cucumbers	2 small
Mushrooms (button)	100 gms
Baby corns	5
Capsicum	1
Carrots	2
Spring onions	2
Onion	1
Chaat masala	2 tsp
Salt and pepper	to taste

Method

1. Blanch carrots and baby corns.
2. Dice all the remaining vegetables into big chunks.
3. Heat a pan and add all the vegetables and sauté for a couple of minutes on high flame.
4. Add salt, pepper and chaat masala.
5. Serve hot.

When you choose fruits and vegetables, look for those with colour, usually the deeper is the colour, more are the antioxidants.

Nutritive Information

CALORIES: **59.4 Cal**   PROTEIN: **0.12 gm**   FAT: **0.29 gm**
CARBOHYDRATE: **40.85 gm**   FIBRE: **2.03 gm**

17 Carrot Salad with Chutney

Ingredients

Carrots	2-3
Green chutney	1 tbsp
Vinegar	2 tsp
Cumin seed powder (roasted)	1 tsp
Garlic paste	1/4 tsp
Salt	to taste
Red chilli powder	1 tsp
Coriander leaves	for garnishing

Method

1. Shred carrots and add green chutney.
2. Mix well, add garlic paste, vinegar, salt, cumin seed and red chilli powders and garnish with chopped coriander.

Coriander leaves are liberally used raw in salads and as toppings in curries, soups etc. Fresh juice can be used in vitamin deficiency, anemia, constipation etc.

Nutritive Information

CALORIES: **14.4 Cal**   PROTEIN: **0.27 gm**   FAT: **0.06 gm**
CARBOHYDRATE: **31.8 gm**   FIBRE: **0.36 gm**

18 Whole Meal Salad

Ingredients

Medium sized cabbage	1/4 piece
Spring onions	3
Capsicum	1
Carrots	2
Tomatoes	2
Lettuce leaves	4
Cucumbers	3
Lemon juice	1 1/2 tbsp
Salt	to taste
Roasted chapatis (cut into pieces)	1 bowl
Pepper	1 pinch

Method

1. Cut all the leafy vegetables into thin strips.
2. Chop other vegetables into small pieces.
3. Add lemon juice, salt and pepper and mix.
4. Just before serving mix in the roasted chapati pieces.
5. Decorate with few leaves of celery or parsley or coriander.

Eat wide variety of foods. While there is no need to worry too much about individual meals, it is a good idea to make sure that by the end of the day you have eaten all kinds of food.

Nutritive Information

CALORIES: **101.4 Cal**   PROTEIN: **4.17 gm**   FAT: **0.56 gm**
CARBOHYDRATE: **47.5 gm**   FIBRE: **4.61 gm**

Cereals

19 Spanish Rice

Ingredients

Basmati/Dehra Dun rice	250 gms
Onion pieces (small)	4 tbsp
Garlic paste	5 or 6 (cloves)
Capsicum pieces	2 tbsp
Tomato purée	500 gms
Boiled carrot pieces	100 gms
Boiled peas	100 gms
Boiled beans	100 gms
Skimmed milk cottage cheese	4 to 6 tbsp (grated)
Salt, red chilli powder and pepper	to taste

Method

1. Wash rice and drain water.
2. Heat a karhai and sauté onions.
3. When onion changes colour, add garlic and rice.
4. Slowly mix it and see rice does not break.
5. Add tomato purée, salt, red chilli powder, pepper and enough water to cook.
6. Cover the vessel with a lid with water on it (if need be add this water to rice).
7. As rice is about to cook, add all the boiled vegetables and capsicum and mix slowly.
8. While serving add grated paneer.

Garlic: Herbalists and naturopaths regard garlic as a miracle food and use it as a *remedy for dozens of complaints, ranging from asthma to arthritis. Daily doses may help to lower blood cholesterol and blood pressure.*

Nutritive Information

CALORIES: **338.5 Cal**   PROTEIN: **20.85 gm** FAT: **2 gm**
CARBOHYDRATE: **83.65 gm**   FIBRE: **7.4 gm**

20 Spinach and Tomato Rice

Ingredients

Basmati rice	500 gms
Water	3 ½ cups
Salt	1 tsp
Ginger	4 slices
Spinach, (chopped)	300 gms
Tomatoes	2 (finely chopped)
Black peppercorns	½ tsp
Cumin seeds	1 tbsp
Coriander seeds	1 tbsp

Dry roast the last 3 ingredients and grind to a fine powder

Method

1. Heat a karhai and roast the ginger slices. Sauté the rice for a while.
2. Transfer all the ingredients to the rice cooker and switch on and cook.

Tomatoes: *Being delicious in salads, tomatoes are extremely good for you. They are good source of both potassium and beta-carotene and they are a useful source of vitamins — C and E, while containing very few calories.*

Nutritive Information

CALORIES: **146 Cal**   PROTEIN: **4.9 gm**   FAT: **0.15 gm**
CARBOHYDRATE: **26 gm**   FIBRE: **0.14 gm**

21 Mustard Rice

Ingredients

Boiled rice	250 gms
Mustard seeds	1 tbsp
Dry red chillis	4 to 5
Roasted gram	1/2 tbsp
Tamarind	1 lemon-size ball
Urad dal	1 tsp
Dry red chillis	2
Curry leaves	few soaked in water

Method

1. Put in the mixie mustard seeds, chillis, roasted gram and grind it.
2. After it is half done, add tamarind along with very little water and grind to a smooth paste.
3. To a pan add urad dal, red chillis and curry leaves.
4. Once they start to splutter add the ground paste and sauté for a few seconds. Take care not to overcook them.
5. Immediately add the cooked rice. Coat evenly and serve hot.

Mustard: Recognised for centuries as a decongestant and expectorant, also antibacterial. Revs up metabolism, burns off extra calories. Warm mustard oil massage on the chest is a very good remedy for congestion caused by colds and sinus problems.

Nutritive Information

CALORIES: **100 Cal**   PROTEIN: **2 gm**   FAT: **0.06 gm**
CARBOHYDRATE: **19.5 gm**   FIBRE: **0.05 gm**

22 Brinjal Rice

Ingredients

Boiled rice	750 gms
Brinjals, chopped into small pieces	250 gms
Medium sized onions	2 (chopped)
Mustard seeds	1/2 tsp
Urad dal	1 tsp
Green chillis	2 (chopped)
Garam masala	1 ½ tsp
Curry leaves	few
Salt	to taste

For the Powder

Coriander (dhania) seeds	1 tbsp
Bengal gram dal	1 tsp
Red chillis	4 to 6

Method

1. Roast the coriander seeds, Bengal gram dal and red chillis till they become light brown in colour and then grind coarsely into a powder and keep aside.
2. Take a karahi and add the mustard seeds and urad dal. When the mustard seeds start crackling add the curry leaves and green chillis.
3. Add the onions and sauté till they become slightly brown.
4. Toss in the chopped brinjals and let them cook for a few minutes.
5. Add garam masala, salt and the prepared powder and sauté for a few minutes.

6. Add boiled rice and mix well.
7. Serve hot with papad, chips or raita.

Brinjal: *There are different types of brinjals available. They are used to cure bile symptoms (only tender ones) and constipation. It can be used in raita, curry, kottu, chutney etc.*

Nutritive Information
CALORIES: **149 Cal** PROTEIN: **4 gm** FAT: **0.95 gm**
CARBOHYDRATE: **29.05 gm** FIBRE: **1.6 gm**

23 Fenugreek-Pea Pulao

Ingredients

Basmati rice	500 gms
Fenugreek leaves	250 gms (chopped)
Frozen peas (matar)	200 gms
Medium tomato	1 (chopped)
Turmeric powder	¼ tsp
Raisins (optional)	2 tbsp
Lime juice	½ tbsp
Water	3 ½ cups
Salt and red chilli powder	to taste

Method

1. Wash and soak rice for 25/30 minutes.
2. Heat a pressure cooker and roast methi leaves for 4-5 minutes on medium flame.
3. Add chopped Tomatoes and cook for a while.
4. Add Turmeric and red chilli powder and cook for a minute
5. Add water, lime juice and salt.
6. Bring the prepared mixture to a boil and add rice.
7. Pressure cook for 3 whistles and serve hot.

Fenugreek: Has antidiabetic powers. Helps control blood sugar and insulin. Also antidiarrhoeal, antiulcer, anticancer, tends to lower blood pressure, helps prevent intestinal gas.

Nutritive Information

CALORIES: **252 Cal**   PROTEIN: **14.05 gm**   FAT: **1.7 gm**
CARBOHYDRATE: **43.2 gm**   FIBRE: **5.5 gm**

24 Mixed Pulao

Ingredients

Rice	500 gms
Poppy seeds (Khus khus)	2 tsp
Cinnamon	2-3 pieces
Cloves	2-3
Cardamom	1
Cumin seeds	1 tsp
Peppercorns	5
Bay leaf	1
Dry red chillis	8 to 10
Onions	3 (sliced lengthwise)
Green peas	100 gms
Kabuli chana (soaked)	100 gms
Jalapeno	50 gms (sliced long)
Vegetables (beans, carrots, capsicum, cauliflower)	400 gms

Method

1. Wash rice and vegetables separately.
2. Grind in a blender poppy and cumin seeds, cinnamon, cloves, cardamom, red chillis, $3/4$ of sliced onions and peppercorns.
3. Heat a cooker and roast bay leaf. Add rest of the onions and sauté till light brown.
4. You may add a few pieces of cloves and cinnamon.
5. Then add vegetables and rice and cook for 2 minutes.
6. Add ground paste and salt to taste.

7. Put 5 glasses of water and pressure cook for 4-5 whistles. After the cooker cools, open the lid and mix with a big spoon.

Rice: *Anti diarrhoeal, anti cancer activity. Like other seeds, contains anticancer protease inhibitors of all grains and cereals, it is least likely to provoke intestinal gas or adverse reactions.*

Nutritive Information
CALORIES: **250 Cal**   PROTEIN: **11.67 gm**   FAT: **2.24 gm**
CARBOHYDRATE: **55.5 gm**   FIBRE: **3.79 gm**

25 Mint Rice

Ingredients

Boiled rice	250 gms
Mint leaves (pudina)	250 gms
Coriander leaves	100 gms
Onion	1
Green chillis	3-4
Cinnamon	2-cm piece
Cloves	3
Curry leaves	2-3
Cumin seeds	½ tsp
Pepper	to taste
Salt	to taste

Method

1. Roast half the quantity of onion, green chillis and curry leaves and keep aside.
2. Add mint leaves and Coriander leaves, cinnamon, cloves and make a fine paste in the mixie.
3. Take a pan, add cumin seeds, and balance onions and the paste into it.
4. Sauté them well.
5. Add cooked rice and salt and pepper to taste.

Mint: Mint is a fragrant, dark coloured green, delicate, thin herb. It is anti-flatulent, anti-spasmodic, muscle relaxant, stimulant that promotes health. It also dissolves gravel in bladder and kidneys, helps the liver to function normally and improves appetite.

Nutritive Information

CALORIES: **178 Cal** PROTEIN: **7.4 gm** FAT: **1.25 gm**
CARBOHYDRATE: **31.6 gm** FIBRE: **2.3 gm**

26 Mushroom Pulao

Ingredients

Mushrooms	200 gms (sliced lengthwise)
Garlic	4 cloves (chopped)
Rice	750 gms (washed and soaked)
Water	2 cups
Spring onions	5 (chopped with greens)
Salt and pepper	to taste
Skimmed milk	100 gms

Method

1. Heat a large flat-bottomed microwave dish at 100% power for 2 minutes.
2. Add garlic and onions and cook at the same power for 2 minutes.
3. Add mushrooms, stir and cook covered at 100% power for 4 minutes.
4. Add salt, pepper, milk and rice with water in which it has been soaked. Microwave uncovered at 100% power for 15 minutes.
5. Reduce the power to 60% and cook covered for 5 minutes.
6. Stand for 5 minutes before serving.

Mushrooms: Mushrooms are edible fungi, which grow in moist places. Because of their flavour and fibre, they are sometimes used in vegetarian meals as substitutes for meat though they have little digestible protein.

Nutritive Information

CALORIES: **236 Cal** PROTEIN: **9.4 gm** FAT: **2.2 gm**
CARBOHYDRATE: **39.2 gm** FIBRE: **1.6 gm**

27 Green Pulao

Ingredients

Basmati rice	250 gms
Cauliflower (florets)	250 gms
Green peas	150 gms
Potatoes	200 gms (thinly sliced)
Cinnamon	2 sticks
Cloves	4-5
Peppercorns	7-8
Bay leaves	2-3
Green cardamoms	2
Onions	2 (thinly sliced)
Green chillis	2 (thinly sliced)
Paste of green coriander leaves	2 tbsp
Green chillis and ginger paste	1 tbsp
Salt	to taste
Garam masala powder	to taste

Method

1. Heat a pan and roast bay leaves, cloves, cinnamon, black pepper for $1/_2$ a minute on medium heat.
2. Add thinly sliced onions, green chillis and sauté till pink. Keep this aside.
3. Sauté all the vegetables for 4-5 minutes. This adds taste to the pulao.
4. Add paste of coriander leaves, green chilli and ginger to it.
5. Add the sautéd onions, garam masala and salt. Stir and then sauté it for 5 minutes.

6. Add washed rice and water (slightly more than 2 cups). Cook on medium heat. Stir rice once while it is getting cooked

Rice: *It is used as a staple cereal by majority of people in India. It is of special value in cases where there is irritation of the tissues of the mouth, oesophagus or stomach and in acute disorders of the kidney.*

Nutritive Information

CALORIES: **253 Cal**   PROTEIN: **20 gm**   FAT: **3.2 gm**
CARBOHYDRATE: **50.9 gm**   FIBRE: **8.2 gm**

28 Hara Bhara Pulao

Ingredients

Mushrooms	10 to 12
Ginger-garlic paste	1 tbsp
Potatoes	2-3 (boiled)
Parboiled rice	400 gms
Onion	1 large (minced)
Spinach, coriander, mint, fenugreek	1 bunch each
Curd (skimmed milk)	250 gms
Salt	to taste
Coriander powder	1 tbsp
Cumin seed powder	1 tbsp
Garam masala powder	2 tsp
Turmeric powder	1 tsp
Red chilli powder	1 tsp
Cardamoms	4
Cinnamon	5-cm piece
Cloves	4

Method

1. Wash and cut mushrooms in halves. Cut the potatoes into cubes and roast. Clean, wash and finely chop the greens. Heat a pan and roast whole spices along with the onion till onion turns golden brown.
3. Add the finely chopped greens, ginger-garlic paste and sauté till dry.
4. Add curd and cook.
5. Put the mushrooms, potatoes, salt and mix well.

6. Add all the masala powders and mix well. Cover and cook on low heat for 10 minutes.
7. Put the parboiled rice on top, dampen a muslin cloth, place over pan and cover and cook for 20 to 25 minutes on low flame.
8. Serve hot with raita of your choice.

Potatoes: *They are considered the most important food product of the human race. They contain very digestive starch and offer rich variety of minerals. Raw potatoes are an excellent source of vitamin C and fair source of vitamin B.*

Nutritive Information

CALORIES: **265 Cal**   PROTEIN: **8.7 gm**   FAT: **2.1 gm**
CARBOHYDRATE: **49.3 gm**   FIBRE: **1.6 gm**

29 Chick Pea Pulao

Ingredients

Rice	250 gms
Water	2 cups
Chick peas (Kabuli chana)	250 gms (boiled)
Onion	1 (chopped)
Garam masala	½ tsp
Turmeric powder	¼ tsp
Salt	to taste

Method

1. Soak rice for 20-25 minutes.
2. Heat a pan, put onion and sauté for 3-4 minutes till light brown in colour. Use water when required.
3. Add the rest of the ingredients and cook for another 2-3 minutes. Add this prepared mixture to rice along with water and cook till rice is done.

Salt: Different varieties of salt are found like (i) Sendha Namak (ii) White Namak (iii) Kala Namak (iv) Alkaline Namak (v) Sambhara Namak. Besides being an edible item, its uses are varied like used in making detergents, chemicals and pesticides.

Nutritive Information

CALORIES: **243 Cal**   PROTEIN: **10.4 gm**   FAT: **0.7 gm**
CARBOHYDRATE: **46.5 gm**   FIBRE: **4.8 gm**

30 Pongal Rice

Ingredients

Rice	250 gms
Water	2 cups
Salt	to taste
Cumin seeds	1 tsp
Peppercorns	3-4
Curry leaves	8-10
Green chillis	5
Ginger	1 tsp (chopped)
Asafoetida	a pinch
Gram dal (chana dal)	100 gms

Method

1. Clean and wash rice properly. Soak it for 20-25 minutes.
2. Then cook rice with gram dal till tender.
3. Heat a saucepan and put asafoetida till it gives a crackling sound. Then add rest of the ingredients and cook for another few minutes.
4. Now pour the prepared mixture of seasonings over the rice along with salt. Serve hot.

Chillis: *Chillis are richer in vitamin-C than citrus fruits, but are unlikely to contribute much to the daily intake as they are usually eaten only in small amounts. They may also help to relieve congestion.*

Nutritive Information

CALORIES: **286 Cal**   PROTEIN: **12.4 gm**   FAT: **3.3 gm**
CARBOHYDRATE: **49.5 gm**   FIBRE: **0.8 gm**

31 Vegetable Khichdi

Ingredients

Rice	250 gms
Water	2 cups
Cauliflower florets	4 (boiled)
Capsicums	2 (chopped and dry roasted)
Potatoes	2 (chopped and boiled)
French beans	100 gms (boiled and cut)
Carrots	2 (boiled and chopped)
Peas	100 gms (boiled)
Turmeric powder	½ tsp
Ginger	½ tsp (chopped)
Chilli powder	½ tsp
Garam masala	½ tsp
Salt	to taste

Method

1. Clean and wash rice. Soak in water for 20-25 minutes.
2. Heat saucepan, add ginger and sauté for a while. Add rice and roast a little.
3. To this add all the vegetables and ingredients. Put water and cook till rice is done. Serve hot.

Cauliflower: *A member of the famous cruciferous family, it contains many of the cancer fighting and hormone regulating compounds.*

Nutritive Information

CALORIES: **299.6 Cal**   PROTEIN: **15.1 gm**   FAT: **2.25 gm**
CARBOHYDRATE: **58.3 gm**   FIBRE: **6.85 gm**

32 Tomato and Pineapple Rice

Ingredients

Rice	100 gms
Water	1 cup
Ginger	¼ tsp (crushed)
Garlic	¼ tsp (chopped fine)
Red chilli sauce	½ tsp
Tomatoes	50 gms (chopped)
Pineapple	50 gms (chopped)
Salt	to taste

Method

1. Clean and wash rice. Soak it in water for 20 minutes. Drain and boil rice till tender. Then cool.
2. Heat a saucepan, add ginger and garlic. Cook for 2 minutes. Add tomatoes and chilli sauce. Cook for another few minutes till tomatoes turn into purée. Use water if required.
3. Now add salt and pineapple. Mix in the boiled rice and stir well for a few minutes.
4. When mixed well serve hot.

Pineapple: Traditional folk medicine credits the sweet, juicy flesh of the pineapple with various healing powers, with some apparent justification. The fruit is a useful source of vitamin C but other than this it provides little vitamins and minerals.

Nutritive Information

CALORIES: **116.5 Cal**   PROTEIN: **2.35 gm**   FAT: **0.58 gm**
CARBOHYDRATE: **13.1 gm**   FIBRE: **0.53 gm**

33 Hara and Safed Rice

Ingredients

Peas	125 gms (frozen)
Coriander leaves	2 tbsp (chopped)
Green chillis	2
Salt	to taste
Rice	½ cup
Water	1 cup
Garam masala	¼ tsp

Method

1. Clean, wash and soak rice for 20 minutes.
2. Mash the peas and make a paste along with green chillis and coriander. Use a mixer for this.
3. Now mix in salt and garam masala.
4. Heat a pan, put in pea paste and cook for a few minutes.
5. Mix rice in it and cook for another few minutes.
6. Add water and stir to mix well. Cover and cook till rice is tender.

Peas : *Green peas contain considerable amount of sugar. Both proteins and carbohydrates are much less.*

Nutritive Information

CALORIES: **267.5 Cal** PROTEIN: **11.33 gm** FAT: **0.4 gm**
CARBOHYDRATE: **54.6 gm** FIBRE: **4 gm**

34 Methi Flavoured Rice

Ingredients

Rice	100 gms
Water	1 cup
Chilli powder	¼ tsp
Fenugreek leaves (methi) chopped finely)	100 gms (washed and
Salt	to taste

Method

1. Clean and wash rice. Soak in water for 20 minutes.
2. Heat a pan, add rice and cook for a few minutes.
3. Add fenugreek leaves, chilli powder and water.
4. Cover and cook till rice is done.

Fenugreek leaves: *Being rich in iron, fenugreek leaves are useful in anaemic conditions. Its leaves have a cooling effect.*

Nutritive Information

CALORIES: **124.5 Cal**   PROTEIN: **4.4 gm**   FAT: **1.05 gm**
CARBOHYDRATE: **21.5 gm**   FIBRE: **0.55 gm**

35 Makai Bhaat

Ingredients

Rice	100 gms
Water	1 cup
Corn (makkai)	50 gms (precooked)
Turmeric powder	¼ tsp
Chilli powder	¼ tsp
Garam masala	¼ tsp
Salt	to taste
Coriander leaves	for garnishing (chopped)

Method

1. Clean and wash rice properly. Soak it in water for 20 minutes.
2. Heat a pan, add rice and corn. Cook for 2-3 minutes.
3. Add water, turmeric and chilli powders, garam masala and salt.
4. Cover and cook till rice is done. Garnish with chopped coriander leaves.
5. Serve with green or tomato chutney.

Corn: *Anti cancer and anti viral activity. Rich source of vitamin A and energy dense foodstuff.*

Nutritive Information

CALORIES: **184.5 Cal**   PROTEIN: **9.75 gm**   FAT: **2.1 gm**
CARBOHYDRATE: **71.8 gm**   FIBRE: **1.35 gm**

36 Flavoured Rice

Ingredients

Rice	50 gms
Water	½ cup
Cloves	1 or 2
Bay leaves	2
Peppercorns	3-4
Cinnamon	2-3 (1" sticks)
Cumin seeds	¼ tsp
Salt	to taste
Garam masala	¼ tsp

Method

1. Soak cleaned and washed rice in water for 20 minutes.
2. Heat a pan. Put cumin seeds and cook till they become dark brown. Pour water and let it boil.
3. Tie cloves, bay leaves, peppercorns and cinnamon in a muslin cloth.
4. Put tied seasoning, rice and garam masala to the boiling water. Cook till rice is done.
5. Serve hot.

Cinnamon: *Cinnamon is used as a condiment and stimulates decongestion. It is also used as an application for toothache and warts.*

Nutritive Information

CALORIES: **174.5 Cal**   PROTEIN: **4.25 gm**   FAT: **0.3 gm**
CARBOHYDRATE: **38.5 gm**   FIBRE: **1.25 gm**

37 Festive Rice Stuffing

Ingredients

Rice	1 ½ cups
Water	3 cups
Salt	¾ tsp
Onion	1 cup (diced)
Garlic	1 tsp (crushed)
Celery leaves	¼ cup (chopped)
Mushrooms	2 ½ cups (sliced)
Curry leaves	2 tbsp
Apple juice	¼ cup
Raisins	½ cup

Method

1. Rinse the rice and drain. Bring salt and water to boil in a medium saucepan. Stir in rice, cover and return to boil. Reduce heat to simmer and cook until all the liquid is absorbed and rice is tender. Transfer the cooked rice to a strainer and rinse quickly with cold water to stop cooking. Drain the rice thoroughly and then transfer to a mixing bowl.

2. Heat a pan and add onion. Cook till onion is soft, then add garlic, mushrooms, celery, and curry leaves. Continue to cook till mushrooms are soft, stirring frequently.

3. Stir in apple juice and cook just to blend. Add the mushroom mixture along with the raisins to the rice and stir to mix.

4. You can also use it as stuffing for capsicums, tomato or brinjal.

Nutritive Information

CALORIES: **213.3 Cal**   PROTEIN: **6.5 gm**   FAT: **0.3 gm**
CARBOHYDRATE: **44.43 gm**   FIBRE: **1.82 gm**

38 Vegetable and Dalia Pulao

Ingredients

Porridge (dalia)	1 cup
Water	2 cups
Mixed vegetables	1 cup (finely chopped) (peas, carrots, french beans, capsicum and cauliflower)
Green chillis	2 (slit lengthwise)
Cumin seeds (jeera)	$1/2$ tsp
Salt and pepper	to taste

Method

1. Semi-boil the vegetables. Drain and keep aside.
2. Heat a pan, add jeera and green chillis.
3. Put in mixed vegetables and cook slightly.
4. Add dalia and water.
5. Then add salt and pepper.
6. Cover with a lid.
7. When cooked serve hot with curd (skim milk).
8. Keep checking the way you check rice.

Dalia: It is made of broken wheat and since it is not refined it provides a lot of fibre which helps in removing constipation and also gives B-vitamins.

Nutritive Information

CALORIES: **198.7 Cal** PROTEIN: **7.6 gm** FAT: **1.7 gm**
CARBOHYDRATE: **39.89 gm** FIBRE: **2.2 gm**

39 Corn Roti

Ingredients

Wheat flour	100 gms
Corn (big) & Carrot	1-1 (shredded)
Cabbage	100 gms (shredded)
Boiled potato	1 (mashed)
Green chillis	3 (finely chopped)
Omum seeds (ajwain)	½ tsp
Red chilli powder	1 tsp
Salt	1 tsp
Coriander leaves	100 gms (chopped)
Garam masala	1 tsp
Mango powder (amchoor)	½ tsp

Method

1. Take wheat flour, add a little water and make a dough like you make for roti and add little salt to it.
2. Heat a pan. Keep the shredded corn in the pan and stir it constantly so that it does not stick to the pan. Do it till it gets cooked.
3. Cool the corn.
4. Mix all the above ingredients and the corn except the dough.
5. Take a dough ball. Make a thick roti. Stuff it with the corn mixture.
6. Then cook it like a normal roti on both sides and serve hot with curd (skimmed milk).

Carrots: A good source of beta-carotene, a powerful anti-cancer, artery protecting, immune boosting, infection fighting, anti-oxidant with wide protective powers.

Nutritive Information

CALORIES: **263.25 Cal**   PROTEIN: **14.8 gm**   FAT: **2.9 gm**
CARBOHYDRATE: **56.5 gm**   FIBRE: **6.4 gm**

40 Dahiwale Aloo ki Subzi aur Urad Dal Roti

Ingredients

For dahiwale aloo ki subzi

Baby potatoes	600 gms (peeled)
Cumin seeds (jeera)	1/2 tsp
Mustard seeds (sarson)	1/2 tsp
Onion seeds (kalonji)	1/2 tsp
Fennel seeds (saunf)	1/2 tsp
Asafoetida (hing)	1/4 tsp
Bay leaves	2
Cloves	3
Cinnamon sticks	2
Curry leaves	3 to 4
Green chilli	1 (slit)
Red chilli powder	2 tsp
Coriander-cumin powder (dhania-jeera)	1 ½ tsp
Turmeric powder (haldi)	½ tsp
Curd (skimmed milk)	250 gms (beaten)
Salt	to taste
Coriander leaves	2 tbsp (chopped)

Method

1. Heat a pan and add cumin, mustard, onion and fennel seeds and asafoetida. When the seeds crackle, add bay leaves, cloves, cinnamon, curry leaves and green chilli and sauté for a few seconds.

2. Add potatoes, chilli, coriander-cumin and turmeric powders and salt and sauté till the masala coats the potatoes evenly.
3. Add ½ cup of water and bring to a boil.
4. Add curd and bring to a boil while stirring continuously so that the gravy does not split. Simmer on low heat till the potatoes are cooked.
5. Garnish with coriander leaves.

Ingredients

For the urad dal roti

Split black lentils (dhuli urad dal)	100 gms
Onion seeds (kalonji)	1 tsp
Asafoetida (hing)	½ tsp
Whole wheat flour	250 gms
Salt	to taste

Method

1. Clean, wash and soak the urad dal for 2 to 3 hours. Drain completely.
2. Purée the dal in a mixer using ¼ cup of water to make a fine paste.
3. Combine onion seeds, asafoetida, wheat flour and salt and knead into a soft dough.
4. Cover the dough with a wet muslin cloth and allow to rest for 10 minutes.
5. Divide the dough into 12 equal portions and roll out each portion into a circle of 75 mm (3") diameter.
6. Prepare the rotis by cooking on both sides.
7. Serve hot with dahiwale aloo ki subzi.
8. A complete, balanced and nutritious meal that contains a combination of both lentils and milk protein.

Nutritive Information

CALORIES: **311.26 Cal** PROTEIN: **17.15 gm** FAT: **3.3 gm**
CARBOHYDRATE: **32 gm** FIBRE: **3.2 gm**

41 Green Pea Roti

Ingredients

For the stuffing

Green peas	500 gms (boiled)
Green chillis	5 (finely chopped)
Cumin seeds (jeera)	1 tsp
Salt	to taste

For the dough

Whole wheat flour (atta)	750 gms
Salt	$1/4$ tsp

For the stuffing

1. Mash the boiled green peas.
2. Roast the cumin seeds.
3. Add the green chillis, sauté for 1 minute and then add the mashed peas and salt.
4. Cook for 1 minute and cool the mixture.

For the dough

1. Sieve the flour with salt.
2. Knead very well and divide into 10 to 12 portions.

Method

1. Take a small portion of the dough, flatten a little and put 1 tbsp of the green peas mixture in the centre. Cover the mixture by drawing up the edges towards the centre. Press on a floured board and roll out into a round.
2. Put the roti on a hot tava, cook for a minute or two and turn once.
3. Repeat for the rest of the dough likewise.

4. Serve hot.

Green chillis are pungent and hot. They are useful as decongestant and digestive. They strengthen the blood clot dissolving system.

Nutritive Information

CALORIES: 178.25 Cal   PROTEIN: 13.25 gm   FAT: 1.8 gm
CARBOHYDRATE: 33.3 gm   FIBRE: 5.9 gm

42 Onion Rice

Ingredients

Rice	500 gms (boiled)
Onions	2
Green chilli	1
Mustard seeds (sarson)	1/4 tsp
Asafoetida powder (hing)	1/4 tsp
Pepper	1/4 tsp
Turmeric powder	little
Curry leaves	few
Salt	to taste
Coriander leaves (dhania)	1 tbsp (chopped)

Method

1. Heat a karahi and put in mustard seeds. After they crackle, put in green chilli.
2. Add the onions and sauté them.
3. Now add asafoetida and turmeric powders, pepper, curry leaves and salt.
4. Add the cooked rice and mix well.
5. Garnish with dhania leaves.

Onion: Thins blood, lowers cholesterol, raises good type HDL cholesterol, wards off blood clots, fights asthma, chronic bronchitis, hay fever, diabetes, and infections.

Nutritive Information

CALORIES: **185.25 Cal**   PROTEIN: **8.05 gm**   FAT: **2.2 gm**
CARBOHYDRATE: **26.9 gm**   FIBRE: **19.2 gm**

43 Rice Roti

Ingredients

Rice	500 gms (boiled)
Wheat flour (atta)	500 gms
Chilli powder	½ tsp
Mango powder	½ tsp
Coriander leaves	1 tbsp (chopped)
Salt	to taste

Method

1. You can also use leftover rice for the recipe.
2. Mix all the ingredients and prepare dough as for parathas.
3. Roll out rotis and roast on a tawa.
4. Serve hot with curd (skimmed milk).

Coriander leaves: *The leaves of coriander strengthen the stomach and promote its digestive action. Also reduces fever.*

Nutritive Information

CALORIES: **125 Cal**   PROTEIN: **2.6 gm**   FAT: **0.55 gm**
CARBOHYDRATE: **24 gm**   FIBRE: **0.5 gm**

44 Akki Roti

Ingredients

Rice flour (akki)	100 gms
Onion	½ (chopped fine)
Sprigs of cilantro (herb)	3-4
Green chilli	1 (minced)
Salt	to taste

Method

1. Mix all the ingredients by adding a little water to make a thick enough mixture to hold in your hands.
2. Heat a tawa or griddle and flatten half of this mixture on it.
3. Cover with a lid and cook on medium flame. Reverse side after 3-4 minutes.
4. Remove when done.
5. Repeat this with the remaining mixture.

Onion: *Onion is a source of energy and acts as a stimulant, increases vigour and vitality, acts as an expectorant and diuretic, slows the heartbeat, prevents flatulence and dyspepsia.*

Nutritive Information

CALORIES: **198 Cal**   PROTEIN: **3.65 gm**   FAT: **1.05 gm**
CARBOHYDRATE: **43.85 gm**   FIBRE: **0.9 gm**

45 Soya Mince Chatpatti Chapati

Ingredients

For the samosa chapati

Flour (maida)	200 gms
Salt	to taste

For filling

Soya mince	150 gms
Onion	1 (chopped)
Capsicum	1 (chopped)
Tomato	1 (chopped)
Coriander leaves	100 gms (chopped)
Peas	100 gms (boiled and minced)
Chilli, garlic and ginger paste	to taste
Cottage cheese (paneer)	250 gms (grated)
Salt and pepper	to taste

For outer covering

Plain flour	750 gms
Salt	to taste

Method

1. Prepare a dough for samosa chapati by mixing flour, salt and water and make samosa chapatis.
2. Boil soya mince and rinse thoroughly. Add all the remaining ingredients for filling and keep aside.
3. Prepare a stiff dough by mixing the ingredients for the outer covering. Divide into 10 portions.

4. Roll out one portion into an extremely thin chapati.
5. Place a samosa chapati on the the big chapati, spread 3 tbsp of filling on top and fold chapati from all sides into a rectangle, enveloping the filling.
6. Bake chapati for 20 minutes, until golden and crisp. Make the rest in the same way.
7. Serve with salad, red chilli and tamarind chutneys.

Capsicum: Capsicum has the remarkable effect of being a powerful stimulant.

Nutritive Information
CALORIES: **269 Cal** PROTEIN: **12.25 gm** FAT: **1.65 gm**
CARBOHYDRATE: **50.05 gm** FIBRE: **4.7 gm**

46 Spicy Delicious Pulao

Ingredients

Basmati rice	250 gms
Cottage cheese (paneer)	50 gms (skimmed milk)
Onions	2 (slit lengthwise)
Tomatoes	2
Peas	250 gms
Potatoes	1 (boiled and cubed)
Cauliflower	50 gms (boiled)
Mushrooms	250 gms
Mint leaves	a few
Bay leaf	1
Cardamoms	2
Cinnamon sticks	2
Cloves	2
Aniseed (saunf)	½ tsp
Salt	to taste

Make into a paste

Ginger	1 2-cm piece
Garlic cloves	4-5
Green chillis	9-10

Method

1. Wash the mushrooms well. Cut them sidewise and sauté them well till they are reduced to ½ the size and keep aside.

2. Cut the cheese into small cubes and sauté them till they turn golden brown in colour and keep aside. Just sauté the mint leaves and keep aside.

3. Cut the tomatoes into small pieces.
4. Heat the pressure cooker and add aniseed, bay leaf, cardamoms, cinnamon and cloves and sauté till they turn golden brown in colour.
5. Add the ginger, garlic and green chilli paste and sauté till the raw smell goes.
6. Then add the slit onions and sauté till they turn light pink in colour.
7. Add tomatoes and sauté well. Later add the potatoes, peas, cauliflower cut into florets and salt. Mix well.
8. Add rice and enough water to cook it in a pressure cooker till well cooked.
9. Finally add the mint leaves, sautéd cottage cheese and mushrooms to the cooked rice. Mix well.
10. Serve hot with raita of your choice.

Aniseed: *The leaves of the plant are useful in relieving gas. They strenghthen the stomach and promote its action.*

Nutritive Information
CALORIES: **376.8 Cal**   PROTEIN: **19.95 gm** FAT: **1.63 gm**
CARBOHYDRATE: **71.73 gm**   FIBRE: **6.3 gm**

47 Ragi Roti with Potato

Ingredients

Ragi flour	150 gms
Green chillis	4-5 (finely chopped)
Potatoes	2 (boiled and mashed)
Coriander leaves	a small bunch, (finely chopped)
Onions	2 (finely chopped)
Cumin seeds (jeera)	2 tbsp
Salt	as per taste

Method

1. Mix all the ingredients and add water, if necessary; to make a firm dough.
2. Heat a tava.
3. Take some dough (about the size of an orange fruit) and nicely spread it in the shape of a roti with your fingers.
4. Now transfer it onto the tava and cook well on both sides.
5. Serve hot with coriander chutney.

Ragi: It is an easily digestible food. High in calcium content. Iodine in ragi is good for diabetics probably because of the slow digestion thereby slow rate of release of glucose.

Nutritive Information

CALORIES: **311 Cal** PROTEIN: **6.45 gm** FAT: **1.5 gm**
CARBOHYDRATE: **69.7 gm** FIBRE: **4.6 gm**

48 Potato Vegetable with Puri

Ingredients
For potato vegetable

Potatoes	5-6 (boiled)
Turmeric powder (haldi)	½ tsp
Salt	1 tsp
Sugar	1 tsp
Lemon juice	1 tsp

For puri

Wheat flour	500 gms
Semolina (rava)	50 gms
Salt	1½ tsp

For seasoning

Green chillis	2-3 (chopped)
Ginger piece	¼" (chopped)
Garlic cloves (lasun)	2
Mustard seeds	¼ tsp
Cumin seeds (jeera)	¼ tsp
Asafoetida (hing)	a pinch
Curry leaves	7-8

For garnishing

Coriander leaves	1 tbsp (chopped)

Method
For potato vegetable
1. Peel boiled potatoes and cut them in small pieces.

2. Crackle cumin and mustard seeds, chopped ginger and crushed garlic in a karahi.
3. On crackling of mustard seeds, add chopped green chillis, asafoetida and curry leaves.
4. Add the boiled potatoes. Stir well.
5. Stir in turmeric powder, salt, sugar and lemon juice and cook for a few minutes.
6. Finally add chopped coriander. Mix thoroughly and let it cook for a couple of minutes more.

For puri
1. Sieve flour with salt and semolina.
2. Knead the dough hard with water. Cover it with a wet cloth and keep aside for ½-1 hour.
3. Before making the puri, knead the dough well and divide it into small balls.
4. Flatten each ball and roll it thick with a rolling pin to approximately 5-cm diameter.
5. Steam the rolled puris in a big idli maker for 10 minutes.
6. Bake at 200° C for 10 minutes.
7. Serve hot with potato vegetable.

Ginger: Has anti-depressant, anti-diarrhoeal and strong anti-oxidant activity, ranks very high in anti-cancer activity.

Nutritive Information

CALORIES: **356 Cal**   PROTEIN: **12.85 gm** FAT: **3.2 gm**
CARBOHYDRATE: **77.4 gm** FIBRE: **2.4 gm**

49 Baked Puri

Ingredients

Whole wheat flour	100 gms
Salt	¼ tsp

Method

1. Mix flour and salt. Add water and prepare a stiff dough. Knead well.
2. Divide the dough into 25 portions.
3. Roll out into thin puris and prick with a fork.
4. Steam the puris for 10 minutes.
5. Arrange the puris on a baking tray.
6. Bake in a hot oven at 200° C for 10 minutes.

Wheat flour: *Good source of B-complex and fibre.*

Nutritive Information

CALORIES: **170.5 Cal**   PROTEIN: **6.05 gm**   FAT: **0.85 gm**
CARBOHYDRATE: **34.7 gm**   FIBRE: **0.95 gm**

50 Masala Puri

Ingredients

Whole wheat flour	100 gms
Coarsely powdered cumin seeds	½ tsp
Coarsely powdered peppercorns	½ tsp
Turmeric powder (optional)	¼ tsp
Salt	¼ tsp

Method

1. Mix all the ingredients. Add water and prepare a stiff dough. Knead well.
2. Divide the dough into 25 portions.
3. Roll out into thin puris and prick with a fork.
4. Steam the puris for 10 minutes.
5. Or arrange the puris on a baking tray and bake in a hot oven at 200^0 C for 10 minutes.

Pepper: *Pepper is a good stimulant and most commonly used during cough and cold.*

Nutritive Information

CALORIES: **174 Cal**   PROTEIN: **5.5 gm**   FAT: **0.45 gm**
CARBOHYDRATE: **36.95 gm**   FIBRE: **0.15 gm**

51 Methi-Papad Subzi with Khakhra

Ingredients

For subzi

Papad	12
Fenugreek seeds (methi)	250 gms
Cumin seeds	1 tsp
Tomatoes	2 (chopped)
Curd (skimmed milk)	100 gms
Ginger & green chillis	2 tsp (crushed)
Coriander leaves	100 gms (chopped)
Salt	to taste
Red chilli powder	to taste
Turmeric powder	to taste
Coriander and cumin powders	to taste

For khakhra

Wheat sprouts	250 gms
Bean sprouts (moong)	250 gms
Curd (skimmed milk)	50 gms
Gram flour (besan)	2 tbsp
Cumin seeds	1 tsp
Salt	to taste

Method

For Subzi

1. Wash and soak the fenugreek seeds in water for 1-2 hours.

2. Cut the papads into pieces.
3. Crackle the cumin seeds.
4. Add fenugreek seeds and sauté for 2 minutes, then add tomatoes, ginger-chillis, curd, turmeric and mix well.
5. When the water gets absorbed then add red chili powder, coriander and cumin powders, ½ cup water, papad pieces and salt.
6. Cook for 5 minutes.
7. Garnish with coriander leaves. Serve hot.

For khakhra

1. Grind sprouted wheat and beans in a mixer and make a fine paste.
2. Add gram flour, curd and salt and make a soft dough.
3. Roll out the dough and make a thin roti (khakhra).
4. Roast on a non-stick tava on slow flame until khakhra becomes crispy.
5. Serve with methi-papad sabzi.

Gram flour: *It is a good anti-diabetic legume flour. It is energy dense and good source of protein.*

Nutritive Information

CALORIES: **274.5 Cal**   PROTEIN: **14.65 gm**   FAT: **2.125 gm**
CARBOHYDRATE: **47.5 gm**   FIBRE: **6.9 gm**

Dals

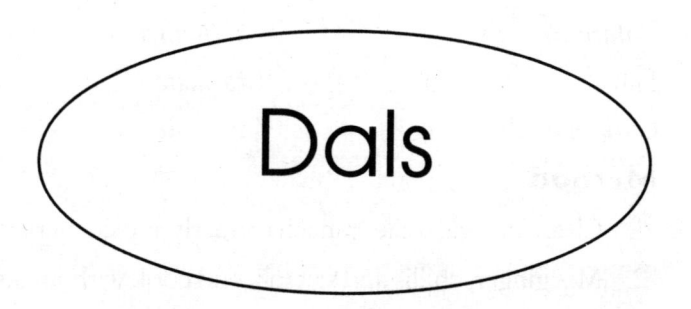

52 Dal-Palak

Ingredients

Spinach (pàlak)	1 bunch
Green gram (moong dal)	100 gms
Green chillis	2 (finely chopped)
Ginger	2-cm piece
Turmeric powder	½ tsp
Garam masala	¼ tsp
Tomato	1 or 2
Potato	1 (boiled)
Salt	to taste
Chilli powder	to taste

Method

1. Clean and wash the spinach properly and cut very finely.
2. Mix ginger, chillis and salt in it and cook without adding water.
3. Remove from flame and keep it warm.
4. Wash the dal thoroughly and cook in the soaked water adding salt, turmeric and chilli powder and garam masala till it turns dry.
5. Now take a bowl and cover the bottom of the bowl with spinach. Then place the dal over the spinach evenly.
6. Garnish with tomato and boiled potato.

Dal-palak is a very nutritious recipe as it contains both pulse and vegetable combination. Dals are known for their rich protein content whereas green leafy vegetables are good sources of vitamins and minerals.

Nutritive Information

CALORIES: **230 Cal** PROTEIN: **10.5 gm** FAT: **1.3 gm**
CARBOHYDRATE: **44.1 gm** FIBRE: **1.9 gm**

53 Dal Chana

Ingredients

Bengal gram (chana dal)	250 gms
Water	6 cups
Salt	2 tsp
Turmeric powder	1 tsp
Garam masala	1 tsp
Onions	2 medium (chopped)
Fenugreek seeds	2 tsp
Ginger	3-cm piece (chopped fine)
Chilli powder	1 tsp

Method

1. Wash the dal properly and soak it for 30 minutes.
2. Separate the water in which dal is soaked and bring this water to boil in a saucepan.
3. Add dal along with salt, turmeric and chilli powders. Bring it to a boil and cook on low flame till the dal is tender.
4. Mix it well with a thick spoon without allowing the dal to get mashed.
5. In a pan, sauté onions and ginger without the use of oil by sprinkling water when required. Add fenugreek seeds and garam masala just before taking it off the flame.
6. Add this mixture to dal and serve either with chapati or rice.

Chana dal: *It is a wholesome diet to which some lemon juice may also be added to make up for the low concentration of abscorbic acid.*

Nutritive Information

CALORIES: **93 Cal**   PROTEIN: **5 gm**   FAT: **1.4 gm**
CARBOHYDRATE: **15 gm**   FIBRE: **0.3 gm**

54 Mixed Dal

Ingredients

(Lentil) (masoor dal)	125 gms
Green gram, (moong dal)	125 gms
Bengal gram (chana dal)	125 gms
Cumin seeds	1 tsp
Onion	1 (chopped)
Garlic cloves	5 (sliced)
Turmeric powder	1 tsp
Chilli powder	1 tsp
Ginger	2-cm piece (chopped)
Coriander leaves	few (chopped)
Garam masala	½ tsp
Salt	to taste

Method

1. Mix all the dals and rinse them.
2. Soak them in water overnight. Next day rinse, drain and cook with sufficient water in the pressure cooker for 20 minutes.
3. Now heat a pan. Add cumin seeds. When they get brown add onion, ginger, garlic, salt, turmeric and red chilli powders and sauté till golden brown using water when required.
4. Add this mixture to the prepared dal and stir.
5. Cook for 5-6 minutes on medium flame. Add garam masala and coriander leaves and serve hot

This recipe is a combination of variety of dals which makes it a good source of proteins.

Nutritive Information

CALORIES: **265.75 Cal**   PROTEIN: **17.25 gm**   FAT: **1.9 gm**
CARBOHYDRATE: **45 gm**   FIBRE: **0.6 gm**

55 Dal Urad

Ingredients

Black gram, whole (urad dal)	125 gms
Hot water	1 cup
Tomatoes	125 gms (sliced)
Onion	1 medium (chopped)
Turmeric & Red chilli powder	½-½ tsp
Garam masala	½ tsp
Fenugreek seeds	¼ tsp
Ginger	2-cm piece (chopped)
Salt	to taste
Coriander leaves	1 tbsp (chopped)

Method

1. Wash dal and allow it to soak for a while.
2. Heat saucepan, put onion, ginger, fenugreek seeds and sauté using water when required till light brown.
3. Add turmeric, salt and chilli powder.
4. Mix well and add sliced tomatoes. Keep on low flame for a few minutes and remove.
5. Put this mixture in drained dal. Keep stirring for 10 minutes and then pour in hot water. Bring it to boil and then let it simmer for 30-40 minutes.
6. Put garam masala. Serve hot garnished with coriander leaves.

Black gram dal is known for its hypoglycemic effect. But when eaten in excess produces flatulence.

Nutritive Information

CALORIES: **142 Cal**   PROTEIN: **7.4 gm**   FAT: **0.55 gm**
CARBOHYDRATE: **27 gm**   FIBRE: **1 gm**

56 Dal Amritsari

Ingredients

Black gram, washed (urad dal)	250 gms
Chick peas (kabuli chana)	75 gms
Kidney beans (rajma)	75 gms
Garlic paste	2 tbsp
Ginger paste	2 tbsp
Onions	100 gms (grated)
Tomatoes	100 gms (chopped)
Milk & Curd (skimmed milk)	1-1 cup
Turmeric & Red chilli powder	1 tsp
Salt	to taste

Method

1. Soak all the dals together overnight.
2. In a cooker, put 2 cups of water along with 1 cup of milk and cook the dals in it till tender.
3. Heat a pan, put in the onions and sauté for 5-6 minutes till golden in colour. Add tomatoes and cook for another 5 minutes. Add the spices and keep cooking.
4. Now add cooked dal and cook for a few more minutes on low flame.
5. Garnish with curd if needed.

This recipe is a combination of various dals which provide healthy nutrition. Dals are good sources of protein and proteins are good body builders.

Nutritive Information

CALORIES: **270 Cal** PROTEIN: **17.8 gm** FAT: **1.03 gm**
CARBOHYDRATE: **47.7 gm** FIBRE: **3.5 gm**

57 Hari Moong Dal Kadhi

Ingredients

Green gram dal	100 gms
Curd (skimmed milk)	100 gms
Gram flour (besan)	50 gms
Red chilli powder	¼ tsp
Coriander powder	¼ tsp
Mango powder (amchoor)	½ tsp
Asafoetida	a pinch
Turmeric powder	¼ tsp
Salt	to taste

Method

1. Pressure-cook the green gram for one whistle.
2. Grind it using the rolling pin.
3. Heat a pan and put in asafoetida and green gram and roast till light brown.
4. Beat curd and add besan to it and churn it vigorously to make a homogeneous mixture.
5. Now add turmeric and red chilli powders. Bring it to a boil and add roasted green gram mixture. Cook on low flame.
6. Add coriander and mango powders and cook for a few minutes. Serve hot.

Green gram: *It is a rich source of protein and phosphorus. It is known for its good digestibility.*

Nutritive Information

CALORIES: **296 Cal**   PROTEIN: **17.05 gm** FAT: **3.05 gm**
CARBOHYDRATE: **54.05 gm**   FIBRE: **2.15 gm**

58 Besan ki Kadhi

Ingredients

Gram flour (besan)	50 gms
Curd (skimmed milk)	250 gms
Green chillis	2
Onion	1 (finely chopped)
Cumin seeds	¼ tsp
Red chilli powder	½ tsp
Asafoetida	1 pinch
Turmeric powder	1 tsp
Coriander leaves	1 tbsp (chopped)
Salt	to taste

Method

1. Mix water with curd. Add gram flour and blend well.
2. Add turmeric powder and blend again.
3. Heat a pan, put in asafoetida and cumin seeds. After a few seconds add red chilli and turmeric powders, green chillis, onion and cook till onion is golden brown. Sprinkle water when required.
4. Now add gram flour mixture. Mix in salt. Bring to a boil and cook till kadhi thickens, stirring continuously.
5. Garnish with coriander leaves and serve hot.

Curd: Curd is a milk product and a good source of calcium.

Nutritive Information

CALORIES: **259 Cal** PROTEIN: **12.25 gm** FAT: **2.85 gm**
CARBOHYDRATE: **46.15 gm** FIBRE: **2.5 gm**

59 Moong Dal Kadhi

Ingredients

Washed green gram (moong dal)	250 gms
Curd (skimmed milk)	125 gms
Gram flour (besan)	1 tsp
Cumin seeds	½ tsp (ground)
Turmeric powder	½ tsp
Asafoetida	to taste
Red chillis (whole)	2
Coriander leaves	1 tbsp (chopped)
Salt	to taste

Method

1. Soak dal in water for about 4 hours. Grind finely.
2. Add asafoetida to the dal and churn it vigorously.
3. Heat a pan. Put in water and let it boil. When water is boiling take the thin mixture of the dal and pour it drop by drop taking it on the edge of your hand and let it drop gently on high boiling water.
4. Take the well-beaten curd in a big container and add double the quantity of water to it. Let it boil for about 15 minutes. Now add besan to it, stirring continuously.
5. When the mixture is boiling vigorously add the dal pieces to it. Boil again.
6. Heat a pan and add asafoetida, cumin seeds and red chillis. Put this in the kadri kadhi. Serve garnished with coriander leaves.

Moong dal kadhi is a good combination of proteins, minerals and vitamins.

Nutritive Information
CALORIES: **203 Cal**   PROTEIN: **8.5 gm**   FAT: **0.4 gm**
CARBOHYDRATE: **19.6 gm**   FIBRE: **0.2 gm**

60 Cabbage Sambhar

Ingredients

Pigeon peas (arhar dal)	100 gms
Cabbage	250 gms (grated)
Drumstick	1 (scraped and cut)
Peas	250 gms (shelled)
Red chillis	3
Mustard seeds	½ tsp
Turmeric powder	¼ tsp
Curry leaves	a few
Tamarind pulp	100 gms
Salt	to taste

Method

1. Cook dal in water with salt and turmeric powder.
2. Add all the other vegetables and tamarind pulp when dal is half cooked.
3. Cook till vegetables are done and remove from fire.
4. Dry roast mustard seeds, curry leaves and red chillis.
5. Put into prepared sambhar.

Cabbage sambar is a nutritious recipe with rare combination. It provides most of the vitamins and minerals.

Nutritive Information

CALORIES: **298 Cal**   PROTEIN: **21.7 gm**   FAT: **2.3 gm**
CARBOHYDRATE: **47.4 gm**   FIBRE: **6.3 gm**

61 Soya Rasam

Ingredients

Soya beans (soaked)	100 gms
Mustard & Cumin seeds	100-100 gms
Sugar	100 gms
Asafoetida (hing)	a pinch
Tomatoes	2 (chopped)
Green chillis	3
Tamarind paste & Rasam powder	1-1 tsp
Salt	to taste
Curry leaves	a few
Coriander leaves	1 tbsp

Method

1. Cook soya beans and blend in a blender.
2. Heat a pan. Crackle mustard seeds.
3. Add cumin, asafoetida and curry leaves.
4. Add cut tomatoes and 3 cups of water.
5. Put the blended soya beans and green chillis.
6. After the tomatoes are cooked add tamarind, salt and sugar.
7. Add rasam powder. Let it boil for 10 minutes.
8. Garnish and serve.

Soya bean: *The miracle golden bean considered as a king of pulses and vegetables. It is rich in calcium, phosphorus and lysine without which proteins are of little value to the human system.*

Nutritive Information

CALORIES: **226 Cal**   PROTEIN: **22 gm**   FAT: **9.85 gm**
CARBOHYDRATE: **12.25 gm**   FIBRE: **2.25 gm**

62 Plain Keerai

Ingredients

Greens (spinach and fenugreek)	2 bundles
Asafoetida (hing)	2 pinches
Mustard seeds	1 tsp
Cumin seeds (jeera)	1 tsp
Sugar	1 tsp
Red chillis	2 -3
Urad dal (washed)	2 tsp
Salt	to taste

Method

1. Cut the roots, take stems and leaves of greens and wash in water till mud is completely removed.
2. You can wash 3-4 times then put the greens in a vessel. Pour a tumbler of water and cover with a lid.
3. After it starts boiling put jeera, sugar, and salt.
4. Then mash the greens nicely or you can churn them in a mixie.
5. Heat karahi, crackle the mustard, red chillis, urad dal, asafoetida and pour it over the green mixture.
6. You can have it with sambar, rice, rasam etc

Asafoetida: It has antibiotic properties and inhibits the growth of microbes.

Nutritive Information

CALORIES: **75 Cal**   PROTEIN: **6.4 gm**   FAT: **1.6 gm**
CARBOHYDRATE: **89 gm**   FIBRE: **1.7 gm**

63 Ripe Mango Kadhi

Ingredients

Medium ripe mangoes	2
Medium onion	1 (chopped lengthwise)
Green chillis	2
Curry leaves	6-8
Coriander seeds	1 tsp
Cumin seeds	2 tsp
Turmeric powder	1 tsp
Red chilli powder	1 tsp
Salt	to taste
Coriander leaves	1 tbsp (finely chopped)

Method

1. Take mangoes, remove skins.
2. Extract juice as well as the seeds.
3. Heat a pan and put in coriander and cumin seeds, green chillis, curry leaves and sauté for 1 minute.
4. Then add onion and sauté for 2 minutes.
5. Add turmeric and red chilli powders, salt and mango juice.
6. Put $1^1/_2$ cups of water.
7. Cook covered for 10 minutes.
8. Garnish with finely chopped coriander leaves.

Mango is known as the king of fruits. It is a good source of beta-carotene which is an anti-oxidant.

Nutritive Information

CALORIES: **124 Cal** PROTEIN: **1.8 gm** FAT: **0.5 gm**
CARBOHYDRATE: **28 gm** FIBRE: **1.3 gm**

64 Tiranga Koumbo

Ingredients

Dry red chillis	5-6
Mustard seeds (sarson)	1 tbsp
Fenugreek seeds	1 tbsp
Asafoetida (hing)	a pinch
Bengal gram dal	2 tbsp
Urad dal	1 tbsp
Sambhar powder	2 tbsp
Curry leaves	a few
Extracted Tamarind water	500 gms
Jaggery	1 little
Salt	to taste

Method

1. Heat a pan, put hing, dry red chillis and then slowly add mustard and fenugreek seeds.
2. Let them splutter. Add Bengal gram and urad dals, curry leaves and sauté till golden brown on medium flame.
3. Add sambhar powder and quickly add tamarind water, jaggery and salt to it.
4. Let it boil till it becomes a little thick.

This recipe is a good appetiser. It is good for stomach and adds flavor to the food.

Nutritive Information

CALORIES: **71.9 Cal**   PROTEIN: **4.48 gm**   FAT: **0.7 gm**
CARBOHYDRATE: **11.94 gm**   FIBRE: **0.21 gm**

65 Dal Bahar

Ingredients

Onion	1 (chopped)
Green chillis	2 (chopped)
Tomato (large)	1 chopped
Ginger	2-cm (chopped)
Rajma	50 gms
Black gram (urad dal)	50 gms
Chana dal	50 gms
Red chilli powder	1 tsp
Salt	to taste

Method

1. Soak all the 3 dals in water for 4-5 hours.
2. Give 5-7 whistles to dals in a pressure cooker.
3. Heat a pan and add chopped onion and green chillis.
4. Add ginger and sauté for 1 minute.
5. Put in tomato, red chilli powder and boiled dals into the pan.
6. Add salt.

Onion: *They are mild acid neutralizers. They are rich in vitamin-C, good in B and fair in A. Raw onions are excellent natural digestive stimulants.*

Nutritive Information

CALORIES: **386.5 Cal**   PROTEIN: **18.3 gm**   FAT: **25.5 gm**
CARBOHYDRATE: **84.4 gm**   FIBRE: **3.65 gm**

66 Tridali Dal

Ingredients

Green moong dal (sabut)	250 gms
Red gram dal (arhar)	250 gms
Bengal gram dal (chana)	250 gms
Ripe tomatoes	3 medium
Ginger	1 tsp (grated)
Green chillis	1 tsp (chopped)
Cumin seeds	$1/2$ tsp
Turmeric powder (haldi)	$1/4$ tsp
Red chilli powder	$1/2$ tsp
Asafoetida (hing powder)	A pinch
Coriander powder	$1/2$ tsp
Coriander leaves	1 tbsp (chopped)
Water	3 cups
Salt	to taste

Method

1. Soak all the three dals in water for 2 hours.
2. Pressure-cook these for 3-4 whistles.
3. Soak the tomatoes in hot water, peel the skin and blend them to make a purée. Keep aside.
4. In a pan, roast the cumin seeds and let them turn a little brown.
5. Add asafoetida and immediately add the puréed tomatoes. Allow to cook for 5 minutes.
6. Now add the turmeric, red chilli and coriander powders, ginger, green chillis, water and salt and allow to cook for another 10 minutes.

7. Now add the pressure-cooked dals and mix well and let it cook for 10 minutes.
8. Sprinkle the chopped coriander on top and serve hot with home made chapatis.

Green chillis: They provide β-carotene and vitamin C in good amount

Nutritive Information

CALORIES: **287 Cal**   PROTEIN: **17.15 gm**   FAT: **2.6 gm**
CARBOHYDRATE: **48 gm**   FIBRE: **1.7 gm**

67 Yummy Dal

Ingredients

Tur dal	250 gms
Green gram dal	100 gms
Tomatoes	2 (chopped)
Green chilli	1 (slit)
Kokum pieces	4
Turmeric powder (haldi)	½ tsp
Cumin seeds (jeera)	½ tsp
Curry leaves	a few
Asafoetida (hing)	a pinch
Salt	to taste
Green coriander leaves	1 tbsp (chopped)

Method

1. Wash the dals and pressure cook with turmeric powder till soft.
2. Heat a pan and add asafoetida, chilli, cumin and curry leaves.
3. When they splutter, add the cooked dal and tomatoes.
4. Check the consistency and if too thick add some water.
5. Add salt to taste and the kokum.
6. Simmer on low heat for 5 minutes and turn off the gas.
7. Garnish with chopped coriander leaves.
8. Serve hot with rice.

Curry leaves: *possess the quality of a herbal tonic. They strenghen the functions of the stomach and promote its action. They are also used as a mild laxative.*

Nutritive Information

CALORIES: **270 Cal**   PROTEIN: **18.7 gm**   FAT: **1.25 gm**
CARBOHYDRATE: **46.2 gm**   FIBRE: **1.2 gm**

68 Dal Balls in Indian Gravy

Ingredients

For dal balls

Red gram dal	250 gms
Bengal gram dal (chana)	250 gms
Green chillis	4 (finely chopped)
Curry leaves	10-15, (chopped finely)
Ginger paste	1 tsp

For gravy

Tamarind	1 lemon-size ball
Asafoetida powder	$1/4$ tsp
Salt	to taste
Sambhar powder	2 tbsp
Turmeric powder	2 pinches

For seasoning

Mustard seeds	1 tsp
Cumin seeds	$1/2$ tsp
Fenugreek seeds	$1/4$ tsp

Method

For dal balls

1. Wash both the dals and pressure cook along with green chillis, curry leaves, ginger paste and a pinch of turmeric with just enough water. If water is more, you'll have difficulty in making the balls.
2. Once it is cooked well, mix the cooked ingredients.
3. Make gooseberry size of balls with the mixture. If you are having

difficulty in making the balls stay together, you can use some flour to bind.

For gravy

1. Soak the tamarind in hot water for a few minutes and make a pulp out of it, by squeezing it. This squeezing can be done 2-3 times to get the whole pulp out of the tamarind.
2. Now, add salt, sambhar powder and turmeric powder.
3. Boil for a few minutes and then put all the dal balls in the gravy.

For seasoning

1. Sprinkle roasted mustard seeds, cumin seeds and fenugreek seeds.

Pulses: *The pulses are considered 'poor man's meat' due to their low price. They are rich in protein, phosphorus and also in vitamin-B.*

Nutritive Information

CALORIES: **240.5 Cal**   PROTEIN: **59.6 gm**   FAT: **1.45 gm**
CARBOHYDRATE: **35.7 gm**   FIBRE: **3.8 gm**

69 Dal Tamarind Curry

Ingredients

Tamarind	2 tbsp
Turmeric powder	a pinch
Asafoetida (hing powder)	a pinch
Salt	to taste
Sambhar powder	1 tsp
Garam masala	1/2 tsp
Mixed dal (boiled)	500 gms
Green chilli	2-3 (finely chopped)
Mustard seeds	½ tsp
Cumin seeds	1/2 tsp
Fenugreek seeds	1/4 tsp

Method

For curry

1. Put the tamarind in a vessel and keep it for boiling. Add turmeric and asafoetida powders and salt and boil it. The pulp should not be very thick. If it is very thick, make it watery by adding some water, so that it can boil and become thick later on.
2. Let it boil for 5 minutes or till it is reasonably thick (it should not be thick like chutney, but should be flowing in consistency).
3. Add sambhar powder and let it boil for 5 more minutes.
4. Now add the dal balls to this gravy and boil for a few minutes.
5. Take off from the gas and season it with mustard, cumin and fenugreek seeds.
6. This curry goes well with plain rice.

Tamarind *is a good appetiser and a good source of calcium, phosphorous and iron.*

For Balls
1. Dry out the excess water from the boiled dal.
2. Add green chilli, garam masala, salt. Mix and shape it into balls.

Nutritive Information

CALORIES: **179 Cal**   PROTEIN: **10.95 gm** FAT: **1.8 gm**
CARBOHYDRATE: **29 gm**   FIBRE: **0.7 gm**

Vegetables

70 Soyabean Sukha

Ingredients

Soyabean chunks	250 gms
Large onion	1 (chopped)
Green chillis	2 (slit)
Tomato	1 (chopped)
Turmeric powder	1 tsp
Chilli powder	1 tsp
Garam masala	1/4 tsp
Salt	to taste
Coriander leaves	few (chopped)
Water	1 cup

Method

1. In a big bowl soak soyabean chunks in water for 15 minutes. Squeeze out all the water and cut the chunks into quarters.
2. Heat a karahi and add onion and sauté till brown.
3. Add cut tomato and slit green chillis. Sauté for 1 minute.
4. Add turmeric and chilli powders, garam masala, salt and stir.
5. Add 1 cup of water and bring to a boil.
6. Add soyabean chunks and simmer for a few minutes till it absorbs the gravy and is cooked.
7. Add coriander leaves to garnish the dish.

Soyabean: It is a legume having a wealth of nutrition and there is no other food that compares with it. It is rich in carbohydrates, vitamins, minerals and proteins. It is a rich source of protein.

Nutritive Information

CALORIES: **168 Cal**   PROTEIN: **12.45 gm**   FAT: **5.2 gm**
CARBOHYDRATE: **18.1 gm**   FIBRE: **1.9 gm**

71 Mushroom-Spinach Subzi

Ingredients

Mushrooms	50 gms
Spinach	½ bunch
Asafoetida (hing)	a pinch
Garlic	3-4 cloves (chopped)
Ginger	½ tsp (chopped)
Red chilli powder	¼ tsp
Coriander powder	½ tsp
Turmeric powder	¼ tsp
Salt	to taste

Method

1. Wash spinach thoroughly and boil in $1/8$ cup of water with a little salt for 5 minutes. Mash it and keep aside.
2. Heat a pan, add asafoetida and cook it till it crackles. Add garlic, ginger and salt and cook for a minute.
3. Wash and remove the stalks of mushrooms. Then mix with ginger and garlic. Cook till mushrooms become tender.
4. Add all the masalas and stir for 1 minute.
5. Add mashed spinach and cook for 5 minutes or till excess water dries up.

Mushrooms: *A longevity tonic, heart medicine and cancer remedy. Helps in preventing and/or treating high blood cholesterol and blood pressure.*

Nutritive Information

CALORIES: **47.5 Cal**   PROTEIN: **3.55 gm**   FAT: **1.1 gm**
CARBOHYDRATE: **0.8 gm**   FIBRE: **5.05 gm**

72 Yam with Lemon

Ingredients

Yam (zimikand)	750 gms (peeled, cubed)
Fresh lemon juice	1 tbsp
Parsley	1 tbsp (chopped)
Salt	to taste
Freshly ground black pepper	to taste

Method

1. Preheat the oven to 375°F.
2. Place the yam in a covered baking dish with just enough water to coat the bottom of the pan.
3. Bake for 45 to 50 minutes until tender.
4. Add lemon juice, parsley, salt and pepper to taste and serve.

People frequently confuse yam with sweet potato. It is actually a different root vegetable. In this country the word yam is used to refer to the sweet potato, and not to any of the distinctively sharp-tasting root vegetables that people from the Caribbean or Africa know. This recipe calls for sweet potatoes.

Nutritive Information

CALORIES: **178 Cal**   PROTEIN: **1.89 gm**   FAT: **0.3 gm**
CARBOHYDRATE: **80.15 gm**   FIBRE: **0.65 gm**

73 Yam with Ginger and Dried Apricots

Ingredients

Large yam (zimikand)	1
Dried apricots	6 (cut in quarters)
Fresh ginger	1-cm piece (finely diced)
Water	1½ cups

Method

1. If the skin on the yam looks firm and smooth, scrub the yam. Otherwise, peel it.
2. Cut the yam into rounds slightly less than 1-cm thick, and cut each round into quarters, or sixths if it is very large.
3. Combine all the ingredients in a small saucepan, cover with 1½ cups of water, bring to a boil, then simmer, covered, for $^1/_2$ an hour.
4. Check the pan and add more water, in small increments if necessary, until the yam is completely cooked, for another 20 minutes or so.
5. Allow whatever liquid is left to boil down until a small amount of sauce is left. Pile into a bowl and serve.

Apricots are quite delicious with yam. Leave the ginger in big pieces and pull it out later, or finely chop it and leave it with the yam, as you wish.

Nutritive Information

CALORIES: **173 Cal**   PROTEIN: **1.25 gm**   FAT: **0.3 gm**
CARBOHYDRATE: **50.25 gm**   FIBRE: **1.85 gm**

74 Pan Umbrellas

Ingredients

Mushrooms	50 gms
Peppercorns	½ tsp (coarsely crushed)
Coriander powder	½ tsp
Garam masala	½ tsp
Ginger	½ tsp (chopped finely)
Garlic	½ tsp (chopped)
Green chillis	3-4 (whole)
Red chilli	1 (whole)
Salt	to taste
Red chilli powder	¼ tsp
Chaat masala	¼ tsp

Method

1. Wash mushrooms properly and cut into half.
2. Heat a pan and put in ginger, garlic, peppercorns and whole green chillis. Cook for a few seconds.
3. Put mushrooms and cook for another 5-6 minutes.
4. Add all the masalas. When mushrooms become tender put salt and cook for 3-4 minutes.
5. Serve garnished with chopped coriander.

Mushrooms are edible fungi which grow in moist places. They are considered a delicacy because of the meat like flavour.

Nutritive Information

CALORIES: **21.5 Cal** PROTEIN: **1.55 gm** FAT: **0.4 gm**
CARBOHYDRATE: **2.15 gm** FIBRE: **0.2 gm**

75 Brinjals in Curd

Ingredients

Brinjals	250 gms
Onion	1 (finely chopped)
Curd (skimmed milk)	1 tbsp (beaten)
Ginger-garlic paste	½ tsp
Coriander powder	½ tsp
Garam masala	¼ tsp
Chilli powder	¼ tsp
Kasoori methi	1 tsp (dried)
Salt	to taste

Method

1. Give four slits in the brinjals without separating from the stalk.
2. Dry-roast them either in a pan or in an oven.
3. Heat a pan. Add ginger-garlic paste and cook for a few seconds.
4. Then add onion and sauté for a few more minutes till it becomes brown in colour.
5. Now add coriander and chilli powders, methi and salt and then add curd. Cook for 5 minutes, stirring continuously till well mixed.
6. Add roasted brinjals and ¼ cup of water. Cover and cook for 5 minutes.
7. Garnish with chopped coriander and garam masala.

Brinjal is a good source of minerals and vitamin B.

Nutritive Information

CALORIES: **49 Cal** PROTEIN: **2.0 gm** FAT: **0.35 gm**
CARBOHYDRATE: **9.55 gm** FIBRE: **1.6 gm**

76 Parwal Ki Subzi

Ingredients

Parwal	250 gms

For stuffing

Potatoes	1 ½ (boiled, mashed)
Green chillis	2 (chopped)
Onion	½ (finely chopped)
Chaat masala	¼ tsp
Cumin seed powder	¼ tsp
Red chilli powder	¼ tsp
Salt	to taste

For curry

Onion	1 (finely chopped)
Tomato	½ (finely chopped)
Ginger	½ tsp (chopped)
Garlic	½ tsp (chopped)
Red chilli powder	¼ tsp
Turmeric powder	¼ tsp
Coriander powder	¼ tsp
Garam masala	¼ tsp
Coriander leaves	1 tbsp (chopped)
Salt	to taste

Method

1. Cut the head of the parwal and scoop out the seeds and the pulp from inside. Scrape its skin a little bit.
2. Sauté in a pan till slightly brown in colour.

3. Combine together the stuffing ingredients and fill into the parwal and keep aside.
4. Heat a pan and sauté the ginger and garlic, add onion and cook for 5 minutes with continous stirring.
5. When onion turns brown, add tomato and spices and sauté for 3-4 minutes.
6. Add ¼ cup of water and bring to a boil. Add parwal and cook for 5 minutes and turn off the heat.
7. Serve garnished with coriander and garam masala.

This recipe is a delicious one. With the stuffing this can be eaten with whole wheat chapatis which provide a good combination of cereals and vegetables.

Nutritive Information

CALORIES: **172 Cal**   PROTEIN: **6.65 gm**   FAT: **0.85 gm**
CARBOHYDRATE: **34.35 gm**   FIBRE: **7.1 gm**

77 Masala Tinda

Ingredients

Tinda	250 gms (scraped and cut into pieces)
Asafoetida (hing)	a pinch
Turmeric powder	¼ tsp
Salt	to taste

For masala

Mango powder	1 tsp
Kashmiri chillis	½ tsp
Black salt	¼ tsp
Cumin powder	1 ½ tsp
Garam masala	¼ tsp
Coriander leaves	for garnishing

Method

1. Heat pan and put in asafoetida and let it sizzle a bit.
2. Add the cut tinda and cook for 3-4 minutes. Cover and cook for another 5 minutes on a low flame till the tindas become tender.
3. Now add all the masalas, stir well and cook covered till tender. Sprinkle water in between when required.
4. Garnish with coriander leaves.

Tinda is an easily digestible vegetable and can be used in stomach disorders, fevers and other digestive problems. This recipe with masalas comes out to be an appealing dish.

Asafoetida is yellow in colour, acrid and bitter in taste. But it should not be used in excess due to its semi toxic effects.

Nutritive Information

CALORIES: **21 Cal** PROTEIN: **1.4 gm** FAT: **0.2 gm**
CARBOHYDRATE: **3.4 gm** FIBRE: **1 gm**

78 Gajar and Nutri Bhaji

Ingredients

Carrots	½ kg (scraped and chopped)
Ginger	1 tbsp (finely chopped)
Asafoetida	a pinch
Cumin seeds	½ tsp
Nutri mince (soyabean)	200 gms
Coriander powder	½ tsp
Turmeric powder	½ tsp
Salt	to taste

Method

1. Heat a karahi, add asafoetida and cumin seeds. Sauté till they give a crackling sound and cumin seeds turn brown.
2. Add ginger, cook for 2 minutes and then add carrots and cook for a few minutes.
3. Add all the masalas and nutri mince and cook covered on slow flame for 3-4 minutes or till tender.

This recipe contains both carrots and soyabean chunks which makes it a nutritous dish. Carrots are good source of beta-carotene which is an anti-oxidant and pro-vitamin A whereas soyabean chunks are a good source of protein.

Nutritive Information

CALORIES: **360 Cal**   PROTEIN: **24.3 gm**   FAT: **10.35 gm**
CARBOHYDRATE: **42.25 gm**   FIBRE: **5.45 gm**

79 Bhindi-Capsicum Subzi

Ingredients

Lady's fingers (bhindi)	250 gms (dried and chopped)
Capsicum	250 gms (deseeded and chopped)
Onions	1 ½ (chopped)
Garlic	2-3 flakes (finely chopped)
Ginger	½ tsp (chopped)
Green chillis	3-4 (deseeded and chopped)
Salt	to taste
Turmeric powder	½ tsp
Coriander powder	½ tsp
Pepper	½ tsp
Mango powder	½ tsp

Method

1. Put ginger, garlic, onions and green chillis in a heated pan. Cook for 2-3 minutes.
2. Now put in chopped lady's fingers and capsicum and cook for 5-6 minutes.
3. Then put all the masalas and cook again for 5 minutes.

Lady's finger and capsicum: *They can be used in salads, curry and sandwich etc. They are used in the treatment of ulcers, rheumatism, arthritis, constipation and diabetes.*

Nutritive Information

CALORIES: **84 Cal**   PROTEIN: **3.8 gm**   FAT: **0.55 gm**
CARBOHYDRATE: **16.25 gm**   FIBRE: **2.5 gm**

80 Spinach in Curd Gravy

Ingredients

Spinach	½ kg (washed and finely chopped)
Curd (skimmed milk)	500 gms
Green chillis	3-4
Small onions	3 (cut in thin slices)
Red chilli (dried)	1
Curry leaves	5-6
Urad dal (soaked)	½ tsp
Onion seeds (kalonji)	½ tsp
Salt	to taste

Method

1. Heat a karahi and put cumin seeds and urad dal along with the curry leaves. Cook for 2 minutes.
2. Add red chilli and onions, sauté for 1-2 minutes. Add green chillis and sauté for another 2-3 minutes.
3. Now add spinach and salt. Cook on a low flame for 4-5 minutes till spinach is cooked.
4. Add curd and increase the flame. Cook for a few seconds and remove.

Spinach *is a rich source of beta-carotene, folic acid and good source of iron.*

Nutritive Information

CALORIES: **184 Cal**   PROTEIN: **4.1 gm**   FAT: **3.65 gm**
CARBOHYDRATE: **19.65 gm**   FIBRE: **0.6 gm**

81 Haryali Kamal Kakri Subzi

Ingredients

Spinach	½ bunch
Lotus stems (kamal kakri)	½ (scraped and washed)
Asafoetida (hing)	a pinch
Red chilli powder	¼ tsp
Turmeric powder	¼ tsp
Salt	to taste

Method

1. Boil spinach in ¼ cup of water with a bit of salt. Mash and keep aside.
2. Cut lotus stem into thin round slices.
3. Heat a karahi and add asafoetida and cook a little. When it gives a crackling sound add lotus stem slices and cook till tender.
4. Add the masalas and the mashed spinach. Cook till liquid dries up. Serve hot with chapati or rice.

Lotus stem *is a rich source of calcium, phosphorus, iron and fibre.*

Nutritive Information

CALORIES: **260 Cal**   PROTEIN: **6.1 gm**   FAT: **2.0 gm**
CARBOHYDRATE: **54.3 gm**   FIBRE: **25.6 gm**

82 Methi Chaman

Ingredients

Fenugreek leaves (methi)	100 gms
Spinach	100 gms
Cottage cheese (skimmed milk)	250 gms
Ginger	½ tsp (chopped finely)
Red chilli powder	½ tsp
Coriander powder	¼ tsp
Garam masala	¼ tsp
Salt	to taste

Method

1. Wash methi leaves and spinach thoroughly and boil in hot salted water for 5 minutes.
2. Drain completely and grind methi-spinach in a mixer to a fine paste.
3. Heat a pan, add the ginger and sauté for a minute. Add cottage cheese cut in cubes.
4. After cooking for 3-4 minutes add red chilli and coriander powders and puréed spinach and methi. Add salt according to taste.
5. Cook for a few minutes on slow flame and then on high flame for another 5 minutes till excess water dries up. Sprinkle garam masala and serve hot.

Methi leaves: They are good source of beta-carotene and iron. Methi seeds are used as anti-diabetic agent and also used in digestive problems.

Nutritive Information

CALORIES: **91 Cal**   PROTEIN: **6.9 gm**   FAT: **1.35 gm**
CARBOHYDRATE: **12.55 gm**   FIBRE: **1.4 gm**

83 Cauliflower with Curd

Ingredients

Cauliflower	1
Onions	4 (chopped)
Garlic	3 flakes
Ginger	2-cm piece (chopped)
Sugar	1 tsp
Curd (skimmed milk)	250 gms
Garam masala	1 tsp
Green chillis	4-5
Coriander leaves	1 tbsp (chopped)
Salt	to taste

Method

1. Heat a pan, cook ginger and garlic for a few seconds and then add onions. Cook till they are brownish pink in colour.
2. Cut cauliflower and mix with onions.
3. Simmer for 5-10 minutes or till cauliflower is slightly tender.
4. Add rest of the ingredients except green chillis and coriander leaves, mix well.
5. Cover and cook for another 5 minutes till cauliflower is done. Garnish with green chillis and coriander leaves and serve.

Cauliflower is a good source of vitamin C and may help to ward off cancer. Cauliflower contains only 28 calories per serving, it is a good component of a balanced slimming diet, filling but not fattening.

Nutritive Information

CALORIES: **154 Cal**   PROTEIN: **9.6 gm**   FAT: **1.5 gm**
CARBOHYDRATE: **24.8 gm**   FIBRE: **2.6 gm**

84 Aloo Chholia Subzi

Ingredients

Chholia (fresh green gram)	100 gms
Potato	1 (boiled and diced)
Onion	1 (finely chopped)
Tomato	1 (chopped finely)
Green chilli	1 (finely chopped)
Red chilli powder	¼ tsp
Turmeric powder	¼ tsp
Salt	to taste
Coriander leaves	1 tbsp (chopped)

Method

1. Heat a pan and put in onions. Cook till golden in colour. Then add chholia and sauté for 2-3 minutes.
2. Cover and cook on low flame till done. Add masalas along with the tomato and boiled and diced potatoes.
3. Cover and cook again on low flame for 10 minutes. Serve garnished with fresh coriander leaves.

Potatoes are best eaten steamed or baked with their skins. The skin contains potassium, calcium, phosphorus & sulphur.

Nutritive Information

CALORIES: **312 Cal** PROTEIN: **11.15 gm** FAT: **2.90 gm**
CARBOHYDRATE: **55.4 gm** FIBRE: **3.05 gm**

85 Kamal Kakri Koftas

Ingredients

For koftas

Lotus stems (kamal kakri)	250 gms
Gram flour	½ tsp
Green chilli	1 (finely chopped)
Chaat masala	½ tsp
Red chilli powder	¼ tsp

For curry

Onions	1 ½ (grated)
Tomato	1 (finely chopped)
Chilli powder	¼ tsp
Garam masala	½ tsp
Turmeric powder	¼ tsp
Coriander powder	½ tsp
Salt	to taste

Method

1. Boil lotus stems in water till tender. Squeeze the water and mash. Mix with other kofta ingredients and make into small balls.
2. Bake these balls in an oven till golden brown.
3. Heat a pan, add onions and sauté till golden in colour. Sprinkle water when required.
4. Add the rest of the curry ingredients and simmer for 10 minutes. Add water if necessary.
5. Put in koftas and cook for 2 minutes. Put in a serving bowl and serve.

Lotus stems: This recipe is an energy booster. Lotus stems have good amount of vitamins and minerals whereas gram flour is a good source of calories.

Nutritive Information

CALORIES: **330.9 Cal**   PROTEIN: **8 gm**   FAT: **11.32 gm**
CARBOHYDRATE: **70.11 gm**   FIBRE: **26.1 gm**

86 Bhindi Gravy

Ingredients

Lady's fingers (bhindi)	250 gms
Cumin powder	1 tsp
Turmeric powder	1 tsp
Red chilli powder	1 tsp
Curd (skimmed milk)	250 gms
Aniseed	1 tsp (roasted and ground)
Coriander powder	½ tsp
Asafoetida	a pinch
Salt	to taste

Method

1. Clean, wash and dry bhindi properly. Cut off the heads and tails of all. Then give a slit lengthwise.
2. Mix all the powders except asafoetida and add a little water to make a thick paste.
3. Now fill this paste in each bhindi. Place them in an oven proof dish and bake till they are crisp and done. Keep aside.
4. Beat the curd vigorously. Put water in a container and bring to boil. Add beaten curd to it and stir.
5. When the mixture comes to a boil, reduce the flame. Cook for sometime. Then put bhindis in it.
6. When bhindis are tender, season with asafoetida and roasted cumin seed powder. Add salt and serve hot.

Aniseed: *Aniseed is favoured in medicine for its properties to relieve flatulence and to remove catarrh and phlegm from the bronchial tube.*

Nutritive Information

CALORIES: **64 Cal** PROTEIN: **4.4 gm** FAT: **0.3 gm**
CARBOHYDRATE: **11 gm** FIBRE: **1.2 gm**

87 Arbi Cooked in Whey

Ingredients

Colocasia (arbi)	100 gms
Whey	100 gms
Bishop's weed (ajwain)	½ tsp
Coriander powder	½ tsp
Red chillis	¼ tsp
Mango powder	¼ tsp
Salt	to taste
Mint leaves	½ bunch

Method

1. Boil or steam arbi in a pressure cooker to make it tender.
2. Heat karahi and put all the spices leaving mint leaves.
3. Now mix in arbi and cook on low flame.
4. Put a cupful of water along with the whey and keep stirring.
5. Let it simmer for half an hour after bringing it to a boil. Before removing from fire add salt.
6. Garnish with freshly chopped mint leaves and serve.

Whey water *is a rich source of protein and vitamins. It is easily digestible and even used in weaning foods.*

Nutritive Information

CALORIES: **97 Cal**   PROTEIN: **3 gm**   FAT: **0.1 gm**
CARBOHYDRATE: **21.1 gm**   FIBRE: **1 gm**

88 Masala Baigan

Ingredients

Small brinjals, (Baigan)	8-10
Potatoes	2 (boiled, peeled and mashed)
Gram flour	2 tbsp (sieved & slightly roasted)
Onions	2 (finely chopped)
Tomatoes	2 (finely chopped)
Cumin powder	1 tsp
Garam masala	1 tsp
Chilli powder	½ tsp
Turmeric powder	½ tsp
Sugar	1 tsp
Salt	to taste
Mango powder	½ tsp
Coriander leaves	1 tbsp (chopped)

Method

1. Give a slit in brinjals lengthwise without cutting the tops.
2. Mix all the ingredients except onions and tomatoes with very little water to make an almost dry filling. Stuff this mixture in the slit brinjals. Tie each with thread.
3. Arrange the tied brinjals in a dish. Steam in a pressure cooker, without weight for 10-12 minutes till tender. Allow to cool.
4. Heat pan and lightly roast onions. Sprinkle water when required. Then add tomatoes, a cup of water with salt and stir.
5. Now add the brinjals, cover and allow simmering on a low flame until the gravy is thick.

6. Sprinkle coriander leaves and serve.

Cumin seeds: *They are a good source of minerals, specially calcium, phosphorous and iron. Other than nutritive value, it has medicinal virtues. They are very beneficial in the treatment of several digesive system disorders such as morning sickness, indigestion, dyspepsia and flatulent colic.*

Nutritive Information

CALORIES: 227.9 Cal   PROTEIN: 7.35 gm   FAT: 1.82 gm
CARBOHYDRATE: 47.11 gm   FIBRE: 3.2 gm

89 Khatte Mitthe Baigan

Ingredients

Small brinjals (baigan)	8-10
Ginger paste	1 tsp
Curry leaves	8-10
Onions	2 (chopped)
Tamarind	3 tbsp
Tomatoes	2 (finely chopped)
Chilli powder	½ tsp
Coriander powder	½ tsp
Cumin powder	½ tsp
Jaggery	20 gms
Salt	to taste
Coriander leaves	1 tbsp (finely chopped)

Method

1. Wash the brinjals and wipe them dry. Make four slits along the length, taking care to keep tops intact.
2. Bake these brinjals in an oven till they are tender.
3. Heat a pan and put onions. Cook till golden brown using water when required. Add ginger and curry leaves and cook for 4-5 minutes.
4. Then add tomatoes, cook for a few minutes and add chilli, coriander and cumin powders, salt, tamarind pulp and jaggery and cook for a few minutes more.
5. To this curry add baked brinjals, coriander leaves and cook until the brinjals are tender. Serve hot.

Tamarind is a fair source of calcium, phosphorous and iron. The leaves of tamarind are stimulating, cooling and antibilious. The bark of tamarind is an astringent and a tonic and it reduces fever.

Nutritive Information

CALORIES: **112.3 Cal** PROTEIN: **2.64 gm** FAT: **0.41 gm**
CARBOHYDRATE: **24.6 gm** FIBRE: **1.9 gm**

90 Mushroom Masala

Ingredients

Mushrooms	250 gms
Onion	1 tsp
Ginger-garlic paste	1½ tsp
Coriander powder	1 tsp
Salt	to taste
Turmeric powder	¼ tsp
Red chilli powder	¼ tsp
Green chillis	2 (cut lengthwise)
Garam masala	½ tsp
Coriander leaves	for garnishing

Method

1. Cut mushrooms into small pieces. Chop onion fine.
2. Heat a pan. Put onion, ginger-garlic paste, red chilli, coriander, and turmeric powders and garam masala.
3. Cook using little water when required till onion powders get brown.
4. Heat a karahi, add green chillis and then add the prepared paste. Cook for a few minutes. Add salt.
5. After cooking for a few minutes add little water. Then add mushrooms.
6. Cook till the gravy becomes thick and mushrooms are done. Add chopped coriander and serve

Mushrooms are an excellent source of vitamin - C, useful source of beta carotene and a good source of bioflavonoids.

Nutritive Information

CALORIES: **68 Cal** PROTEIN: **3.7 gm** FAT: **0.85 gm**
CARBOHYDRATE: **9.85 gm** FIBRE: **0.7 gm**

91 Pea Koftas in Greenlake

Ingredients

Gram flour (besan)	250 gms
Milk	4 tsp
Peas	100 gms (shelled)
Cumin seeds	1 tsp
Salt	2 tsp
Pea paste	250 gms
Onion	1 (chopped)
Garlic paste	1½ tsp
Green chilli paste	1 tsp
Ginger paste	½ tsp
Coriander leaves	2 tbs (chopped fine)
Cinnamon	2 pieces
Black cardamom	1
Pomegranate powder	1 tsp
Tomato and onion rings	for garnishing

Method

1. Mix the gram flour with 1 tsp salt, water, 4 tsp milk and make a dough. Make small balls and flatten them one by one in your palm. Stuff few peas in each and turn them into balls again.
2. Boil water in a saucepan and cook all the prepared balls in boiling water for 10-15 minutes. Drain and keep aside.
3. Heat a pan and put in chopped onion and cumin seeds. Cook using little water if required, until light brown.
4. Add the paste of garlic, green chillis, ginger, coriander leaves,

cinnamon and cardamom and cook for a few minutes.
5. Now add the peas paste, salt, pomegranate powder and cook for another 10 minutes.
6. When it is done arrange it in a dish and dip the prepared balls in it. Garnish with tomato and onion rings. Serve hot.

Green pea koftas in green coloured gravy adds freshness on the dining table and promotes one towards vegetarianism.

Nutritive Information

CALORIES: **327.5 Cal** PROTEIN: **19.65 gm** FAT: **2.85 gm**
CARBOHYDRATE: **56.05 gm** FIBRE: **4.65 gm**

92 Masaledar Aloo with Baby Corn

Ingredients

Potatoes	250 gms (diced)
Baby corn	250 gms (diced)
Onions	2 (chopped)
Tomatoes	2 (chopped)
Red chillis (whole)	4-5
Tamarind	25 gms (soaked in water)
Salt	to taste

Method

1. Boil red chillis in water for sometime and make a fine paste, using a little water. Keep aside.
2. Boil diced potato and baby corns separately and keep aside.
3. Heat a pan, add onions and sauté until golden brown, sprinkling water when required. Then add chopped tomatoes and continue cooking.
4. When tomatoes are cooked, add the red chilli paste, tamarind water and cook for a minute.
5. Now add potatoes, baby corn and salt. Cook for two minutes and serve hot.

Corn vegetable gives variety in menu. This recipe provides sufficient nutrients along with taste and flavour.

Nutritive Information

CALORIES: **292 Cal** PROTEIN: **8.4 gm** FAT: **1.3 gm**
CARBOHYDRATE: **61.9 gm** FIBRE: **3.7 gm**

93 Bharva Hari Mirch

Ingredients

Green peppers	5 big (slit and remove centre)
Gram flour	250 gms (sieved and lightly roasted)
Mustard seeds	1 tsp
Asafoetida	a pinch
Chilli powder	1 tsp
Onions	2 (finely chopped)
Garam masala	½ tsp
Salt	to taste
Jaggery	2 tbsp
Tamarind pulp	2 tbsp
Turmeric powder	$1/2$ tsp
Coriander leaves	$1/2$ tbsp (chopped)

Method

1. Soak peppers in water for 15 minutes. Drain off the water.
2. Roast mustard seeds till they pop. Add asafoetida, chopped onions and stir till dry. Remove from heat.
3. Add chilli powder, garam masala, salt, jaggery, tamarind pulp, turmeric powder and coriander leaves. Mix well using little water. Stuff this mixture in peppers.
4. Place these green peppers in a shallow vessel. Sprinkle any remaining mixture on top. Pressure cook without weight for about 5 minutes or till peppers are tender.
5. Grill in a hot oven till browned. Garnish with chopped coriander leaves.

Tamarind is a fair source of calcium, phosphorous and iron. The leaves of tamarind are stimulating, cooling and antibilious. The bark of tamarind is an astringent and a tonic and it reduces fever.

Nutritive Information

CALORIES: **270.8 Cal**   PROTEIN: **17.29 gm** FAT: **3.46 gm**
CARBOHYDRATE: **63.35 gm**   FIBRE: **7.05 gm**

94 Khatti Mitthi Subzi

Ingredients

Carrots	100 gms
Beans & Cabbage	75-75 gms
Capsicum	75 gms
Pineapple	50 gms
Garlic	50 gms (chopped)
Tomato sauce	2 tbsp
Red colour	a pinch (optional)
Salt	to taste
Cornflour	2 tbsp
Sugar	3 tbsp
Chilli sauce & Chilli powder	¼-¼ tsp

Method

1. Cut vegetables and boil in water for 5 minutes.
2. Heat a pan, put chopped garlic, cut vegetables and cook for a few minutes.
3. Then add tomato sauce, colour, salt, sugar, chilli sauce, chilli powder, pineapple pieces and sauté for 5 minutes. Add 4 cups of water and cook the vegetables.
4. When boiling, add dissolved cornflour to the vegetables.
5. When the gravy thickens add salt and mix well.
6. Remove from heat and serve.

Nothing will benefit human health and increase the chances for survival of life on earth as much as the evolution to a vegetarian diet.

Nutritive Information

CALORIES: **212 Cal**   PROTEIN: **7.45 gm**   FAT: **1.05 gm**
CARBOHYDRATE: **43.1 gm**   FIBRE: **4.15 gm**

95 Capsicum Curry

Ingredients

Capsicum	½ kg
Garlic	1 whole
Curry leaves	2 sprigs
Cinnamon sticks	2
Cumin seeds	1 tsp
Coriander seeds	2 tbsp
Onions	2 (chopped)
Ginger paste	1 tsp
Salt	2 tsp
Coriander leaves	for garnishing
Roasted chana dal	250 gms

Method

1. Cut the capsicums into fours, lengthwise, to three fourths of their total length.
2. Mix chana dal, few garlic cloves and blend them into a fine paste.
3. Mix coriander and cumin seeds, ginger, cinnamon, salt, onions, remaining garlic cloves and blend them into a fine paste.
4. Heat a wide pan and put in the onion mixture. Cook until brown sprinkling water when needed.
5. Add the chana dal-garlic paste and capsicums to the onion mixture.
6. Add some water, if required, and cook on low flame until the capsicums are tender. Serve hot.

Capsicum: *Capsicum has the remarkable effect of being a powerful stimulant. In spite of being pungent, it does not blister the mouth or throat.*

Nutritive Information

CALORIES: **199 Cal**   PROTEIN: **7.2 gm**   FAT: **1.3 gm**
CARBOHYDRATE: **40 gm**   FIBRE: **3.5 gm**

96 Red Bean Chilli

Ingredients

Beans (Lobia)	500 gms
Cumin seeds	1 tsp
Dried oregano	1 tsp
Chilli powder	1 to 2 tbsp
Bay leaves	2
Onion	1 (finely diced)
Garlic cloves	2 (minced)
Tomatoes	500 gms (chopped)
Freshly chopped cilantro	3 tbsp
Green bell pepper	1 (diced in small squares)
Vinegar	to taste

Method

1. Sort and rinse the beans, then soak overnight in water. Drain off the soaking water from the beans and cover them generously with fresh water in a large pot to at least a few centimetres above the beans. Boil vigorously for 5 minutes. Usually a lot of scum will rise to the surface. Skim off what you can, then lower the heat.

2. Toast the cumin seeds and the oregano very briefly in a dry pan, then grind them in a mortar and pestle to break up the seeds. Add them to the beans along with the chilli powder, bay leaves, onion and garlic. Cook over a medium heat until the onion is soft, about 15 minutes, then add the chopped tomatoes. Add the diced pepper, then lower the heat and allow the beans to simmer gently until they are well cooked, about an hour.

3. Once the beans have cooked, the flavour of the chilli will continue

to soften and develop. Just before you serve it, stir in some vinegar to sharpen the taste.

This dish will keep well in the refrigerator for several days. In fact, the flavours will keep improving. Check the seasoning when you reheat it and add an extra splash of vinegar, if desired.

Nutritive Information

CALORIES: **199 Cal**   PROTEIN: **7.2 gm**   FAT: **1.3 gm**
CARBOHYDRATE: **40 gm**   FIBRE: **3.5 gm**

97 Mushrooms in Tomato Sauce

Ingredients

Mushrooms	500 gms (sliced)
Onions	100 gms (chopped)
Ginger and garlic paste	1 tbsp
Tomatoes	2 (skinned and chopped)
Turmeric powder	1 tsp
Green chillis	4 (slit lengthwise)
Salt	to taste
Capsicum	1 (juliennes)
Coriander leaves	2 tbsp (chopped)
Garam masala	½ tsp

Method

1. Heat a pan, add onions, ginger-garlic paste and cook till onions are light brown in colour.
2. Add tomatoes, turmeric and chilli powders, green chillis, salt and stir for 2-3 minutes. Also add mushrooms, stir well adding little water, if required. Simmer till done.
3. Now add capsicum, cover and cook for 2 minutes on low heat. Sprinkle garam masala and cook for another 2 minutes.
4. Serve hot garnished with coriander leaves.

Tomato sauce: *It is a mixture of tomato, onion, garlic and sugar, salt, garam masala and preservatives like sodium benzoate and acetic acid.*

Nutritive Information

CALORIES: **125 Cal**   PROTEIN: **5.85 gm**   FAT: **1.25 gm**
CARBOHYDRATE: **21.15 gm**   FIBRE: **2.3 gm**

98 Taj Mahal Hari Gobi

Ingredients

Mustard seeds	1 tsp
Cumin seeds	½ tsp
Garlic	1 clove (minced)
Jalapeno pepper	½ (deseeded & finely chopped)
Ginger	1 tsp (finely grated)
Onion	1 (chopped)
Broccoli florets (HariGobi)	800 gms
Tomatoes	1 (chopped)
Vegetable stock or water	¼ cup
Salt	to taste
Pepper	¼ tsp

Method

1. Heat a saucepan and add mustard and cumin seeds. Cook, stirring continuously until crackling sound comes.
2. Stir in garlic, chopped pepper, ginger and onion and sauté the mixture slowly stirring frequently for 8-10 minutes, until onion turns golden in colour.
3. Add broccoli, tomatoes and stock, cover and cook till broccoli is tender but crisp. Add salt and pepper to taste and serve.

Broccoli: *Excellent source of vitamin C, useful source of beta-carotene. Contains folate, iron and potassium. May help to protect against cancer.*

Nutritive Information

CALORIES: **111 Cal** PROTEIN: **7.4 gm** FAT: **1.55 gm**
CARBOHYDRATE: **15.75 gm** FIBRE: **3.1 gm**

99 Carrot Gazpacho

Ingredients

Garlic	3 cloves (peeled)
Onion	1 (chopped)
Capsicum	1 (deseeded & cubed)
Jalapeno pepper	1 (minced)
Cucumbers	2
Tomatoes	6
Parsley	50 gms (chopped)
Basil	50 gms (chopped)
Carrot juice	750 gms
Cold water	1 cup
Vinegar	3 tbsp
Ground cumin	2 tsp
Salt	1 tsp

Method

1. Turn the food processor on and drop the garlic through the feed tube to process finely.
2. Add the onion to the bowl and process with a pulse action until minced. Add capsicum and process finely.
3. Transfer the mixture to a large bowl and stir in jalapeno pepper.
4. Place the cucumbers in the processor and process with a pulsating action until they are finely diced. Add to the onion mixture.
5. Now purée the tomatoes and add them to the onion and cucumber mixture along with the remaining ingredients.
6. Boil the mixture for 10 minutes.

7. Cool and chill overnight.

Parsley: It is a herb which is used mostly for flavouring in salads, soups etc. Eaten raw, it is helpful in maintaining normal action of the adrenal and thyroid gland.

Nutritive Information

CALORIES: **144 Cal** PROTEIN: **8.5 gm** FAT: **1.6 gm**
CARBOHYDRATE: **23.9 gm** FIBRE: **4 gm**

100 Lentil Stuffed Tomatoes

Ingredients

White rice	100 gms
Red lentil	100 gms
Boiling water	1 cup
Onion	1 (chopped)
Fresh mint	1 tbsp (chopped)
Salt	to taste
Pepper	1/4 tsp
Tomatoes	8
Garlic	1 clove (crushed)

Method

1. Rinse rice and lentils in a strainer. Cook in boiling water for 10 minutes over slow flame.
2. Heat a pan, add onion and sauté till golden brown, sprinkling water when required. Mix in lentil mixture, garlic and mint. Season with salt and pepper.
3. Slice the top of tomatoes and keep aside. Scoop out the middles. Fill tomato shells with lentil mixture and replace the tops.
4. Place in baking dish, chop reserved tomato middles and sprinkle around stuffed tomatoes.
5. Bake in a preheated oven at 230^0 C for 10-15 minutes.
6. Remove from oven and serve.

Tomatoes: *Good source of carotenoids and potassium. Useful source of vitamins C & K.*

Nutritive Information

CALORIES: **414.5 Cal**   PROTEIN: **18.4 gm**   FAT: **1.15 gm**
CARBOHYDRATE: **72.55 gm**   FIBRE: **2.05 gm**

101 Green Beans Stew

Ingredients

Tomato paste	3 tbsp
Green beans	100 gms (cut into 2-cm pieces)
Water	½ cup
Onion	1 (cut into rings)
Capsicum	1 (chopped)
Salt	½ tsp
Turmeric	¼ tsp
Pepper	¼ tsp

Method

1. Heat pan, stir in tomato paste. Cook for a while and keep aside.
2. In a saucepan, put green beans and water. Arrange onion rings and capsicum in layers over beans. Sprinkle turmeric and salt and pepper over the vegetables.
3. Top with tomato paste. Cook covered over medium heat until vegetables are tender and all the water has evaporated.

***Green beans** supply protein, high in soluble fibre. Provide beta-carotene which the body converts to vitamins A and also contain some iron, niacin, vitamins C and E.*

Nutritive Information

CALORIES: **182 Cal**   PROTEIN: **9.99 gm**   FAT: **1.4 gm**
CARBOHYDRATE: **45.2 gm**   FIBRE: **3.5 gm**

102 Tomato Sar

Ingredients

Tomatoes (large)	2
Beetroot	1 tsp (cooked, chopped/grated)
Onions	1 large/2 small
Green chillis	3
Garlic	2 tsp (chopped)
Ginger	1 tsp (chopped)
Salt	to taste
Cumin powder	1/2 tsp
Coriander powder	1/2 tsp
Garam masala	1/4 tsp
Pepper	1/4 tsp
Red chilli powder	1/4 tsp
Curry powder	1/2 tsp
Sugar	a pinch
Water	1 cup
Coriander leaves	to garnish

Method

1. Chop onions and tomatoes, slit green chillis.
2. In a pressure pan add garlic and ginger. Sauté for a few minutes.
3. Add onions and sauté till translucent.
4. Add all the other ingredients except water.
5. Stir for a minute.
6. Add water and pressure-cook for 5 minutes.

7. Garnish with coriander leaves and serve hot with rice or as it is.

Tomato sar: *A carotene rich hot and spicy tomato preparation. It may be eaten with any cereal preparation or also can be eaten as an accompaniment with a snack on wheat bread cubes.*

Nutritive Information

CALORIES: **70 Cal**   PROTEIN: **2.1 gm**   FAT: **0.3 gm**
CARBOHYDRATE: **14.7 gm**   FIBRE: **1.4 gm**

103 Cauliflower Curry

Ingredients

Cauliflower (stalks and leaves)	1 (chopped finely)
Onion, small	1 (chopped finely)
Lime or lemon juice	3-4 tbsp
Mustard seeds	$1/2$ tsp
Cumin seeds	$1/2$ tsp
Dried red chilli	1
Turmeric powder	$1/2$ tsp
Asafoetida	a pinch
Chilli powder	to taste
Salt	to taste
Curry leaves	few

Method

1. Heat a pan.
2. Add mustard and cumin seeds, dried red chilli and turmeric powder.
3. When the seeds start to splutter, add the finely chopped onion.
4. When the onion gets brown, add the cauliflower stalks and leaves.
6. Add chilli powder, asafoetida and salt and stir.
7. Let this cook on medium heat until stalks are tender.
8. Add curry leaves towards the end.
9. Sprinkle lemon juice when ready to serve.

A dry n spicy cauliflower preparation. Presence of the stalks in the vegetable not only incorporates additional fibre but also increases the iron content.

Nutritive Information

CALORIES: **80 Cal**   PROTEIN: **3.8 gm**   FAT: **0.5 gm**
CARBOHYDRATE: **15.1 gm**   FIBRE: **1.8 gm**

104 Palak Paneer

Ingredients

Spinach (palak)	2 bunches
Onions, medium	2 (chopped)
Tomatoes, medium	2
Ginger/garlic paste	2 tbsp
Green chillis	4
Tofu	½ kg
Milk (skimmed)	½ tbsp
Kasoori methi & Coriander powder	½-½ tsp
Coriander & Cumin seeds	½-½ tsp
Cloves	½ tsp
Salt	to taste

Method

1. Parboil spinach. Drain, cool and make a paste in the blender/ mixer.
2. In a pan roast cumin and coriander seeds and cloves.
3. Put chopped onions, ginger and garlic paste and green chillis and sauté till onions are golden brown.
4. Now put the chopped tomatoes and let them cook.
5. Add salt and coriander powder and cook.
6. Add spinach paste and tofu (drained and cut into cubes).
7. Add some milk and let it cook.
8. Just before serving, add some garam masala and kasoori methi for flavour.

A low fat and cholesterol free palak paneer which contains handful amount of iron, good quantity of carotene and proteins.

Nutritive Information
CALORIES: **312 Cal**   PROTEIN: **25.7 gm**   FAT: **10.75 gm**
CARBOHYDRATE: **28.05 gm**   FIBRE: **3.85 gm**

105 Baby Corn and Palak

Ingredients

Spinach (palak)	1 big bunch
Baby corn	250 gms (diced)
Onion	1
Garlic cloves	2-3
Ginger	2 cm piece
Green chillis	2
Cinnamon stick	1
Bay leaves & Cloves	2-2
Cumin seeds & Garam masala	½-½ tsp
Salt	to taste

Method

1. Roughly chop palak, onion, garlic, ginger and green chillis.
2. Add a spoonful of water to the above mixture and cook for 1 whistle in a cooker.
3. Cool and grind it into a paste in a mixer.
4. Add cumin seeds, cinnamon, bay leaves and cloves and cook.
5. Add baby corn and sauté for 5 minutes.
6. Add the palak mixture, salt and garam masala powder and sauté for 2-3 minutes.
7. Serve hot with parathas.

Corn: *Yellow corn has vitamin A content that can be found in no other grain product.*

Nutritive Information

CALORIES: **201 Cal**   PROTEIN: **7.9 gm**   FAT: **1.7 gm**
CARBOHYDRATE: **38.6 gm**   FIBRE: **3.1 gm**

106 Spicy Vegetable Lapsi

Ingredients

Lapsi	400 gms
Mustard seeds (sarson)	½ tsp
Cumin seeds (jeera)	½ tsp
Asafoetida (hing)	¼ tsp
Red chillis	2
Onion	1 (chopped)
Garlic paste	½ tsp
Tomato, large	1 (finely chopped)
Chilli powder	½ tsp
Turmeric powder (haldi)	½ tsp
Mixed vegetables (carrots, peas, cauliflower)	250 gms (chopped)
Salt	to taste
Garam masala	½ tsp

For garnishing

Coriander leaves	2 tbsp (chopped)

Method

1. In a pan roast lapsi till golden in colour and keep aside.
2. Heat a pan and add the mustard and cumin seeds. When they crackle, add asafoetida.
3. Add red chillis and onion and sauté for 3 to 4 minutes.
4. Add the garlic paste and tomato and sauté for 3 to 4 more minutes.
5. Add the chilli and turmeric powders and mixed vegetables and mix well.

6. Add lapsi, garam masala, salt and enough water (approx. 3 cups of water) and pressure-cook.
7. Garnish with chopped coriander.

Coriander: The pungent leaves are used in curries, salads and sauces. In herbalism small fresh bunches are eaten as tonic for the stomach and heart.

Nutritive Information

CALORIES: **41.75 Cal**   PROTEIN: **16.7 gm**   FAT: **1.85 gm**
CARBOHYDRATE: **73.3 gm**   FIBRE: **6.55 gm**

107 Methi-Paneer

Ingredients

Onions	2 medium (sliced)
Kasoori methi	40 gms
Cottage cheese (skimmed milk)	400 gms (cubed)
Cumin seeds	1 tsp
Pepper	1 tsp
Salt	to taste

Method

1. Heat a pan. Add cumin seeds and crackle. Add onions and cook for 5 minutes. Let the onions become transparent.
2. Now add cottage cheese cubes, kasoori methi, pepper and salt and cook for another 5 minutes.

Dry paneer dish which is fast to cook and good to eat. Can be served hot either with chapati, paratha or may be even taken as an evening snack.

Nutritive Information

CALORIES: **157 Cal** PROTEIN: **10.6 gm** FAT: **1.2 gm**
CARBOHYDRATE: **26.3 gm** FIBRE: **1.7 gm**

108 Green Onion Subzi

Ingredients

Green/spring onions	3 bunches (cut in 1-cm pieces)
Medium potatoes	2 (cut in 1-cm cubes)
Tomatoes	6 (halved)
Mustard seeds	1 tsp
Turmeric powder	$1/8$ tsp
Chilli powder	$1/2$ tsp

Method

1. Heat a pan and add the mustard seeds.
2. When mustard seeds crackle add the vegetables and sauté for 1 minute.
3. Then add chilli and turmeric powders and sauté for 5 minutes.
4. Add $1/2$ cup of water and cover until potatoes are tender and the vegetable is dry.
5. Serve with khichdi.

A low fat, low cholesterol and a low calorie vegetable preparation containing enough of carotene and vitamin C and a good amount of fibre. It is an ideal vegetable preparation for the heart patients.

Nutritive Information

CALORIES: **70 Cal**   PROTEIN: **2.1 gm**   FAT: **0.3 gm**
CARBOHYDRATE: **14.7 gm**   FIBRE: **6.8 gm**

109 Soang

Ingredients

Potatoes	6-7 (boiled, cubed)
Onions	4-5 (chopped)
Tamarind juice	3 tbsp
Salt	to taste
Red chilli powder	to taste

Method

1. Heat a pan and add the onions, sauté till brown.
2. Then slow the gas and add red chilli powder, tamarind juice and little water. Simmer for 2 minutes.
3. Add the cubed potatoes and salt. Let it simmer on low flame for 5 minutes.

As per its uncommon name, having an uncommon flavour in a dry potato preparation. It may be served as a vegetable or as tea time snack.

Nutritive Information

CALORIES: **147 Cal** PROTEIN: **2.8 gm** FAT: **0.2 gm**
CARBOHYDRATE: **33.7 gm** FIBRE: **6.4 gm**

110 Tomato Chokha

Ingredients

Tomatoes	500 gms
Pepper	1 tsp
Onion	1 (finely chopped)
Garlic cloves	3 (chopped)
Salt	to taste

Method

1. Boil or roast tomatoes for about 10 minutes.
2. Drain off water and peel tomatoes, then mash them.
3. Add onion and pepper and mix well.
4. Heat a pan, add garlic and roast until light brown, taking care not to burn it.
5. Take off from the fire and mix with the tomatoes.
6. Serve with roti.

A quick and easy to cook and serve tomato preparation which is high in carotene, vitamin C and fibre. The same recipe may be tried out with raw mangoes.

Nutritive Information

CALORIES: **70 Cal**   PROTEIN: **2.1 gm**   FAT: **0.3 gm**
CARBOHYDRATE: **19.7 gm**   FIBRE: **6.8 gm**

111 Cauliflower in Gravy

Ingredients

Cauliflower	½ kg
Tomatoes	¼ kg
Garam masala	2 tsp
Red chilli powder	1 tsp
Turmeric powder	½ tsp
Cumin seeds (jeera)	½ tsp
Skimmed milk	250 gms
Coriander leaves (for garnishing)	100 gms
Salt	to taste

Method

1. Purée tomatoes well by blending in a mixer and set aside.
2. Cut cauliflower in 5-cm florets. Add a little salt, turmeric and garam masala powders and set aside for 10 minutes.
3. Heat a non-stick pan. Add jeera and allow it to crackle.
4. Add the cauliflower florets and roast until light brown.
5. Add the rest of the garam masala red chilli and turmeric powders.
6. Add skimmed milk and tomato purée and bring the subzi to a boil.
7. Add salt to taste.
8. Switch off the gas and garnish with coriander leaves.

Patients with heart disease because of their vegetarian eating pattern cut down on the protein content in the diet. But with skimmed milk's gravy in this vegetable prepartion a good amount of protein content is maintained in their diet.

Nutritive Information

CALORIES: **86 Cal**   PROTEIN: **6.8 gm**   FAT: **1.5 gm**
CARBOHYDRATE: **11.2 gm**   FIBRE: **2.8 gm**

112 Raw Banana Subzi

Ingredients

Raw bananas	4
Asafoetida (hing)	2 pinches
Red chillis	3-4
Peppercorns	a few
Urad dal	1 tsp
Mustard seeds	1 tsp
Chana dal	1 tsp
Curry leaves	a few
Salt	to taste
Juice of one lime	optional
Coriander leaves	optional (finely chopped)

Method

1. Steam the raw bananas for 7-8 minutes.
2. Peel and grate the steamed bananas.
3. Heat a karahi and add asafoetida.
4. Add the red chillis, peppercorns and urad dal. Roast until the dal is pink. Keep aside.
5. Powder all the roasted ingredients together.
6. Again heat a karahi and add the mustard seeds and let them splutter.
7. Add the chana dal and sauté until pink.
8. Add the curry leaves, grated bananas, salt and powdered spices.
9. Stir gently taking care not to mash the bananas.
10. Sauté for a few more minutes.

11. Add the lime juice (optional) and stir gently.
12. Garnish with chopped coriander leaves (optional).

Green bananas are known as plantains and are indigestible, inpalatable when eaten raw. They are rich in tanin so they taste bitter though some of this flavour disappears on cooking.

Nutritive Information

CALORIES: **187.9 Cal**   PROTEIN: **5.68 gm**   FAT: **1 gm**
CARBOHYDRATE: **39.14 gm** FIBRE: **0.61 gm**

113 Navratan Korma

Ingredients

Fresh curd (skimmed milk)	250 gms
Cottage cheese (skimmed milk)	50 gms (grated)
Fresh soft (skimmed milk)	2 tbsp
Flour	½ tbsp
Tomato purée	2 tbsp
Peas	250 gms (boiled)
Carrot	1 (cubed and boiled)
Green chillis	2-3
Small apple	1 (cut in cubes)
Orange	1 (sliced)
Pineapple slices	2
Raisins	15-20
Cherries	2-3
Salt	to taste

Dry grind

Cumin seeds	½ tsp
Poppy seeds (khus khus)	1 tsp
Cardamoms	2

Method

1. Grind green chillis, fresh cottage cheese to a fine paste and keep aside.
2. Heat a pan, add green chilli-cottage cheese paste, dry masalas, tomato purée and sauté for 2-3 minutes.

3. Add carrot, peas, curd, flour and mix well.
4. Add all the fruits except cherries, raisins, salt and stir and take off the fire.
5. Garnish with cherries and grated paneer before serving.

A colourful and nutritious preparation having most of the ingredients in raw or pure state which promotes a pure mind.

Nutritive Information

CALORIES: **327.8 Cal**   PROTEIN: **7.4 gm**   FAT: **1.15 gm**
CARBOHYDRATE: **81.6 gm**   FIBRE: **3.15 gm**

114 Vegetable Rissoto

Ingredients

Vegetable stock	1ltr
Sticky rice	500 gms
Mixed vegetables (of your choice)	250 gms
Cottage cheese (skimmed milk)	2 tbsp (grated)
Pepper	½ tsp
Salt	to taste
Coriander leaves	few (for garnishing)

Method

1. Wash and soak the rice for 10 minutes, then drain off the water.
2. Pour the vegetable stock in a pan and keep it warm on low gas.
3. Heat another pan on medium flame and add the mixed, chopped vegetables and sauté for a few minutes.
4. Add the rice and salt to taste and sauté for 2 minutes or till the moisture evaporates.
5. Add 1 cup of vegetable stock and increase the heat, keep adding ladle by ladle of the stock to the rice till over or till the rice turns soft like thin khichdi. Turn off the heat
6. Pour into a serving dish, sprinkle grated cottage cheese over it and garnish with coriander leaves.

The least fattening foods are those with the maximum water content in them. For example fresh vegetables contain a large percentage of water.

Nutritive Information

CALORIES: **202.9 Cal**   PROTEIN: **4.01 gm**   FAT: **0.31 gm**
CARBOHYDRATE: **41.94 gm**   FIBRE: **1.3 gm**

115 Tomato Gojju

Ingredients

Tomatoes (medium size)	3
Onions (medium size)	2 (chopped)
Coriander leaves	few
Mustard seeds	½ tsp
Urad & Gram dal	½-½ tsp
Turmeric powder	¼ tsp
Red chilli & Rasam powder	1-1 tsp
Asafoetida (hing)	1 pinch
Sugar	½ tsp
Salt	to taste
Coriander leaves	1 tbsp (chopped)

Method

1. Chop onions, tomatoes, coriander leaves and keep aside.
2. Heat a karahi, add mustard seeds and roast till they crackle.
3. Add urad and gram dals and roast until golden brown.
4. Add onions and sauté until golden brown.
5. Now add tomatoes, turmeric, chilli rasam powders, salt, sugar, asafoetida and 1 small cup of water. Allow to cook until done.
6. The mixture should become semi thick in consistency.
7. Garnish it with coriander leaves.
8. Serve it with dosa, chapati, poori, roti or rice.

A different kind of tomato chutney and the presence of pulses adds protein to the dish.

Nutritive Information

CALORIES: **141.9 Cal**   PROTEIN: **6.58 gm**   FAT: **1 gm**
CARBOHYDRATE: **26.64 gm**   FIBRE: **1.67 gm**

116 Spring in Provence

Ingredients

Mixed vegetables (beans, peas, cauliflower, carrots)	500 gms
Onions	2 (sliced into big pieces)
Tomato	1 (diced into big pieces)
Oregano leaves	few
Water	3 cups

Method

1. Cut and boil all the vegetables in water so that they soften (excluding tomatoes and onions).
2. Heat a pan and add the onions. When they turn brown, add tomatoes and cook them for a minute till they start releasing juices.
3. Remove the pan from heat.
4. Pour the contents of the pan and boiled vegetables in a baking tray.
5. Cook in a pre-heated oven (350°C) for 20 minutes. Then turn on the oven to boil for another 3 minutes.
6. Take out the tray and garnish it with fresh oregano leaves.
7. Serve hot.

A multi-coloured vegetable preparation having a good amount of fibre helps in preventing constipation.

Nutritive Information

CALORIES: **140.2 Cal** PROTEIN: **8.5 gm** FAT: **1.58 gm**
CARBOHYDRATE: **20.58 gm** FIBRE: **5.12 gm**

117 Besan Bhindi

Ingredients

Lady's fingers (bhindi)	500 gms
Red chilli powder	1 tsp
Turmeric powder	$^1/_2$ tsp
Coriander powder	1 tsp
Gram flour	2 tbsp
Lemon juice	1 tbsp
Salt	to taste

Method

1. Wash and wipe the bhindis, and after removing the stalks, divide them lengthwise.
2. Mix all the ingredients with the slit bhindis.
3. Bake the bhindis in the oven for 20 minutes.
4. When done serve hot.

Bhindi is a vegetable liked by almost all age groups and thus this dish caters to all tastes.

Nutritive Information

CALORIES: **151.9 Cal** PROTEIN: **11.75 gm** FAT: **1.52 gm**
CARBOHYDRATE: **37.81 gm** FIBRE: **6.1 gm**

118 Tandoori Phoolgobi

Ingredients

Cauliflower (phoolgobi)	250 gms
Ginger	5-cm piece
Green chillis	2-3 no.
Cumin seeds	1 tsp
Garlic (optional)	3-4 flakes
Salt	3/4 tsp
Chilli powder	¼ tsp
Red colour	a little
Lemon juice	1 tsp
Capsicums	2
Onions	2
Tandoori masala	2 tsp

Method

1. Grind ginger, garlic, green chillis, and cumin seeds to a fine paste.
2. Add chilli powder, lemon juice, red colour and keep aside.
3. Cut gobi into 2-cm pieces.
4. Boil it in salted water for 2-3 minutes. Do not boil much, it should be a little firm.
5. Marinate the gobi in 3/4 of the ginger-garlic paste.
6. Keep the marinated gobi in the grill for 5 minutes on high power till the paste is dry and gobi is soft.
7. Cut onions and capsicums into fine rings.
8. Roast onions and capsicum rings for a few minutes till onions turn transparent.

9. Add the balance ginger-garlic paste and sprinkle salt and tandoori masala.
10. Serve hot.

An oil free tandoori gobi preparation with lots of flavour. Other vegetables like carrot, bean etc. may be added to it to incorporate more colour, fibre and carotene.

Nutritive Information

CALORIES: **101 Cal**   PROTEIN: **4.3 gm**   FAT: **0.5 gm**
CARBOHYDRATE: **20 gm**   FIBRE: **2.6 gm**

119 Masaledar Karela

Ingredients

Small bitter-gourds (karelas)	250 gms
Large onions	2 (sliced fine)
Tamarind pulp	100 gms
Cumin powder	1 tbsp
Ginger & Garlic paste	1-1 tbsp
Turmeric & Chilli powder	1-1 tsp
Salt	to taste

Method

1. Slit the karelas lengthwise in the centre, so as to keep them whole.
2. Scoop out a little centre portion of the karelas without letting them break into two pieces. Mix it with ginger and garlic pastes, salt and cumin powder well.
3. Stuff the karelas with this mixture and gently press them to close the opening.
4. Heat a pan and sauté onion till light brown.
5. Add turmeric powder and stir well.
6. Place the karelas in the pan and cook on low heat till done.
7. Add tamarind pulp, salt and chilli powder. Cook for a few minutes more till the gravy is thick.
8. Serve with rice.

Karela is a blood purifier, activates the spleen and it is highly beneficial in diabetes. It is a purgative, appetiser, disgestive, anti-flatulent and has healing capacity.

Nutritive Information

CALORIES: **75 Cal**   PROTEIN: **2.8 gm**   FAT: **0.3 gm**
CARBOHYDRATE: **15.3 gm**   FIBRE: **1.4 gm**

120 Dum Phoolgobi

Ingredients

Small cauliflowers (Phoolgobi)	4
Small onions	2 (peeled and grated)
Ginger	1-cm piece (peeled and finely shredded)
Garlic cloves	2 (peeled and grated)
Medium tomatoes	4 (chopped)
Green chilli optional)	1 (finely chopped,
Coriander powder	1 ½ tsp
Turmeric powder	½ tsp
Chilli powder	¼ tsp
Salt	1 tsp
Cottage cheese (skimmed milk)	1 tbsp (grated)
Coriander leaves	1 tbsp (chopped)

Method

1. Clean cauliflowers, removing all leaves and trim stalks. Part the florets in a few places for the spices to seep in.
2. Heat a karahi and add ginger and garlic. Sauté for 20 seconds.
3. Add onions and sauté until light brown.
4. Add all the spices and tomatoes.
5. Cover the florets with the paste, pushing some of it in between the florets.
6. Place in a baking dish, cover with foil and cook at 225^0 C for 30-40 minutes.

7. Sprinkle grated cheese on top and put it back in the oven uncovered for 10 minutes.
8. Take out of the oven, place on a serving dish and sprinkle chopped coriander leaves.
9. Serve hot with chapati.

Cauliflower like other fibrous vegetables, may cause flatulence as the cellulose is broken down in the gut. Eating it with spicy accompaniments such as garlic, ginger, ground coriander and cumin will ease digestive discomforts.

Nutritive Information

CALORIES: **165 Cal**   PROTEIN: **9.69 gm**   FAT: **1.7 gm**
CARBOHYDRATE: **26.9 gm**   FIBRE: **3.4 gm**

121 Broccoli Curry

Ingredients

Broccoli (Hari gobi)	100 gms (chopped into small pieces)
Onion	1/2 (chopped)
Green chilli	1 (slit lengthwise)
Salt	to taste
Garam masala	1 tsp
Coriander-cumin powder	1/2 tsp
Asafoetida powder	a pinch
Chilli powder	1 tsp
Turmeric (optional)	1 tsp

Method

1. Microwave the chopped broccoli in a microwave proof dish for 4 minutes (It will turn into bright green).
2. Add all the remaining ingredients and mix well.
3. Microwave again for 3-4 minutes.
4. A crisp broccoli curry is ready in just minutes.

Broccoli: The tender flower heads or florets of broccoli are richer in beta-carotene than the stalks and deeper the colour the higher their nutritive value. The freshness of broccoli is indicated by crisp, easily shaped stalks.

Nutritive Information

CALORIES: **102 Cal**   PROTEIN: **4.9 gm**   FAT: **0.6 gm**
CARBOHYDRATE: **18.2 gm**   FIBRE: **1.8 gm**

122 Capsicum in Soya Sauce

Ingredients

Capsicum	250 gm
Big onions	3-4
Potatoes	2
Soya sauce	2 tbsp
Green chilli sauce	to taste
Salt	to taste

Method

1. Cut deseeded capsicums and potatoes lengthwise, medium size.
2. Cut onions lengthwise finely.
3. Heat a pan and add the onions and sauté till pink in color.
4. Now add potatoes and sauté till half cooked. (If they stick to the vessel while cooking, keep water on the lid and pour this hot water in it).
5. Now add soya sauce, very little salt if required (since soya sauce is salty) and capsicums. Cook well.
6. If you require this to be spicy then add green chilli sauce, according to taste. Cook till done.

Soya sauce: *It is made from fermenting soya beans, is an extremely concentrated source of sodium..*

Nutritive Information

CALORIES: **171 Cal**   PROTEIN: **4.1 gm**   FAT: **0.5 gm**
CARBOHYDRATE: **37 gm**   FIBRE: **2 gm**

123 Masala Aloo Bhindi

Ingredients

Lady's fingers (bhindi)	200 gms
Potatoes	2
Big onion	2
Coriander leaves	250 gms
Green chillis	2
Ginger	5-cm piece
Garlic cloves	6-7
Tomatoes	2
Salt	to taste
Red chilli powder	1 tsp
Turmeric powder	1 tsp
Coriander powder	4 tsp

Method

1. Wash and dry lady's fingers with paper tissue, then cut off the stems and the pointed ends.
2. Now make deep horizontal cuts in the middle for the stuffing and keep aside.
3. Wash and peel the potatoes, cut medium round pieces.

For stuffing

4. Grind to paste one onion, one tomato, ginger, garlic, fresh coriander leaves. Now add all the dry masalas to this paste.
5. Stuff the bhindi with this masala.
6. In a pan, add one sliced onion. Sauté till it gets transparent.
7. Then add one finely chopped tomato. After two minutes add

potatoes and finally add the stuffed bhindi (arrange it on the potatoes so the bhindi won't fall apart). Cover it and simmer on low flame. Turn it occasionally so it won't stick.

8. When it's half done, add the remaining stuffing, if any is left. Let it cook for 10 minutes on low flame, covered.
9. When the potatoes are done your bhindis are ready.
10. Serve with roti or paratha.

Coriander: *The leaves of coriander strengthen the stomach and promote its action. They relieve flatulence, increase secretion and discharge of urine and reduce fever. It helps in the removal of catarrh matters and phlegm from the bronchial tubes.*

Nutritive Information

CALORIES: **202 Cal**   PROTEIN: **5.6 gm**   FAT: **0.6 gm**
CARBOHYDRATE: **43.7 gm**   FIBRE: **3 gm**

124 Punjabi Vegetable

Ingredients

Tomatoes	2 (chopped)
Mixed vegetables	450 gms
Curd (skimmed milk)	100 gms
Tomato purée	2 tsp
Red chilli powder	2 tsp
Punjabi masala	1 tsp
Salt	to taste

Method

1. In a pan put chopped tomatoes.
2. Then add masala and mixed vegetables.
3. Afterwards put curd and tomato purée.
4. Mix all together and cook till done.

Tomatoes: Two medium-sized tomatoes contain only around 22 calories between them — a fact that makes them a useful element in any weight reducing diet.

Nutritive Information

CALORIES: **232 Cal**   PROTEIN: **5.3 gm**   FAT: **0.7 gm**
CARBOHYDRATE: **51.3 gm**   FIBRE: **3.8 gm**

125 Quick Brinjal Curry

Ingredients

Brinjals	250 gms (cut in long thin pieces)
Garlic cloves	4 (chopped fine)
Red chilli powder	1/2 tsp
Turmeric powder	1/2 tsp
Salt	to taste
Mustard seeds	1/2 tsp
Curry leaves	few

Method

1. Heat a pan, add mustard seeds and allow them to splutter.
2. Add brinjal pieces and cook well.
3. Put in garlic and sauté.
4. Then add turmeric and red chilli powders and salt and mix well.
5. Cook on low flame by covering with a lid.
6. When it is cooked, add curry leaves and mix once.

Brinjals: *Some recipes of brinjals call for salting before cooking to draw out the bitter juice and reduce moisture. This makes the flesh more dense so that less fat is absorbed during cooking.*

Nutritive Information

CALORIES: **24 Cal**   PROTEIN: **1.4 gm**   FAT: **0.3 gm**
CARBOHYDRATE: **4 gm**   FIBRE: **1.3 gm**

126 Pumpkin Pachadi

Ingredients

Red pumpkin	100 gms (cut into 1-cm cubes)
Thick curd (skimmed milk)	250 gms (well-beaten)
Onion	1 (chopped fine)
Tomato	1 (chopped fine)
Chilli powder	$1/_2$ tsp
Fresh coriander leaves	2 tbsp (for garnishing)
Mustard seeds	$1/_2$ tsp
Split urad dal	$1/_2$ tsp
Dry red chillis	2-3
Curry leaves	few
Asafoetida (hing)	a pinch
Salt	to taste

Method

1. Keep the red pumpkin in a microwave bowl and microwave it for 3-4 minutes covered.
2. Mash the cooked red pumpkin well. Let it cool.
3. After it cools add curd, salt, chilli powder, chopped onion and tomato and mix well.
4. Heat a pan, add asafoetida, red chillis, mustard seeds, curry leaves and urad dal. When it turns slightly brown add to the curd-pumpkin mixture
5. Garnish with coriander leaves and serve.

Pumpkin *is a good source of beta-carotene and vitamin E and thus easily digested.*

Nutritive Information

CALORIES: **124 Cal**   PROTEIN: **6 gm**   FAT: **0.5 gm**
CARBOHYDRATE: **23.9 gm**   FIBRE: **2.1 gm**

127 Bombay Potatoes

Ingredients

Waxy potatoes	1 kg (peeled)
Panch phoran spice mix	1 tsp
Ground turmeric	3 tsp
Tomato paste	2 tbsp
Curd (skimmed milk)	1 ¼ cups

Panch Phoran mix: Mix equal quantities of cumin seeds, fennel seeds, mustard seeds, nigella seeds, fenugreek seeds

Salt	to taste
Cilantro	(chopped fresh)

Method

1. Put the whole potatoes into a large saucepan of salted water and bring them to a boil. Simmer until cooked but not too soft (about 15 minutes).
2. Heat a saucepan and add the panch phoran, turmeric, tomato paste, curd and salt. Bring to a boil and simmer uncovered for 5 minutes.
3. Drain the potatoes and cut each into 4 pieces.
4. Add potatoes to the pan and cook covered. Transfer to a casserole dish. Cover and cook in a pre-heated oven at 350°F for about 40 minutes, until the potatoes are tender and the sauce has thickened a bit.
5. Sprinkle with cilantro.

Curd is a *useful source of calcium and phosphorus. Contains B2 and B12 vitamins. May help to replace valuable bacteria in the gut killed by antibiotics and boost the immune system.*

Nutritive Information
CALORIES: **243 Cal**   PROTEIN: **5.7 gm**   FAT: **0.3 gm**
CARBOHYDRATE: **49.8 gm**   FIBRE: **0.8 gm**

128 Stuffed Veggie Pita

Ingredients

Onion	1 (chopped)
Tomato	1 (chopped)
Green chilli	1 (chopped)
Cottage cheese (skimmed milk)	50 gms
Spinach chopped	75 gms (chopped)
Chilli powder and chilli sauce or ketchup	75 gms
Salt	to taste
Pita bread	

Method

1. Take a deep non stick pan and put chopped green chilli and then add chopped onion on medium high gas.
2. After 1 minute add chopped spinach and sauté it for 1 minute.
3. Add chopped tomato, chilli powder and salt and turn off the gas after 1 minute and let it cool.
4. After 30 seconds, add $1/2$ cup cottage cheese.
5. Take pita bread and cut it in 2 pieces.
6. Spread chilli sauce or ketchup inside the pita bread crust.
7. Then add the mixture you have made and stuff it in the pita bread.
8. Now sauté the pita bread on a non stick pan till it is toasted.

Pita bread is a flat bread which is sometimes split to form a pocket into which a variety of fillings are placed.

Nutritive Information

CALORIES: **125 Cal**   PROTEIN: **6.6 gm**   FAT: **1.1 gm**
CARBOHYDRATE: **22.2 gm**   FIBRE: **2 gm**

129 Baked Vegetable Bonanza

Ingredients

Carrot	1
French beans	8
Fresh green peas	25 gms
Medium-sized cauliflower	25 gms (cut into florets)
Green chillis	2 (finely cut)
Tomatoes for decoration	2
Boiled noodles	100 gms
Skimmed milk	200 gms
Plain flour	2 tbsp
Pepper	½ tsp
Cumin seeds	¼ tsp
Salt	to taste
Cottage cheese (skimmed milk)	1 tbsp (grated)

Method

1. Cut the vegetables into small pieces and boil with little salt and pepper in one cup of water.
2. In a pan add the cumin seeds and the finely cut green chillis.
3. Then add the flour and cook for 2 minutes without browning and stirring throughout.
4. Remove from the heat and gradually add skimmed milk and mix until it is well blended.
5. Return to heat and cook slowly stirring throughout until the sauce thickens.

6. Add the boiled vegetables with the remaining vegetable stock and the boiled noodles and pepper and salt. Mix well.
7. Put it in a baking dish.
8. Sprinkle grated cottage cheese.
9. Cut tomatoes into slices and divide the slices into two and arrange them like a flower all around the edges of the baking dish.
10. Bake at 204⁰ C for 10 minutes.

Peas are a rich source of thiamin, good source of vitamin C, contain fibre, protein phosphorus.

Nutritive Information

CALORIES: **372.3 Cal**   PROTEIN: **24.6 gm**   FAT: **2.45 gm**
CARBOHYDRATE: **83.75 gm**   FIBRE: **7.95 gm**

130 Masala Arbi

Ingredients

Colocasia (arbi)	½ kg (medium size)
Onions	2 (large)
Tomatoes	2 (medium)
Tamarind pulp	50 gms
Cardamoms	3
Bay leaves	2
Curry leaves	10 to 12
Mustard seeds	½ tsp
Cumin seeds	½ tsp
Fenugreek seeds	½ tsp
Ginger-garlic paste	1 tbsp
Chilli powder	1 tsp
Turmeric powder	½ tsp
Coriander powder	1 tsp
Cumin powder (jeera)	1 tsp
Garam masala	1 tsp
Coriander leaves	a handful (chopped)
Water	2 to 3 cups
Salt	to taste

Method
Step 1

1. Boil the arbi, peel the skin and cut into 4-cm lengthwise or breadthwise pieces and keep aside (do not over boil them otherwise they get pulpy).

2. Cut the onions into thin slices, add cardamoms, 2 bay leaves and boil in enough water till the onions become transparent.
3. Sieve the excess water and let the onions cool for sometime and then grind until smooth in a mixie.

Step 2

1. Heat a pan and add cumin, mustard and fenugreek seeds. Let them splutter, then add curry leaves and stir for a few seconds.
2. Add the onion paste, stir and let it cook for a minute.
3. Add ginger-garlic paste.
4. Now add the chopped tomatoes, salt, chilli, turmeric, coriander, cumin powders and stir for some time.
5. Let it cook for 2 to 3 minutes and add 2 cups of water. Stir for few seconds and let it come to a boil.

Step 3

1. When the gravy comes to a boil, add tamarind pulp and stir, and let it cook. (Note: if you want more gravy you can add another cup of water now and then let it cook for a minute and check for the salt and tamarind juice, if it's less sour you can add some more pulp.)
2. Now add the boiled colocasia, garam masala and chopped coriander.
3. Cook till the gravy is thick.

Curry leaves *posseses the qualities of a herbal tonic. They strengthen the functions of the stomach and promote its action. They are also used as a mild laxative.*

Nutritive Information

CALORIES: **361 Cal**   PROTEIN: **3.6 gm**   FAT: **0.6 gm**
CARBOHYDRATE: **78 gm**   FIBRE: **4.4 gm**

131 Raw Mango Curry

Ingredients

Raw mangoes	4
Asafoetida powder (hing)	1 tsp
Red chilli powder	2 tsp
Turmeric powder	½ tsp
Mustard seeds	½ tsp
Salt	to taste

Method

1. Cut the raw mangoes very fine into tiny squares. Heat a degchi and add the mustard seeds. Allow them to splutter.
2. Add hing powder and switch off the gas.
3. Then add the cut raw mangoes, turmeric and chilli powders and salt.
4. Serve it immediately as it tastes best when it is crisp.
5. It tastes best with curd, skimmed milk and rice.

Raw mangoes are a rich source of beta-carotene which the body can convert to vitamin A. Rich source of vitamins.

Nutritive Information

CALORIES: **44 Cal**   PROTEIN: **0.7 gm**   FAT: **0.1 gm**
CARBOHYDRATE: **10.1 gm**   FIBRE: **1.2 gm**

132 Shahi Cauliflower Korma

Ingredients

Cauliflower (small)	1
Cottage cheese (skimmed milk)	125 gms (grated)
Onion	25 gms
Peas	250 gms
Tomatoes	4-5 (chopped fine)
Curd (skimmed milk)	125 gms
Coriander leaves	few (chopped)
Ginger	25 gms (chopped fine)
Cumin seeds	1 tsp
Garam masala	25 gms
Salt	to taste

Method

1. Roast the pieces of cauliflower and grated paneer till they get light brown in colour.
2. Take a pan and roast onion, ginger and spices and chopped tomatoes in it.
3. Now put one cup of water. When it boils add paneer and cauliflower.
4. Boil peas in 2 cups of water and curd. When ¼ cup of water is left then mix it into the prepared vegetables and add salt according to taste.
5. Now cook for 1 minute and garnish it with chopped coriander and garam masala.

Cauliflower is a member of the cancer fighting cruciferous family. It is a rich source of nutrients including vitamin C.

Nutritive Information

CALORIES: **226 Cal**   PROTEIN: **18.9 gm**   FAT: **0.95 gm**
CARBOHYDRATE: **38.25 gm**   FIBRE: **6.3 gm**

133 Haryali Makkai

Ingredients

Spinach (palak)	1 bunch
Corn	1 tin
Garlic	1 tbsp (chopped)
Ginger	1 tbsp (chopped)
Tomatoes	4
Onions	2

Method

1. Boil the palak and blend it in a mixie.
2. Make a paste of onions and tomatoes.
3. In a karahi put ginger and garlic.
4. Then add the paste of onions.
5. When golden brown add tomato-onion mixture and cook for 10 minutes.
6. Add palak and corn.
7. Cook for 10 minutes.

Corn is suitable for gluten free diet and is a good source of potassium and useful source of iron.

Nutritive Information

CALORIES: **221 Cal**   PROTEIN: **8.8 gm**   FAT: **1.9 gm**
CARBOHYDRATE: **42.2 gm**   FIBRE: **3.9 gm**

134 Aloo Tamatar Subzi

Ingredients

Potatoes	1 kg (finely sliced)
Tomatoes	1 kg (chopped)
Curry leaves	6-7
Lemon juice	2 tbsp
Green chillis	2
Coriander leaves	½ a bunch (chopped)
Achaar masala	1 packet

Method

1. Heat a pan. Add chopped tomatoes and achaar masala. Cook for sometime.
2. Sauté the sliced potatoes in a pan. Add them to the tomato and achaar masala mix.
3. Allow it to simmer on low heat for 3-5 minutes. Add the lemon juice and garnish with coriander leaves. Serve hot.

Potatoes considered a favourite of the children is an energy dense food-stuff.

Nutritive Information

CALORIES: **362.5 Cal**   PROTEIN: **8.5 gm**   FAT: **1.25 gm**
CARBOHYDRATE: **74.5 gm**   FIBRE: **5 gm**

135 Healthy Tofu Scramble

Ingredients

Tofu (firm or extra firm)	250 gms (grated or diced finely)
Carrots	100 gms (washed, peeled and chopped finely)
Spinach leaves	100 gms (washed, drained and chopped)
Onion	50 gms (chopped finely)
Salt	to taste
Curry powder	1 tsp

Method

1. Add the chopped onions to a hot pan.
2. Sauté for a 1 minute, till the raw smell disappears.
3. Add the grated tofu and sauté for 3-4 minutes.
4. Add the curry powder and salt and sauté for 2 minutes.
5. Now add the chopped carrots and spinach and sauté for another 2 minutes.
6. Remove from fire and serve hot.

Tofu is high in protein, low in saturated fats. Good source of calcium and a useful source of vitamin E. May help to protect against some forms of cancer and heart disease.

Nutritive Information

CALORIES: **302.6 Cal** PROTEIN: **46.5 gm** FAT: **1.68 gm**
CARBOHYDRATE: **44.8 gm** FIBRE: **4.85 gm**

136 Soya Subzi

Ingredients

Nutri nuggets	800 gms
Preboiled peas	500 gms
Preboiled carrots	500 gms (diced)
Cottage cheese (skimmed milk)	500 gms (grated)
Onions	4 (grated)
Tomatoes	6 (grated)
Green chillis	4 (finely cut)
Ginger	1 tbsp grated
Fresh coriander	few (finely cut)
Cumin seeds (jeera)	½ tsp
Turmeric powder	½ tsp
Coriander powder	½ tsp
Cumin powder	½ tsp
Mango powder	½ tsp
Chana masala	½ tsp
Red chillis	to taste
Garam masala	½ tsp (freshly ground)
Skimmed milk	500 ml
Water	4 cups
Black pepper	a pinch
Salt	to taste

Method

1. Mix skimmed milk and water in a bowl and soak nutri nuggets in it for 7 minutes. Keep aside.

2. In a karahi on the second burner meanwhile put onions and roast along with jeera, ginger, green chillis until brown.
3. Add turmeric, coriander, cumin powders, salt, garam masala, chana and mango powders, red chilli and cook until they are slightly fried and not over done.
4. Now add grated tomatoes to this masala and keep stirring until the masala is done. Please do not add any water to this as the tomatoes leave enough juice.
5. Now add the Nutri nuggets which had been presoaked and cook on high flame stirring till water dries up.
6. Reduce the flame and add the boiled peas, diced carrots, cottage cheese to it and stir till the entire mixture mixes well and all the ingredients get the colour.
7. Spread in a serving dish and sprinkle freshly cut coriander leaves, black pepper and a little garam masala. Serve hot.

Carrots *are an excellent source of beta carotene, the plant form of vitamin A which is needed for healthy vision as well as for the maintenance of the mucous membrane.*

Nutritive Information

CALORIES: **319 Cal**   PROTEIN: **26 gm**   FAT: **5.27 gm**
CARBOHYDRATE: **46.43 gm**   FIBRE: **7.55 gm**

137 Soya Curry

Ingredients

Soya	¼ kg
Onions	2
Mustard seeds	½ tsp
Ginger	2-cm piece
Garlic cloves	3
Red chilli powder	2 ½ tsp
Turmeric powder	¼ tsp
Salt	to taste

Method

1. Boil and cut the soya.
2. Cut the onions, crush the ginger and garlic.
3. Take a pan, put some mustard seeds and then onions to sauté till little brown and then add soya.
4. Lastly add turmeric powder, crushed ginger and garlic, red chilli powder and salt and cook till done.

A very nutritious and protein rich curry. Can be used as accompaniment to rice or chapati.

Nutritive Information

CALORIES: **266 Cal**   PROTEIN: **22.8 gm**   FAT: **9.85 gm**
CARBOHYDRATE: **21.55 gm**   FIBRE: **2.45 gm**

138 Tofu Sambharia

Ingredients

Potatoes	4-5
Onions	4-5
Green chillis (big)	2
Medium sized tomatoes	4
Small brinjals (optional)	4
Tofu	200 gms
Sprouted beans (moong)	300 gms
Chilli powder	1 tsp
Garam masala	1 tsp
Cumin powder	1 tsp
Coriander powder	2 tsp
Ginger-garlic paste	1 tsp
Sugar	½ tsp
Gram flour (besan)	100 gms
Coriander leaves	for garnishing (chopped)
Salt	to taste

Method

1. In a bowl take tofu, sprouted moong and add chilli powder, garam masala, coriander and cumin powders, ginger-garlic paste, sugar, besan, few chopped coriander leaves and salt to taste.
2. Mix well, slit all the vegetables to fill with the stuffing.
3. Stuff all the vegetables and boil them for 6-7 minutes. Take sambharia out and let it cool for a few minutes.
4. Take a pan and heat it.

5. Season it with mustard and cumin seeds and when they start popping add sambharia and sauté it.
6. Sambharia is ready. Serve hot with parathas and green chutney.

Tofu is a soft, cheese like food made by curdling fresh hot soya milk with a coagulant. It is also known as soyabean curd.

Nutritive Information

CALORIES: **365 Cal**   PROTEIN: **27.75 gm**   FAT: **4.1 gm**
CARBOHYDRATE: **101.3 gm**   FIBRE: **4.1 gm**

139 Soya Bean Bhaji or Nutrela

Ingredients

Soya chunks	½ kg pack
Onions	8 (chopped)
Tomatoes	6 (chopped)
Green chillis	4 (chopped)
Kashmiri red chilli powder	2 tsp
Coriander powder	3 tsp
Garam masala powder	to taste
Salt	to taste
Water	1 ½ glasses
Coriander leaves	1 tbsp

Method

1. Soak soya chunks in warm water and give 1 minute boil.
2. Remove from warm water and keep aside.
3. In a karahi put chopped onions and green chillis. Sauté till golden brown.
4. Squeeze soya chunks nicely and add to onions.
5. Then put in chopped tomatoes and all dry masalas.
6. Mix it very nicely till the bhaji turns golden brown. Add salt.
7. Put 1 ½ glasses of water. Pressure-cook for 5 whistles.
8. Garnish it with chopped corianders leaves.

Soya chunks *are rich in potassium and a useful source of magnesium, phosphorus, iron, folate and vitamin E. It contains manganese, vitamin B6 and thiamin.*

Nutritive Information

CALORIES: **248 Cal**   PROTEIN: **20 gm**   FAT: **5.45 gm**
CARBOHYDRATE: **34.63 gm**   FIBRE: **3.73 gm**

140 Mushrooms in Curd

Ingredients

Mushrooms (fresh)	200 gms
Onions	2 (chopped fine)
Omum seeds (ajwain)	1 tsp
Ginger	2-cm piece (chopped)
Green chillis	2 (chopped)
Garam masala powder	1 tsp
Red chilli powder	¾ tsp
Coriander powder (dhania)	1 tsp
Fresh curd (skimmed milk)	75 gms
Salt	to taste

Method

1. Wash and cut mushrooms into 'T' shaped slices. Each into 4 slices.
2. Heat a non-stick pan. Add ajwain and sauté for 3 seconds.
3. Add onions, green chillis and ginger. Cook till onions turn light golden.
4. Add mushrooms, cover and cook till done, stirring occasionally.
5. Add chilli and dhania powders.
6. Blend beaten curd, garam masala and salt and add.
7. Cook till curd dries up and coats the mushrooms.
8. Serve hot.

Mushrooms: *Dried fungi have more intense flavour than their fresh counterparts and they generally contribute more to the flavour than to the bulk of food.*

Nutritive Information

CALORIES: **140 Cal**   PROTEIN: **9.3 gm**   FAT: **1.75 gm**
CARBOHYDRATE: **18.75 gm**   FIBRE: **1.5 gm**

141 Tandoori Aloo

Ingredients

Baby potatoes	250 gms
Curd (skimmed milk)	1 tbsp
Kasoori methi (dried fenugreek leaves)	¼ tsp
Salt	to taste

For the paste

Kashmiri chillis	4
Garlic cloves	2

Method

1. Wash the potatoes thoroughly, pierce them with a fork and place them all around the circumference of the microwave turn table. Place a glass of water in the centre to prevent the potatoes from getting wrinkled.
2. Microwave on HIGH for 5 to 6 minutes until the potatoes are soft.
3. Heat a glass bowl, add the ground paste and salt and mix well. Microwave on HIGH for 1 minute.
4. Add the potatoes, curd and Kasoori methi and microwave on HIGH for 2 minutes.
5. Serve hot.

Baby potatoes are high carbohydrate food which contain both protein and fibre. They also supply us with a significant amount of vitamin C and potassium which we need.

Nutritive Information

CALORIES: **97 Cal**   PROTEIN: **1.6 gm**   FAT: **0.1 gm**
CARBOHYDRATE: **22.6 gm**   FIBRE: **0.4 gm**

142 Broccoli Masala

Ingredients

Big crown of broccoli (Harigobi)	1
Green gram dal (moong)	3 tbsp
Dried red chillis (1 cm pieces)	3-4
Curry leaves	5-6
Cumin seeds	1 tsp
Mustard seeds	$1/2$ tsp
Salt	to taste
Lime juice	as per taste

Method

1. Cut broccoli into florets and clean well.
2. Clean and soak moong dal in water for about 15 minutes.
3. Heat a karahi.
4. Add the mustard seeds.
5. Once the seeds splutter, add cumin seeds, red chillis and curry leaves.
6. Drain the moong dal and add to the karahi.
7. Keep stirring, since the moong dal will stick to the karahi.
8. Add ¼ cup of water, stirring from time to time till the moong dal is half cooked.
9. Add the broccoli florets and salt to taste.
10. Stir well. Cover and cook till the broccoli is tender, stir occasionally. Adjust salt at this point.
11. When the broccoli and moong dal is cooked to the texture you want, remove from fire.

12. Squeeze in the lemon/ lime juice and mix well.

Broccoli: *The tender flower heads, or florets of broccoli are richer in beta- carotene than the stalks and the deeper the colour, the higher the nutritive value. The freshness of broccoli is indicated by crisp, easily shaped stalks.*

Nutritive Information

CALORIES: **66 Cal** PROTEIN: **5.9 gm** FAT: **1.3 gm**
CARBOHYDRATE: **7.6 gm** FIBRE: **2 gm**

143 Radish Leaves Dal Curry

Ingredients

Bunch of fresh radish leaves	2
Red gram dal (arhar)	250 gms
Green chillis	6 (cut fine)
Garlic cloves	6 (chopped fine)
Onions	2 (chopped)
Tomatoes	2 (chopped)
Cumin seeds	2 tsp
Tamarind pulp	2 tsp
Curry leaves	5-6
Turmeric powder	1 tsp
Salt	to taste

For seasoning

Mustard seeds	1 tsp
Cumin seeds	1 tsp
Garlic	3 flakes (finely chopped)
Coriander leaves	few
Water	2 cups

Method

1. Combine arhar dal, chopped onions, green chillis, garlic, tomatoes, turmeric powder, curry leaves and cumin.
2. Pressure cook the above ingredients for two whistles.
3. Make a paste of the cooked ingredients by grinding it in a mixie to form a fine paste, or it can also be mashed finely by using a wooden spoon.

4. Add 2 tamarind pulp.
5. Crackle mustard and cumin seeds. Add garlic. Cook till light brown in colour. Add the above paste.
6. Boil for 5 minutes.
7. Finally add chopped coriander leaves.

Radish leaves *low in fat and calories. Useful source of vitamin C. They are used as diuretic in herbal medicine.*

Nutritive Information

CALORIES: **181.75 Cal**   PROTEIN: **11.48 gm**   FAT: **1.13 gm**
CARBOHYDRATE: **31.5 gm**   FIBRE: **2.78 gm**

144 Versatile Soya

Ingredient

Soya beans   *300 gms*

Method

1. Soak the beans in water for at least 12 hours.
2. Drain all the water and wash the soaked beans.
3. Grind the soaked beans in a blender to a smooth paste using 4 cups of water.
4. Strain to extract the milk.
5. Boil this milk, remove from the flame.
6. Strain the soya bean curd through a muslin cloth placed on a strainer.
7. Press the beaten curd and put some weight on it so that all the water is drained out. Use this Tofu instead of paneer in any recipe. It is low fat and healthier than paneer.

Nutritive Information

CALORIES: **206 Cal**   PROTEIN: **17.9 gm**   FAT: **5.15 gm**
CARBOHYDRATE: **26.93 gm**   FIBRE: **2.73 gm**

145 Lemony Mushroom

Ingredients

Button mushrooms	500 gms
Green chillis	4 (finely chopped)
Lemon juice	1 tbsp
Coriander powder	1 tsp
Chaat masala	2 tsp
Ginger-garlic paste	1/2 tsp
Tomato	1 (finely chopped)
Onion	2 tsp (chopped)
Salt	to taste

Method

1. Chop the mushrooms and cook them on medium flame for 2 minutes. Remove and keep aside.
2. In the same karahi, sauté onion for 1 minute and then add tomato, ginger-garlic paste, chaat masala, green chillis and coriander powder. Cook for 1 minute.
3. Let it cool and then add lemon juice.
4. Add the cooked mushrooms and toss in the hot karahi for 30 seconds.
5. The dish is ready to serve.

Lemon juice *is an excellent source of vitamin C, which helps to maintain the immune system. May help to relieve rheumatism.*

Nutritive Information

CALORIES: **80 Cal**   PROTEIN: **5.22 gm**   FAT: **0.81 gm**
CARBOHYDRATE: **5.41 gm**   FIBRE: **0.46 gm**

146 Lajawaab Gobi

Ingredients

Cauliflower (phoolgobi)	500 gms
Curd (skimmed milk)	250 gms
Ginger paste & Kasoori methi	2-2 tsp
Red chilli paste &Garam masala	1-1 tsp
Cottage cheese (skimmed milk)	100 gms (grated)
Salt	to taste
Coriander leaves	2 tsp (chopped fine)

Method

1. Break cauliflower into florets and place in a bowl with curd, chilli paste, kasoori methi and ½ tsp salt.
2. Mix well and marinate for 10 minutes. Now remove cauliflower florets, keep aside on a plate.
3. Heat karahi. Put curry leaves. Now pour the curd mixture and stir. Once the curd starts drying up add ginger paste and sauté for a few minutes.
4. Now add the gobi pieces and sauté on low heat for 6 minutes.
5. Add salt if needed.
6. Now pour 1 ¼ cups of water and simmer till done.
7. Once gravy thickens add grated cottage cheese, garam masala, and coriander leaves.
8. Serve hot with rotis.

Cottage cheese is a good source of protein and a rich source of calcium, important source of B12 for vegetarians. May help to fight tooth decay.

Nutritive Information

CALORIES: **88 Cal** PROTEIN: **7.6 gm** FAT: **0.6 gm**
CARBOHYDRATE: **13.2 gm** FIBRE: **1.2 gm**

147 Mushroom Paradise

Ingredients

Mushroom	200 gm
Curd (skimmed milk)	250 gms
Garlic-ginger paste	2 tsp
Pepper	½ tsp
Onions	2 sliced
Cloves, Cinnamon, Cardamom	2-3 each
Cumin seeds	½ tsp
Lemon juice	1 tbsp
Coriander and mint leaves	2-3 tbsp (chopped)
Salt	to taste
Basmati rice	500 gms

Method

1. Clean, chop mushrooms into halves and marinate them in curd, a little salt, pepper and 1 tsp of garlic-ginger paste for 10 minutes.
2. Meanwhile in a heavy bottom vessel add cumin seeds and whole garam masala. Sauté for a few seconds.
3. Add the onions and sauté till pinkish in colour.
4. Add 1 tsp garlic-ginger paste and add soaked mushrooms along with curd. Cook on high flame till mixture is almost dry.
5. Add pre-soaked rice, lemon juice and 3 ½ cups of water. Add coriander and mint leaves and cook on low flame till rice is done.

Curd is a fermented form of milk. It is good for heart ailments, for senile state in preventing and delaying degeneration of body, purifies blood, keeps digestive system healthy.

Nutritive Information

CALORIES: **154 Cal**   PROTEIN: **3.1 gm**   FAT: **0.15 gm**
CARBOHYDRATE: **10.15 gm**   FIBRE: **0.3 gm**

148 Besanwali Shimla Mirch

Ingredients

Capsicums (Shimla mirch)	5
Gram flour	2 tbsp
Coriander powder	1 tsp
Turmeric powder & Haldi	½-½ tsp
Salt	to taste
Caraway seeds (Shahjeera)	a pinch
Asafoetida	a pinch
Fennel seeds	a pinch
Cumin seeds	a pinch
Sugar	to taste

Method

1. Cut capsicum into pieces.
2. Take gram flour in a pan and roast a little.
3. Take gram flour pan and add cumin and caraway seeds, asafoetida and fennel.
4. Add capsicum to the pan and sauté.
5. Add turmeric, chilli and coriander powders, salt, sugar and again sauté.
6. Add the gram flour and ½ tsp of water to it.
7. Cook for 10 minutes and serve hot.

Shimla mirch causes the stomach to secrete a mucus which protects its lining against irritants such as acid, aspirin or alcohol.

Nutritive Information

CALORIES: **60 Cal** PROTEIN: **3.01 gm** FAT: **0.65 gm**
CARBOHYDRATE: **10.39 gm** FIBRE: **1.39 gm**

149 Potato-Onion Delight

Ingredients

Potatoes	6
Onions	4
Large tomatoes	2
Green chillis	4-5
Ginger	2-cm piece (finely chopped)
Coriander leaves	few (chopped)
Turmeric powder	½ tsp
Red chilli powder	to taste
Coriander powder	1 tsp
Garam masala and salt	to taste
Dal masala	½ tsp
Cumin seeds	1 tsp
Tomato (to garnish)	1
Long spring onion	1 (to garnish)

Method

1. Peel the potatoes and onions.
2. Cut them in long (French fries type) and thin pieces.
3. Soak the potatoes in water, take out and spread on a muslin cloth.
4. Slit the green chillis lengthwise. Cut the tomatoes also in long pieces.
5. Simultaneously, put the gas on and heat a non-stick karahi.
6. Start roasting onions and potatoes till golden brown in colour.
7. Take them out on a brown paper.
8. In a karahi add cumin, turmeric, coriander and red chilli powder.

After they crackle, add the roasted potatoes, onions, ginger and green chillis.

9. After cooking for a minute, add tomatoes, garam masala and dal masala to it. Toss all the ingredients and cover the karahi. Turn off the gas after half a minute.
10. Pour the subzi in a serving dish. Garnish with chopped coriander leaves and a tomato basket or long pieces of tomatoes and / or onion flowers. Serve with hot chapatis.

A simple, quick, easy vegetable preparation for the homemaker when no other vegetable is available.

Nutritive Information

CALORIES: **167 Cal**   PROTEIN: **3.01 gm**   FAT: **0.65 gm**
CARBOHYDRATE: **10.39 gm**   FIBRE: **1.39 gm**

150 Jhatpat Matar Paneer

Ingredients

Onion, garlic, ginger paste	2 tbsp
Frozen peas cottage cheese (skimmed milk)	250 gms
Tomato purée	1 packet
Salt	1 tsp
Pao bhaji masala	1 tsp
Cumin seeds	½ tsp
Asafoetida powder	½ tsp
Turmeric powder	½ tsp
Coriander leaves	a few

Method

1. Add the cumin to a heated pan. When it starts spluttering add asafoetida and turmeric powders.
2. Add onion-garlic-ginger paste. Cook it on low flame.
3. Then add salt and pao bhaji masala. Cook it for 2 to 3 minutes on low flame.
3. Add peas and cottage cheese. Cook it on low flame for 3 to 4 minutes.
4. Serve it hot after garnished with coriander leaves (finely chopped) with chapatis, paranthas or thepalas.

This paneer matar subji is quick and easy to make. Addition of pao bhaji masala to it instead of normal garam masala gives it an additional taste, flavour and aroma.

Nutritive Information

CALORIES: **215 Cal** PROTEIN: **16.9 gm** FAT: **0.6 gm**
CARBOHYDRATE: **42.1 gm** FIBRE: **2.6 gm**

151 Methi Capsicum Subzi

Ingredients

Capsicums	4
Fenugreek leaves (methi)	500 gms (chopped fine)
Gram flour	2 tbsp
Cumin & Omum seeds	½-½ tsp
Garam masala powder	½ tsp
Turmeric powder	¼ tsp
Lemon juice	1 tsp
Salt	to taste
Coriander leaves & Green chillis	few (chopped)

Method

1. Heat a pan and add gram flour. Roast it until it turns golden in colour. Let it cool.
2. Add fenugreek, cumin, omum, green chillis, garam masala, turmeric, lemon juice and salt to taste. Mix well with roasted gram flour.
3. Pierce the capsicums with the thumb making 3 holes all round its walls, keeping the top intact.
4. Stuff the mixture into the capsicums through these holes.
5. Place the stuffed capsicums in a non-stick pan and cover the pan.
6. Cook on a medium flame, turning the capsicums at intervals until all sides are cooked.
7. Serve hot garnished with coriander.

A combination of both fenugreek and capsicum gives this vegetable a green and fresh look and addition of gram flour not only improves flavour but also increases the protein content of the entire vegetable.

Nutritive Information

CALORIES: **115.2 Cal** PROTEIN: **7.78 gm** FAT: **1.76 gm**
CARBOHYDRATE: **15.28 gm** FIBRE: **2.4 gm**

152 Vegetable Chow Chow

Ingredients

Carrots (sliced into thin long wedges)	2
Beans (cut into thin long pieces)	10-15
Capsicum (sliced into thin long strips)	1 large
Onions (cut into lengthwise pieces)	1
Tomato (cut into small pieces)	1
Ginger-garlic paste	1 tsp
Cornflour	3 tbsp
Salt	to taste
Black pepper	to taste
Vinegar	$1/4$ tsp
Ajinomoto	a pinch
Soya sauce	$1/4$ tsp

Method

1. Mix the cornflour with water and make it into a smooth paste.
2. Take a non-stick karahi and put 2-3 cups of water. Bring to a boil and add the cornflour mixing continuously taking care that no lumps are formed.
3. Add ginger-garlic paste, salt and pepper. If the gravy seems too thick you can add more water.
4. Put in carrots and beans and boil for 2-3 minutes. Then add the capsicum and onions and boil for 2-3 minutes.
5. In the end add chopped tomatoes and vinegar.

6. If you wish you can add ajinomoto and soya sauce. Boil for $^1/_2$ a minute.
7. Remove and serve with hot steamed rice.

Vegetable chow chow is a snack as well as a nutritious dish and easy to prepare.

Nutritive Information

CALORIES: **77 Cal**   PROTEIN: **1.9 gm**   FAT: **0.55 gm**
CARBOHYDRATE: **14.8 gm**   FIBRE: **2.09 gm**

153 Bhindi with Mustard Paste

Ingredients

Lady's fingers (bhindi)	500 gms
Green chillis	7-8 pieces
Turmeric powder	1 tsp
Sugar	1 tsp
Coriander leaves for garnishing	
Mustard seeds (grind to paste with few green chillis and little water)	3 tbsp
Salt	to taste

Method

1. Slit the lady's fingers. Keep aside.
2. Take a karahi, and sauté the lady's fingers nicely till the raw smell comes out.
3. Add turmeric green chillis cut in slits, salt and sauté again.
4. When it is $3/4$ cooked put in mustard paste.
5. Cook till the paste gets evenly coated on the lady's fingers.
6. Lastly put in sugar and coriander leaves. Cook for a while.

Addition of sugar and mustard paste makes this preparation different and adds more flavour to it. To add more crispness and crunch to it, one can prepare this vegetable in the microwave oven too.

Nutritive Information

CALORIES: **175 Cal**   PROTEIN: **9.5 gm**   FAT: **1 gm**
CARBOHYDRATE: **3.2 gm**   FIBRE: **6 gm**

154 Lasuni Baigan

Ingredients

Brinjals (baigan)	4 (big)
Garlic cloves	5 (crushed)
Coriander leaves	few (chopped)
Plain curd (skimmed milk)	250 gms
Tomato purée	1 tbsp
Tomato	1 sliced
Pepper	1 tsp
Chilli powder	1 tsp
Salt	to taste

Method

1. Cut the brinjals into long juliennes (1cm x 3 cms) and roast them for 10 minutes over light to medium flame.
2. Once cooked sprinkle some salt and pepper and keep aside in a dish.

For the sauce

3. Pour the curd in a blender. Add coriander leaves, crushed garlic, tomato purée, salt and chilli powder and blend until finely done.
4. Pour the sauce over the cooked brinjals in the dish and garnish with sliced tomatoes.

This brinjal preparation in curd sauce makes it different from normal brinjal preparations, moreover coriander and tomato purée brings in a colourful green and red combination in the curd sauce.

Nutritive Information

CALORIES: **77 Cal** PROTEIN: **5.3 gm** FAT: **0.7 gm**
CARBOHYDRATE: **12.6 gm** FIBRE: **2.6 gm**

155 Yummy Karela

Ingredients

Bitter gourds (small)	½ kg
Onions (big)	3
Potatoes	2 (cut in long chips)
Salt	to taste
Red chilli powder	1 tsp
Mango powder	1 tbsp
Turmeric powder	½ tsp
Garlic paste	1 tbsp

For masala

Coriander seeds	250 gms
Fennel seeds	100 gms
Fenugreek seeds	1 tbsp

Method

1. Roast the masala items separately and make a fine powder. It can be stored in the fridge for a long time.
2. Chop onions finely. Add salt, chilli powder, mango powder, garlic paste, turmeric powder and the dry masala powder (2 ½ tbsp) and mix well.
3. Scrape the bitter gourds and slit them from top to bottom (not through). Fill with the onion mixture and apply the remaining masala on the potatoes.
4. Heat a karahi on medium flame and keep the bitter gourds with the open ends upward.
5. After 5 minutes add the potatoes and mix slowly and cover. Stir once after 5 minutes.

Presence of various spices in the vegetable extracts bitterness from the bitter gourd. It is an ideal vegetable preparation for diabetic patients but only when potatoes are excluded from this recipe.

Nutritive Information

CALORIES: **197 Cal**   PROTEIN: **6.0 gm**   FAT: **0.6 gm**
CARBOHYDRATE: **42.1 gm**   FIBRE: **2.6 gm**

156 Cauliflower Ghar Jaise

Ingredients

Cauliflower (separated into florets)	1
Potatoes (cut into medium sized pieces)	2
Peas	100 gms (shelled)
Chilli-ginger paste	1 tbsp
Garam masala	1 tbsp
Coriander leaves	few (chopped)
Mustard & Cumin seeds	½-½ tsp
Asafoetida (hing)	a pinch
Turmeric powder	½ tsp
Salt	to taste
Sugar	½ tsp

Method

1. Heat a non-stick pan. Add the mustard and cumin seeds, asafoetida and turmeric.
2. Add cauliflower, peas and potatoes and mix well.
3. Add salt. Mix well and add a little water and cover. Cook till the veggies are done (but not mashed).
4. The water should all get evaporated.
5. Add the chilli-ginger paste, sugar and garam masala. Mix well.
6. Add coriander leaves and serve hot.

A hot n spicy cauliflower preparation. This vegetable can be served with chapati and paratha and may be used as a stuffing in sandwiches.

Nutritive Information

CALORIES: 250 Cal   PROTEIN: 14.0 gm   FAT: 1 gm
CARBOHYDRATE: 46.5 gm FIBRE: 6.8 gm

157 Doda Nu Shak

Ingredients

Corn on the cobs	4
Onions	3
Tomatoes	2-3
Curd (skimmed milk)	100 gms
Red chilli and garlic paste	2-3 tbsp
Gram flour	1 tbsp
Turmeric powder	½ tsp
Cumin powder	1 tsp
Sugar	1 tsp
Garam masala	½ tsp
Coriander leaves	2 tbsp (chopped fine)
Salt	to taste

Method

1. Cut each corn into 3-4 pieces and pressure cook.
2. Chop onions finely and grate the tomatoes.
3. Mix red chilli-garlic paste, turmeric, salt and cumin powder with 3 tbsp of water.
4. Heat a pan and sauté onions till golden brown.
5. Then add grated tomatoes and cook for 2 minutes on low flame.
6. Add red chilli-turmeric paste and cook for 1-2 more minutes.
7. Then add cooked corn and little water from the pressure cooker to make some gravy.
8. Boil for 5 minutes.

9. Mix gram flour with curd and add to the curry. Boil for another minute. Remove the gravy from fire.
10. Add sugar and garam masala. Stir well.
11. Garnish with coriander leaves.

Sugar enhances the taste of some foods. Almost an immediate source of energy.

Nutritive Information

CALORIES: **199 Cal**   PROTEIN: **8.7 gm**   FAT: **1.7 gm**
CARBOHYDRATE: **37.75 gm**   FIBRE: **3.0 gm**

158 Brinjal in Curd

Ingredients

Brinjal	1
Onions	2 (chopped)
Garlic cloves	2 (crushed)
Ginger	1 tbsp (chopped)
Coriander powder	1 tsp
Black pepper	¼ tsp
Turmeric powder	½ tsp
Cumin powder	1 tsp
Salt	1 tsp
Curd (skimmed milk)	250 gms
Sugar	to taste

Method

1. Roast the brinjal, when cool, peel and cut into cubes.
2. Sauté the onions in a karahi. Add ginger, garlic, coriander, pepper, turmeric, cumin and salt.
3. Cook for several minutes. Add the brinjal cubes. Cook for about 5 minutes.
4. Just before serving, stir in the curd and sugar. Serve with Basmati rice.

Garlic is a proven broad spectrum antibiotic that combats bacteria, intestinal parasites and viruses. Garlic lowers blood pressure and blood cholesterol. It boosts the immunes system.

Nutritive Information

CALORIES: **74 Cal** PROTEIN: **2.6 gm** FAT: **0.4 gm**
CARBOHYDRATE: **15.1 gm** FIBRE: **1.9 gm**

159 Mixed Vegetable Bake

Ingredients

Tomato	1
Onion	1
Capsicum	1
Carrot	1
Potato	1
French beans	8-10
Baby corns	2-3
Banana (raw)	1
Plain flour	1 tbsp
White vinegar	1 tbsp
Soya sauce	½ tsp
Sugar	½ tsp
Salt	to taste
Green chillis	3 (finely chopped)
Cottage cheese (skimmed milk)	½ cup

Method

1. Peel (where required) and chop all vegetables separately into big chunks.
2. Combine potato, beans, baby corn, banana, carrot.
3. Boil them in salted water till tender but not mushy.
4. Drain, hold under running water in a colander and keep aside.
5. Heat a pan, add onion and capsicum, stir till tender.
6. Add green chillis, tomato, vinegar, soya sauce, salt, sugar.

7. Stir and cook for a minute. Add boiled vegetables.
8. Stir and sprinkle flour all over. Toss.
9. Transfer to a casserole, crumble and sprinkle paneer.
10. Bake in a hot oven till the vegetables sizzle.
11. Serve hot with garlic buns or warm bread.

The bountiful earth offers you an abundance of pure food and provides for meals obtainable without slaughter and bloodshed.

Nutritive Information

CALORIES: **395.5 Cal** PROTEIN: **10.05 gm** FAT: **1.35 gm**
CARBOHYDRATE: **86.2 gm** FIBRE: **6.2 gm**

160 Tasty Aloo

Ingredients

Potato chips	500 gms
Sauce	50 gms
Capsicums, onions, tomatoes, ginger	500 gms (finely chopped)
Cottage cheese (skimmed milk)	50 gms

Method

1. Mix all the ingredients and put in the microwave for 2 minutes.
2. Serve hot.

A quick, easy and spicy preparation containing almost all the food groups.

Nutritive Information

CALORIES: **107.3 Cal**   PROTEIN: **1.94 gm**   FAT: **0.16 gm**
CARBOHYDRATE: **24.65 gm**   FIBRE: **0.54 gm**

161 Paneer Schezwan

Ingredients

Cottage cheese/paneer (skimmed milk)	250 gms
Tomatoes	2
Capsicum	2
Onions	2
Cumin seeds (jeera)	1 tsp
Tomato-chilli sauce	1 tbsp
Salt	to taste

Method

1. Cut the vegetables and paneer into cubes.
2. Heat a karahi and put in jeera.
3. When it splutters, put paneer and capsicum.
4. Stir and cook for 2 minutes.
5. Add onions and tomatoes.
6. Stir and cover.
7. Let it cook for 2 minutes.
8. Add salt and sauce.
9. Paneer schezwan is ready to eat.

An oil-free paneer preparation which resembles karahi paneer in colour. Flavour and texture goes well with roomali roti, naan or parantha.

Nutritive Information

CALORIES: **152 Cal**   PROTEIN: **8.4 gm**   FAT: **0.8 gm**
CARBOHYDRATE: **24.2 gm**   FIBRE: **1.4 gm**

162 Bharwa Tinde

Ingredients

Tinda (small size)	8
Coriander powder	1 tbsp
Cumin powder	1 tbsp
Onion (big)	1 (chopped fine)
Coriander leaves	250 gms
Curry leaves	1 tbsp
Mustard seeds	$1/2$ tsp
Red chilli powder	2 tsp
Turmeric	$1/2$ tsp
Salt	to taste
Sugar	1½ tsp
Curd (skimmed milk)	250 gms

Method

1. Cut the tindas from top in squares and deseed.
2. Mix the ingredients together and fill in the tindas and close them with their respective square pieces.
3. Heat a pan and splutter the mustard seeds and curry leaves. Add little turmeric and chilli powders. Then add the stuffed tinda and the remaining masala. Cook for 15 min.
4. Add one bowl of beaten curd and keep it in the microwave for 10 minutes.

Bharwa tinda is a low calorie dish and since tinda is low in fibre so it can be given in stomach disorders after removing the masalas.

Nutritive Information

CALORIES: **71 Cal**   PROTEIN: **2.6 gm**   FAT: **0.3 gm**
CARBOHYDRATE: **14.5 gm**   FIBRE: **1.6 gm**

163 Gajar Koshimbir

Ingredients

Carrots (gajar)	3
Coriander leaves	few (chopped fine)
Green chillis	2-3
Lime juice	to taste
Sugar and salt	to taste

For seasoning

Mustard seeds (sarson)	½ tsp
Curry leaves	few

Method

1. Grate gajar. Keep aside.
2. Add chopped green chillis, salt and sugar to the gajar and mix thoroughly.
3. Sprinkle coriander leaves and lime juice over it.
4. Season with mustard seeds and curry leaves.
5. Serve at room temperature.

A beta-carotene rich preparation and presence of green chillis and curry leaves gives this salad preparation a contrasting colour. It may also be used as a stuffing in parantha.

Nutritive Information

CALORIES: **48 Cal**   PROTEIN: **0.9 gm**   FAT: **0.2 gm**
CARBOHYDRATE: **10.6 gm**   FIBRE: **1.2 gm**

164 Tofu Green Bean Curry

Ingredients

Green beans	125 gms
Tofu (firm tofu recommended)	200 gms
Mushrooms (sliced)	6 to 8
Green onions	2 (cut pieces into 1 cm)
Curry paste	1 tbsp
Light soya sauce	1 tbsp
Skimmed milk	1 to 1 ½ cups
Sugar	2 tsp
Fresh red chillis	3 (diced)
Salt	to taste

Method

1. Heat the skimmed milk in a pot until it starts to boil. Then add in the curry paste, soya sauce, red chillis, sugar and salt. Mix well.
2. Add in mushrooms and tofu, and bring to a boil.
3. Add the green beans, and let it simmer until the beans are cooked. Add the green onions. Cook for a minute or so and serve.

*This firm and solid **tofu** is high is protein and calcium than other forms of tofu.*

Nutritive Information

CALORIES: **190 Cal**   PROTEIN: **19.2 gm**   FAT: **2.2 gm**
CARBOHYDRATE: **27.6 gm**   FIBRE: **1.8 gm**

165 Tofu balls in Spinach Sauce

Ingredients

Extra firm tofu	1 pack
Fresh spinach	750 gms
Flour (maida)	2 tbsp
Cornflour	1 tbsp
Egg (white)	1
Chilli powder	1 tsp
Turmeric powder	½ tsp
Cumin seeds	½ tsp
Garlic cloves	6 (medium)
Ginger	1 tbsp (minced)
Bay leaves	2
Dry chilli pods	2
Salt and black pepper	to taste

Method

1. Wash and cook spinach with little water. Let it wilt completely.
2. Drain tofu of its water content and mash it into a coarse paste.
3. Combine egg white, flour, cornflour, chilli powder, turmeric and salt and make it into balls.
4. Roast small balls. Set aside on paper towel.
5. Grind cooked spinach into desired consistency (free flowing paste).
6. Roast cumin seeds, bay leaves and chilli in it.
7. Crush garlic and add into the minced ginger.
8. Add the spinach mixture slowly. Cook for a minute. Adjust salt and black pepper to taste. Your dish is ready.

9. To serve, fill half of the serving bowl with spinach sauce and add the roasted tofu balls on top of it. You can garnish the recipe with fine julienne cut carrots.

Extra firm tofu: *A gravy preparation having tofu balls dipped in it makes up for the demand of extra firm i.e. more dense and solid form of tofu.*

Nutritive Information

CALORIES: **358 Cal**   PROTEIN: **24.71 gm**   FAT: **7.46 gm**
CARBOHYDRATE: **47.61 gm**   FIBRE: **6.57 gm**

166 Vegetable Chunks in Tomato Gravy

Ingredients

Potatoes (scrubbed clean)	2
Capsicum	1
Cucumbers (small)	2
Tomato	1
Onion	1
Baby corns	2
Carrot	1
Cauliflower florets	4-5
Spring onion	1
Coriander	1 tbsp (chopped finely)
Cabbage	1 tbsp (thinly shredded)

For gravy

Tomatoes	4 (dipped in boiling water for 5 minutes)
Ginger-garlic	1 tsp (grated)
Onion	1 (finely chopped)
Water	1½ cups
Cornflour mixed in ½ cup of water	1 tbsp
Red chilli powder	1 tbsp
Sugar	2 tsp
Clove-cinnamon powder	2 tsp
Salt	to taste

Method

1. Skin tomatoes. Purée or grate.
2. Put ginger, garlic and chopped onion in a heated non-stick pan.
3. Sauté for a minute. Add tomato purée, and other gravy ingredients, stirring continuously.
4. Bring to boil. Simmer for about 7-8 minutes, keep aside.
5. Vertically quarter the potatoes, capsicum, cucumber, baby corn (keep whole if very small), tomato carrot and onion.
6. Cook the vegetables in steam till firm but done.
7. Pour the gravy in a casserole.
8. Place the assorted vegetables in it and press down gently.
9. Garnish with cabbage, coriander and spring onion.
10. Grill till gravy sizzles.
11. Serve hot with roti or toasted brown bread.

Cucumber is low in calories. It is refreshing and a natural diuretic.

Nutritive Information

CALORIES: **179 Cal**   PROTEIN: **4.8 gm**   FAT: **1.2 gm**
CARBOHYDRATE: **38.55 gm**   FIBRE: **2.9 gm**

167 Chinese Hot and Sour Onions

Ingredients

Onions (large)	2
Red chillis	3
White vinegar	1 ½ tsp
Brown vinegar	1 ½ tsp
Pepper	3-4 pinches
Sugar	¼ tsp
Salt	to taste

Method

1. Peel and halve onions, chop each half into eight chunks.
2. Slice chillis thin diagonally.
3. Sauté chillis and onions for 3-4 minutes.
4. Add all the other ingredients. Sauté for further 2 minutes.
5. Serve hot with rice or bread.

As the name and ingredients suggest a hot, sour and spicy Chinese preparation, goes equally well with any pasta like noodles, spaghetti or macaroni etc. It may also be eaten as a salad.

Nutritive Information

CALORIES: **59 Cal**   PROTEIN: **1.2 gm**   FAT: **0.1 gm**
CARBOHYDRATE: **12.6 gm**   FIBRE: **0.6 gm**

Zero Oil Raita

168 Roasted Brinjal Raita

Ingredients

Curd (skimmed milk)	250 gms (beaten)
Brinjal	1 (small)
Spring onion	3 (chopped)
Green chillis	2-3 (finely chopped)
Roasted cumin powder	½ tsp
Chaat masala	½ tsp
Coriander leaves	1 tbsp (chopped)
Salt	to taste

Method

1. Roast the brinjal over low flame until brown.
2. Keep turning for even cooking.
3. Cool, peel and mash the brinjal.
4. Add the rest of the ingredients, mix well.
5. Garnish with coriander leaves and serve.

Brinjal is low in calories, gives a chilling effect to the stomach.

Nutritive Information

CALORIES: **84.4 Cal**   PROTEIN: **6.78 gm**   FAT: **0.335 gm**
CARBOHYDRATE: **13.76 gm**   FIBRE: **0.39 gm**

169 Tomato Raita

Ingredients

Curd (skimmed milk)	250 gms
Tomatoes	100 gms
Red chilli powder	½ tsp
Cumin powder	1 tsp
Coriander	1 bunch (chopped)
Salt	to taste

Method

1. Peel and cut tomatoes finely.
2. Mix all the ingredients in the curd including the chopped coriander.
3. Stir well and serve cold.

Tomato *is an acidic fruit. It is the best and most useful of fruits because of its richness in vitamins.*

Nutritive Information

CALORIES: **95.5 Cal**   PROTEIN: **8.15 gm**   FAT: **0.35 gm**
CARBOHYDRATE: **15.1 gm**   FIBRE: **0.7 gm**

170 Radish Raita

Ingredients

Curd (skimmed milk)	250 gms
Radish	1 (scraped & grated)
Green chilli	1 (finely chopped)
Coriander leaves	1 tsp
Red chilli powder	¼ tsp
Chaat masala	¼ tsp
Salt	to taste

Method

1. Beat the curd well.
2. Finely chop the coriander leaves.
3. Mix all the ingredients together and serve.

Radish, low in calories and fat, is popular as a snack with slimmers.

Nutritive Information

CALORIES: **81 Cal**   PROTEIN: **6.60 gm**   FAT: **0.35 gm**
CARBOHYDRATE: **13.2 gm**   FIBRE: **1.7 gm**

171 Bathua Raita

Ingredients

Curd (skimmed milk)	500 gms
Bathua	250 gms
Roasted cumin seed powder	2 tsp
Asafoetida	a pinch
Red chilli powder	1 tsp
Salt	to taste

Method

1. Wash bathua with fresh water thoroughly and boil it.
2. Blend in a mixi.
3. Beat the curd well and put bathua paste in it. Add all the other ingredients too.
4. Serve cold.

Bathua, a green leafy vegetable, is a good source of beta-carotene, iron, B- complex vitamins etc.

Nutritive Information

CALORIES: **147.5 Cal**   PROTEIN: **15.5 gm**   FAT: **1.25 gm**
CARBOHYDRATE: **18.7 gm**   FIBRE: **2 gm**

172 Cucumber Raita

Ingredients

Curd (skimmed milk)	1 cup
Cucumber	1
Pepper	¼ tsp
Sugar	½ tsp
Salt	to taste

Method

1. Peel the cucumber and grate it.
2. Beat the curd well till smooth.
3. Put beaten curd in a bowl and add all the ingredients.
4. Mix well and serve cold.

Cucumber is rich in potassium and phosphorus. It is a good blood purifier and builder and a good nerve, brain and skin food. It is cooling, healing and soothing.

Nutritive Information

CALORIES: **52.5 Cal**   PROTEIN: **2.6 gm**   FAT: **0.125 gm**
CARBOHYDRATE: **10.195 gm**   FIBRE: **0.1 gm**

173 Papaya Raita

Ingredients

Curd (skimmed milk)	½ cup
Papaya	1 cup (chopped)
Red chilli powder	¼ tsp
Roasted cumin powder (jeera)	¼ tsp
Mint powder	¼ tsp
Salt	½ tsp

Method

1. Peel papaya and cut into small pieces.
2. Beat the curd, add salt, chilli, jeera and mint powders and papaya pieces.
3. Mix well, chill and serve.

Papaya is a highly potent and efficacious fruit. It is recommended in constipation, digestive disorders and kidney stones.

Nutritive Information

CALORIES: **46.5 Cal**   PROTEIN: **1.85 gm**   FAT: **0.15 gm**
CARBOHYDRATE: **9.5 gm**   FIBRE: **0.8 gm**

174 Sweet Raita

Ingredients

Curd (skimmed milk)	100 gms
Castor sugar	1 tbsp
Dates	30 gms (chopped fine)
Apple	50 gms (chopped)

Method

1. Beat the curd well till it is smooth.
2. Add sugar and mix well.
3. Add chopped dates and apple to it.
4. Chill and serve in a bowl.

Dates are a wholesome energy fruit, easily digested and assimilated.

Nutritive Information

CALORIES: **91.7 Cal**   PROTEIN: **2.96 gm**   FAT: **0.47 gm**
CARBOHYDRATE: **21.44 gm**   FIBRE: **1.61 gm**

175 Rice Flakes in Chilled Sweet Curd

Ingredients

Chilled sweet curd (skimmed milk)	200 gms
Rice flakes(poha)	150 gms
Cucumber	2 tbsp
Apple	1 (cut into pieces)

Method

1. Take the rice flakes in a sieve and wash them until they get a little soft.
2. Keep aside for 5 minutes to drain away the extra water.
3. Take the chilled sweet curd and mix it with a spoon.
4. Add the washed rice flakes and mix well.
5. Add cucumber and apple and mix.
6. Serve the mixture in small bowls.

Rice flakes are a low salt, low fat, low cholesterol food and a boon for those who have been advised low salt diet. When taken with curd it cures stomach upset.

Nutritive Information

CALORIES: **642.26 Cal**   PROTEIN: **9.36 gm**   FAT: **1.26 gm**
CARBOHYDRATE: **156.10 gm**   FIBRE: **1.19 gm**

176 Carrot Raita

Ingredients

Thick fresh curd (skimmed milk)	800 gms
Carrots	2-3 (grated)

For the tempering

Dry red chillis	4-5
Mustard seeds	a few
Curry leaves	a few
Salt	to taste

Method

1. Whisk the curd till it becomes smooth.
2. Add the carrots and mix well.
3. Roast mustard seeds, curry leaves and red chillis.
4. Pour over the curd and mix well.
5. Finally add salt and serve cold.

Carrot is healing, nourishing and soothing, builds up fresh blood and also purifies it.

Nutritive Information

CALORIES: **120.5 Cal**   PROTEIN: **7.15 gm**   FAT: **0.45 gm**
CARBOHYDRATE: **22.1 gm**   FIBRE: **1.2 gm**

177 Spring Onion Raita

Ingredients

Curd (skimmed milk)	250 gms
Spring onion	1 bunch
Salt	to taste

Method

1. Clean, wash and cut the spring onion into small pieces.
2. Heat a pan and sauté spring onion for a minute after adding a pinch of sugar.
3. Add to the curd along with salt and mix well.
4. Chill it well and serve along with any spicy pulao or biryani.

Spring onion helps to lower blood cholesterol level and reduces the risk of coronary heart disease. Prevents blood clotting.

Nutritive Information

CALORIES: **117 Cal**   PROTEIN: **6.8 gm**   FAT: **0.3 gm**
CARBOHYDRATE: **21.8 gm**   FIBRE: **0.6 gm**

178 Cabbage Raita

Ingredients

Curd (skimmed milk)	150 gms
Skimmed milk	4 tbsp
Cabbage	150 gms (grated)
Salt	to taste
Small green chilli	1 (chopped fine)

Method

1. Mix everything together, chill and serve.

Raw cabbage is highly effective in the healing of stomach, duodenal and peptic ulcers. It is valuable for strengthening alkali reserves in the body.

Nutritive Information

CALORIES: **98.5 Cal**   PROTEIN: **7.7 gm**   FAT: **0.35 gm**
CARBOHYDRATE: **16.1 gm**   FIBRE: **1.5 gm**

179 Ginger Pickle

Ingredients

Ginger	1/2 cup (grated)
Green chillis	1/2 cup
Garlic	1/2 cup
Tamarind juice	250 gms
Jaggery	2 cups
Onions	2 (chopped)

Method

1. Sauté ginger till brown. Keep aside.
2. Heat a karahi, sauté onions till brown and then add green chillis and garlic.
3. Cook a little and then add ginger, tamarind and jaggery.

Ginger is Anti-depressant, anti-diarrhoeal, strong antioxidant and ranks very high in anti-cancer activity.

Nutritive Information

CALORIES: **2089.6 Cal**   PROTEIN: **16.78 gm** FAT: **7.2 gm**
CARBOHYDRATE: **500.06 gm** FIBRE: **15.96 gm**

180 Beetroot Pickle

Ingredients

Large beetroots	2 (boiled)
Red chilli powder	1 tsp
Small mustard seeds (rai)	1 ½ tsp
Salt	1 ½ tsp

Method

1. Peel and cut beetroots into pieces.
2. Add salt, chilli and rai and mix well.
3. Let it marinate for 10 minutes and your pickle is ready.

Beetroot is an intensive blood purifier and helps to build up red blood corpuscles. It is believed to be a natural and helpful stimulant to the heart by virtue of its richness in minerals, potassium and manganese needed for strengthening heart muscles.

Nutritive Information

CALORIES: **86 Cal**   PROTEIN: **3.4 gm**   FAT: **0.2 gm**
CARBOHYDRATE: **17.6 gm**   FIBRE: **1.8 gm**

181 Lotus Stem Pickle

Ingredients

Lotus stems (bhein)	500 gm
Mustard seeds	½ tsp
Onion seeds (kalonji)	½ tsp
Chilli powder	1 tsp
Turmeric powder	¼ tsp
Dry fenugreek (kasoori methi)	1 tsp
Potato	1 (boiled and diced)
Sugar	½ tsp
Coriander powder	1 tsp
Garam masala powder	½ tsp
Salt	1 tsp
Mango powder (amchoor)	1 tsp
Aniseed powder (saunf)	1 tsp
Ginger juliennes	1 tsp
Lemon juice	2 tsp

Method

1. Scrape and wash lotus stems and cut them diagonally into thin slices.
2. Boil them with a pinch of salt till tender. Drain.
3. Heat a karahi. Add the mustard seeds and kalonji. When they splutter, add the chilli and turmeric powders, kasoori methi and stir well.
4. Add the lotus stems and diced potato. Cook on low heat for 4 minutes.
5. Add salt, sugar, coriander, mango and garam masala powders and cook for 2 minutes.

6. Mix in the aniseed powder and ginger juliennes and remove from heat.
7. Sprinkle with lemon juice.

Aniseed possesses a sweet, aromatic taste when crushed, a characteristic agreeable smell and is used for flavouring food, confectionery, bakery products, beverages and other liquors.

Nutritive Information

CALORIES: **1224.2 Cal** PROTEIN: **21.4 gm** FAT: **7.39 gm**
CARBOHYDRATE: **269.41 gm** FIBRE: **125.2 gm**

182 Ber Ka Lajawab Achaar

Ingredients

Zizyphus (ber)	½ kg
Black salt powder	1 tsp
Black pepper	2 tsp
Jaggery, crushed	5 tbsp
Salt	to taste

Method

1. Deseed ber and add all the masalas.
2. Mix and keep in the sun for 5 days.

Black pepper *is stimulant, pungent, aromatic, digestive and a tonic for the nerves.*

Nutritive Information

CALORIES: **687.65 Cal**   PROTEIN: **5.45 gm**   FAT: **2.93 gm**
CARBOHYDRATE: **161.17 gm**   FIBRE: **1.49 gm**

183 Low Calorie Lime Sweet Pickle

Ingredients

Good quality yellow limes	20
Jaggery	250 gms (grated)
Red chilli powder	25 gms
Salt	2 tbsp

Method

1. Soak the lime in water for a day and keep in the fridge.
2. Next day, throw the water and add fresh water and soak again and refrigerate for another day.
3. On the 3rd day also change the water, soak and refrigerate.
4. On the 4th day, cut the limes and remove seeds.
5. Put the limes, jaggery, chilli powder and salt in the mixie and grind to a coarse paste.
6. Your pickle is ready.
7. It will taste better if it is matured for 2-3 days.

Lime is a rich source of natural vitamin C. Serves as a prophylactic by building up general resistance of the body.

Nutritive Information

CALORIES: **941.0 Cal**   PROTEIN: **4.3 gm**   FAT: **3.7 gm**
CARBOHYDRATE: **226.5 gm**   FIBRE: **1.5 gm**

184 Mixed Vegetable Pickle

Ingredients

Carrots	1 kg
Cauliflower	250 gms
Red chillis	12
Curry leaves	8
Vinegar	250 gms
Salt	2 tsp
Large piece ginger	1
Garlic pods	2
Green chillis	18-20
Turmeric powder (haldi)	1 tsp
Fenugreek seeds (methi)	1/2 tsp
Cumin seeds (jeera)	2 tsp
Peppercorns	8
Sugar	50 gms
Small mustard seeds (rai)	2 tsp

Method

1. Clean and cut the vegetables lengthwise into thin strips. Add salt and keep aside.
2. Grind the red chillis, green chillis, haldi powder, methi seeds, ginger, 1 ½ pods garlic, jeera, peppercorns and rai in little vinegar.
3. Roast the remaining garlic and curry leaves till they give out an aroma.
4. Add the ground masala and mix well.
5. Then add sugar and remaining vinegar.
6. Add vegetables and cook on a low fire till done.

7. Cool and bottle.

Nutritive Information

CALORIES: **645.5 Cal** PROTEIN: **19.98 gm** FAT: **4.94 gm**
CARBOHYDRATE: **129.5 gm** FIBRE: **18.4 gm**

185 Capsicum Pickle

Ingredients

Capsicum	500 gms
Mustard seeds	1 tbsp
Sugar	1 tsp
Fenugreek seeds (methi)	1 tsp
Cumin seeds (jeera)	1 tsp
Red chillis	20
Ginger	2-cm piece
Garlic	1 pod
Vinegar	100 gms
Salt	to taste

Method

1. Roast fenugreek, mustard and cumin seeds together.
2. Soak red chillis in vinegar. When soft grind them into a paste with the roasted ingredients, ginger and garlic.
3. Wash and dry the capsicum. Cut into half, remove the seeds, and thinly slice.
4. Heat a karahi and roast the ground masala. Add salt, sugar and sliced capsicums.
5. Mix well. Cook on a low fire in an open vessel.
6. Cook till capsicums change colour.

Capsicum has the remarkable effect of being a powerful stimulant. In spite of being pungent it does not give blisters in the mouth or throat.

Nutritive Information

CALORIES: **252.15 Cal**   PROTEIN: **11.4 gm**   FAT: **7.7 gm**
CARBOHYDRATE: **35.07 gm**   FIBRE: **5.64 gm**

186 Mango Pickle

Ingredients

Mango	1 (chopped)
Salt	to taste
Red chilli powder	$1/2$ tsp
Turmeric	$1/4$ tsp

For the seasoning

Asafoetida (hing)	a pinch
Mustard seeds	to taste

Method

1. Heat a karahi, add the mustard seeds.
2. When they begin to splutter add the hing.
3. Remove from fire.
4. Mix all the ingredients well and store in an air-tight glass jar.

Raw mangoes are used for making pickles and in cooking as well as in salads.

Nutritive Information

CALORIES: **46 Cal**   PROTEIN: **0.85 gm**   FAT: **0.2 gm**
CARBOHYDRATE: **10.1 gm**   FIBRE: **1.4 gm**

187 Green Chilli Pickle

Ingredients

Green chillis (fresh)	250 gms
Asafoetida (hing)	small pinch
Salt	1 tsp
Vinegar	100 gms
Fenugreek seeds (methi)	$1/2$ tsp
Fennel (meethi saunf)	$1/2$ spoon

Method

1. First clean the chillis and separate the stems. Cut from the centre and put them aside (Do not use iron) in a pan.
2. Heat a karahi and put in hing, saunf, methi and then chillis and salt and mix well.
3. Now add vinegar. Mix, cover and cook on low flame. After 5 minute put aside the cover.
4. Cook on high flame.
5. After 5 minutes switch off the gas.
6. Cool and keep in a glass jar.

Green chilli is a fair source of vitamin C. Opens up sinuses and air passages, breaks up mucus in the lungs.

Nutritive Information

CALORIES: **82.49 Cal** PROTEIN: **8.036 gm** FAT: **1.67 gm**
CARBOHYDRATE: **8.82 gm** FIBRE: **17.216 gm**

188 Green Chilli and Lemon Pickle

Ingredients

Green chillis	50 gms
Lemons	½ kg
Salt	to taste
White vinegar	250 gms
Sugar	a pinch
Nutmeg (ground)	2 tsp

Method

1. Wash the green chillis and lemons thoroughly.
2. Cut the green chillis in the centre, leaving them intact at the end.
3. Have glass jars ready for preserving the pickle.
4. Cut the lemons in two halves, fill each lemon with enough salt and then press the two halves together and place them carefully in the glass jar.
5. Now fill in salt in the green chillis and place these in the glass jar also.
6. Close the lid tightly.
7. Leave the pickle jar in a warm place for a week or when you feel that the lemon and chillis are getting softer and absorbing the salty mixture.
8. Lastly add a pinch of sugar and nutmeg.
9. Enjoy your delicious and spicy achaar.

You cannot keep good health without fresh fruits. Lemon is the prince among fruits.

Nutritive Information

CALORIES: **304.7 Cal** PROTEIN: **6.55 gm** FAT: **4.84 gm**
CARBOHYDRATE: **58.12 gm** FIBRE: **11.9 gm**

189 Puli-Inji or Khatta Meetha Adrak ka Achaar

Ingredients

Green chillis	15 (cut into small pieces)
Fresh ginger	50 gms (cut into small pieces)
Tamarind	20 gms
Jaggery	to taste

For seasoning

Turmeric powder

Salt	to taste

Mustard seeds, urad dal,
hing powder, curry leaves

Method

1. Soak tamarind in water and extract juice.
2. To a karahi add mustard seeds. After they crackle, add urad dal, curry leaves and hing.
3. Once dal is golden brown, add ginger, green chillis, turmeric powder and salt. Sauté for 6-7 minutes.
4. Then add the tamarind extract and let it boil.
5. Once cooked add the jaggery.

Depending on individual taste, the quantity of green chillis, ginger and tamarind can be adjusted.

Nutritive Information

CALORIES: **98.8 Cal** PROTEIN: **2.64 gm** FAT: **0.65 gm**
CARBOHYDRATE: **20.53 gm** FIBRE: **4.36 gm**

190 Tomato Pickle

Ingredients

Ripe tomatoes	1 kg (diced)
Small mustard seeds (rai)	50 gms (powder)
Vinegar	250 gms
Green chillis	100 gms
Ginger & Garlic	20-20 gms (ground)
Red chilli powder & Cumin seeds	1-1 tbsp
Salt	to taste
Asafoetida	1/4 tsp
Fenugreek seeds	1 tsp

Method

1. Heat a karahi, add asafoetida, cumin seeds. When brown add ginger paste.
2. Roast and then add garlic paste.
3. Add fenugreek seeds. Roast again.
4. Add the diced tomatoes and cook for some more time till the water evaporates.
5. Now add green chillis (cut into big pieces) and cook for another 5 minutes.
6. Add salt, red chilli powder and vinegar. Stir well and take off the fire.
7. When cool add rai powder, mix well and store in an airtight container.
8. The pickle is ready to eat after a week.

Tomatoes a major source of lycopene, awesome anti-oxidant and anti-cancer agent.

Nutritive Information
CALORIES: **527.4 Cal**   PROTEIN: **22.9 gm**   FAT: **22.59 gm**
CARBOHYDRATE: **56.26 gm**   FIBRE: **16.38 gm**

191 Carrot and Chilli Pickle

Ingredients

Carrots	250 gms
Green chillis	4-5
Salt	to taste
Broken mustard seeds	1 tbsp
Lemon juice	2 tbsp

Method

1. Wash and scrape the carrots. Cut them into long thin strips about 2-cm size pieces.
2. Wash and cut the green chillis as well.
3. Mix all the ingredients in a large bowl.
4. This pickle can be eaten on the same day but tastes good after a day and can be kept for a week in the refrigerator.

Carrots have high soluble fibre which depresses blood cholesterol.

Nutritive Information

CALORIES: **215.65 Cal** PROTEIN: **6.7 gm** FAT: **6.75 gm**
CARBOHYDRATE: **31.57 gm** FIBRE: **7.12 gm**

192 Sada Bahar Aam ka Achaar

Ingredients

Raw mangoes	1 kg (cut into pieces)
Salt	180 gms
Aniseed (saunf)	100 gms
Turmeric powder (haldi)	4 ½ gms
Fenugreek seeds (methi)	5 ½ gms
Onion seeds (kalaonji)	6 ½ to 7 gms
Red chilli powder	7 ½ gms
Asafoetida powder (hing)	a pinch

Method

1. Put all the dry masalas in a large bowl.
2. Add the mango pieces and mix well.
3. Heat a griddle or tawa and roast the hing.
4. When it starts to smoke put the glass container in which you want to store the pickle upside down on the tawa. Keep it for a minute or till the smoke gets fully filled in the container.
5. Transfer the masala coated mango pieces into the glass container. Cover and keep it overnight.
6. Fast, easy to make and tastes really good.
7. You can increase the quantity of the red chilli powder if you want it more hot.

Fennel being a mild expectorant, is used as an ingredient of beverages and liquors. It is a popular flavouring agent.

Nutritive Information
CALORIES: **45.1 Cal**   PROTEIN: **0.85 gm**   FAT: **0.35 gm**
CARBOHYDRATE: **12.1 gm**   FIBRE: **1.3 gm**

Zero Oil Chaat

206 Bread Chaat

Ingredients

Sweet curd (skimmed milk)	½ ltr
Potatoes-boiled and cubed	2
Chaat masala, Cumin seeds	to taste
Red chilli powder	to taste
Green chillis	2-3
Fresh coriander leaves	a few
Tamarind & Green chutney, Salt	to taste

For garnishing

Chaat masala	to taste
Bread slices	6

Method

1. Take 2 bread slices, apply green chutney on each of them and make a sandwich. Cut out the brown sides.
2. Place the sandwich in a plate and make aloo masala in which mash or cube the aloo and add chaat masala, salt, red chilli powder, cumin seeds, green chillis and coriander and mix together.
3. Then spread or sprinkle the aloo masala over the sandwich.
4. Pour 2-3 tbsp of each, tamarind chutney and green chutney over the aloo spread.
5. Then pour whole lot of curd on the sandwich so that it covers the sandwich and garnish it with chaat masala, little tamarind and green chutneys

Tamarind – *Ripe fruit or tamarind pulp has an important role in culinary preparations in the country. Ripe fruit is appetising, laxative, anti-helminthic..*

Nutritive Information
CALORIES: **523.6 Cal**   PROTEIN: **47.02 gm**   FAT: **0.51 gm**
CARBOHYDRATE: **57.01 gm**   FIBRE: **0.67 gm**

207 Flakes Chaat

Ingredients

Cornflakes/any other flakes	500 gms
Onion (optional)	1
Tomato (big)	1
Celery (optional)	50 gms
Coriander	for garnishing
Salt/chilli powder	to taste

Method

1. Chop the vegetables as desired.
2. Sauté onions till pink.
3. Add tomatoes and celery and sauté for a minute.
4. Add salt and chilli powder.
5. Add the flakes, sprinkle very little water and sauté for $1/2$ a minute.
6. Transfer to a serving plate and garnish with coriander.

This recipe is ready to eat with less preparation time. It contains good amount of fibre and B-carotene. Fibre is good for bowel movement and also helps in excreting cholesterol.

Nutritive Information

CALORIES: **283.2 Cal** PROTEIN: **10.26 gm** FAT: **1.92 gm**
CARBOHYDRATE: **53.6 gm** FIBRE: **4.2 gm**

208 Idli Chaat

Ingredients

Idlis	30-40 pieces
Idlis cut into small pieces	10 to 12
Potatoes (boiled)	2
Onions	2 (cut to pieces)
Sev used for bhel	to taste
Coriander leaves	a few
Tomato	1
Cucumber cut to small pieces	1
Green chutney used for bhel	to taste
Tamarind chutney	to taste
Small green chillis cut to pieces	a few

Method

1. Cook idlis and let it cool.
2. Arrange the idlis on a plate.
3. Add potatoes, onion, chutneys and top with coriander leaves.

Idli chaat is a delicious dish which can be even made by left over idlis which cannot be consumed as such.

Nutritive Information

CALORIES: **1064.30 Cal**   PROTEIN: **36.3 gm**   FAT: **3.08 gm**
CARBOHYDRATE: **366.02 gm** FIBRE: **2.34 gm**

209 Curry Chaat

Ingredients

For Curry

Buttermilk (skimmed milk)	1 ltr
Besan	200 gms
Green chilli	2-3 (chopped)
Ginger	1 small piece
Black pepper	a pinch
Salt	to taste

For Chaat

Bhel papdi	10-12 pieces
Sprouted and boiled moong	50 gms
Sprouted and boiled moth	50 gms
Sprouted and boiled black chana	50 gms
Sprouted and boiled green chana	50 gms
Garam masala	to taste

For Kofta:

Soaked chana dal	50 gms
Palak	50 gms (cut into small pieces)
Red mirchi powder	1 tsp
Dhania powder	$1/4$ tsp
Salt	to taste
Hing	a pinch
Shredded cabbage, carrot, capsicum, coriander	for decoration

Method

For Curry

1. Add all ingredients and put it on steam for 30 minutes.

For Chaat

2. Crush the papdi into small pieces.
3. Make a tadka of moth, moong, black and green chana. Add masala to it and put 4-5 drops of lemon juice and garam masala.

For Kofta

4. Grind dal and mix palak. Add masala and then roast it.

Way To Serve Curry Chaat

5. Take a bowl, put papdi, then the chaat and cut the koftas into two pieces and put it on the chaat. Put the curry and in the end put the cabbage, carrot and capsicum and coriander.

Sprouting of the grams enhances the micronutrients like vitamin C, B-complex, calcium and iron. Vitamin C has wound healing and anti-oxidant properties. Calcium is good for bones, teeth and blood clotting.

Nutritive Information

CALORIES: **1869.21 Cal**   PROTEIN: **69.36 gm**   FAT: **6.7 gm**
CARBOHYDRATE: **369.25 gm**   FIBRE: **5.1 gm**

210 Instant Garnished Easy Dosa

Ingredients

Rice flour	500 gms
Urad flour	250 gms
Eno	$1/2$ tsp
Salt	to taste
Coriander leaves	200 gms
Onions	200 gms

Method

1. Mix the rice flour, urad flour and half tsp of Eno. This makes the mixture for dosas.

2. Heat a non-stick (tawa) and make dosa — adding about a spoon of onions for each dosa while it is on the tawa.

3. Remove the dosa. Sprinkle finely chopped coriander leaves on the folded dosa.

These instant dosas can be eaten with any chutney or sambhar. They are easy to prepare and any seasonal veg. like carrots, beans, cabbage, tomato can be added to it.

Nutritive Information

CALORIES: **486.26 Cal**   PROTEIN: **20.3 gm**   FAT: **1.1 gm**
CARBOHYDRATE: **236.01 gm**   FIBRE: **0.56 gm**

211 Stuffed Marvel

Ingredients

Onion	1
Mushrooms	250 gms (sliced)
Powdered sugar	2 tsp
Egg whites	3
Salt	1/2 tsp
Black pepper powder	1/8 tsp
White vinegar	1 tsp
Skimmed milk	1 tbsp
Atta (made into a dough)	500 gms

Method

1. Heat a non-stick frying pan over the cooking range at medium heat and add thinly sliced onions and sugar and brown them or cook them till they are softened.
2. Add sliced mushrooms and vinegar and cook for another 4-5 minutes or till the mushrooms are cooked. Transfer them to a bowl.
3. Beat 3 egg whites, milk, salt and black pepper powder till stiff peaks are formed.
4. Heat the non-stick frying pan and put the egg mixture. Flatten the mixture to an equal level and put the onion mixture on half of the eggs and close with a lid and allow cooking. Fold the egg and remove to a plate and cut into 4 equal parts.
5. Make a very thin chapati from atta. Put one part of egg dish and close the dish with the chapati using water as glue. It will be in the shape of a rectangle.
6. Arrange on a baking dish covered with aluminium foil and put in a

preheated oven at 400 ⁰ C and keep checking till cooked. Turn to bake the other side.

7. Serve hot with tomato sauce.

This dish is a palatable diet for those who love eating eggs but also want to avoid cholesterol by excluding yellow portion of the egg.

Nutritive Information

CALORIES: **392.26 Cal**　　PROTEIN: **19.29 gm**　FAT: **1.3 gm**
CARBOHYDRATE: **156.32 gm**　FIBRE: **2.42 gm**

212 Bread Bahar

Ingredients

Bread	6 slices
Onion small	1
Tomatoes medium	2
Green chills	3-4
Curry leaves	few
Cumin seeds (jeera)	few
Black mustard seeds	few
Haldi	a pinch
Salt	to taste
Coriander leaves	for garnishing
Lemon juice	1 (optional)

Method

1. Cut the bread slices into 1 x 1 inch square pieces and keep them aside.
2. Chop onion, tomatoes and green chills.
3. Heat a kadai and add jeera, mustard seeds, curry leaves and haldi. Let it splutter.
4. Put onion and sauté.
5. Add chopped chillis and then chopped tomatoes and let them cook properly. Put salt and sauté.
6. Put diced bread pieces and mix well. Let it cook for a few minutes. Garnish with lemon juice (optional) and chopped coriander.

Bread bahar is an easy to prepare snack. But when bread is not available, left over chapaties could also be used.

Nutritive Information
CALORIES: **356 Cal** PROTEIN: **2.86 gm** FAT: **4.8 gm**
CARBOHYDRATE: **73 gm** FIBRE: **1.10 gm**

213 Banana Bread

Ingredients

Flour	500 gms
Whole wheat flour	100 gms
Baking powder	1 tbsp.
Baking soda	1/4 tsp.
Bananas (very ripe)	4 (mashed)
Apple juice concentrate	100 gms
Vanilla extract	2 tsp.
Raisins	100 gms
Egg whites	3
Water	2/3 cup

Method

1. Preheat the oven to 350°F. Mix all dry ingredients together. In a separate bowl, combine all the wet ingredients.
2. Fold the dry ingredients into the wet ones. Do not overmix or the bread will not rise.
3. Pour the batter into non-stick loaf pan or one that has been sprayed with vegetable oil.
4. Bake for 1 hour. Cool, slice, and serve.

This quick bread is perfect for snacks, even breakfast.

Nutritive Information

CALORIES: **204 Cal**   PROTEIN: **16.3 gm**   FAT: **0.7 gm**
CARBOHYDRATE: **110.8 gm**   FIBRE: **2.2 gm**

214 Potato Pancakes

Ingredients

Egg whites	2
Onions	300 gms (finely minced)
Flour	2 tbsp
Salt	1 tsp.
Freshly ground black pepper	$1/2$ tsp.
Peeled potatoes	1¼ pounds
Apple sauce	as required

Method

1. Preheat the oven to 450^0F and have a non-stick baking sheet ready.
2. Measure out all the ingredients besides the potatoes.
3. Then grate the potatoes; there should be 3 cups. Squeeze out all the excess moisture and combine with the other ingredients. (It is important to have all the other ingredients ready because the potatoes will quickly turn gray upon exposure to the air.)
4. Using $1/3$ cup of the mixture, form into thin flat cakes on the baking sheet. Bake for 14 minutes, then turn the pancakes over and bake an additional 2 minutes until golden brown.
5. Serve with apple sauce.

Potato pancakes gives a good flavour with apple concentrate and is a good snack

Nutritive Information

CALORIES: **150 Cal**   PROTEIN: **4.3 gm**   FAT: **0.3 gm**
CARBOHYDRATE: **50.95 gm**   FIBRE: **0.47 gm**

215 Spicy Vegetable Lapsi

Ingredients

Lapsi (daliya)	1 $^1/_2$ cup
Small mustard seeds (rai)	$^1/_2$ tsp
Cumin seeds (jeera)	$^1/_2$ tsp
Asafoetida (hing)	$^1/_2$ tsp
Red chillis	2
Onion	1 (chopped)
Garlic paste	$^1/_2$ tsp
Tomato, large	1 (finely chopped)
Chilli powder	$^1/_2$ tsp
Turmeric powder (haldi)	$^1/_2$ tsp
Mixed vegetables (carrots, peas, cauliflower)	1 cup (chopped)
Salt	to taste
Garam masala powder	½ tsp
Coriander	2 tbsp for garnishing

Method

1. In a pan roast lapsi till golden in colour and keep aside.
2. Heat a pan and add the mustard and cumin seeds. When they crackle, add asafoetida.
3. Add the red chilli and onion. Sauté for 3 to 4 minutes.
4. Add the garlic paste and tomato and sauté for 3 to 4 more minutes.
5. Add the chilli and turmeric powders mixed vegetables and mix well.
6. Add lapsi, garam masala, salt and enough water (approx. 3 cup water) and pressure-cook.

7. Garnish with chopped coriander.

Spicy vegetable lapsi, which is one of the nutritious and colourful snacks if taken with curd or dal can then be a complete meal.

Nutritive Information

CALORIES: **245.6 Cal** PROTEIN: **4.9 gm** FAT: **0.3 gm**
CARBOHYDRATE: **50.95 gm** FIBRE: **3.9 gm**

216 Spicy Steamed Idli

Ingredients

Idli pieces	12

For Stuffing

Sprouted moong	50 gms
Ginger	1 inch
Coriander leaves	250 gms
Green chillis	6
Cumin & Coriander seeds powder 1-1 tsp	
Gur	1 tbsp
Lemon	1
Salt	$1/_2$ tsp
Haldi	a pinch

For outer coat

Rice flour	100 gm
Cumin seeds	a pinch
Salt	a pinch
Water	1 cup

For garnish

Curry leaves, Chips of lemon, Clove (laung)	a few

Method

Make stuffing

1. Make paste of ginger, coriander leaves, chillis in a blender. Keep aside.
2. Heat a pan and add the sprouted moong and above paste in it. Cook for 10-12 minutes until the moong is well cooked.

3. Add turmeric powder, salt, gur, and coriander and cumin powders. Mix well and cook for 5-6 minutes.
4. After it is well cooked remove from the flame, cool it in a plate and mash half the stuffing. Do not mash it fully.
5. Make small sections and keep it aside.

Make the outer covering

6. Heat water, salt, cumin seeds. When it starts boiling add rice flour. Mix very well. It will become hard and difficult to stir, but knead it in the water using a spoon.
7. Heat for 10-15 minutes until flour is fully cooked. It becomes little shiny when it is cooked. Remove from the flame.
8. When it is cool knead it well in a plate. Well cooked dough will be absolutely non-sticky; it will stick to your fingers while kneading it.
9. Make small sections and keep aside.

How to proceed

10. Take the idli mould and put the rice dough in its small section and press against the walls. Make a hallow covering. Use water to spread the dough.
11. Put the stuffing inside and fill it well.
12. Cover the base, the open area with the dough again.
13. Remove from the mould.
14. For other idlis repeat the process.
15. After all the idlis are made, put them in a pressure cooker without the whistle and steam them for 15 minutes.
16. Remove them from the cooker and garnish with clove sticks, curry leaves and lemon chips.
17. Serve hot.

When there is no sambhar and chutney, spicy steamed idli is a good option to eat. One can alter its filling as per their liking.

Nutritive Information

CALORIES: **356 Cal**   PROTEIN: **2.86 gm**   FAT: **4.8 gm**
CARBOHYDRATE: **73 gm**   FIBRE: **1.10 gm**

217 Yummy Basket

Ingredients
For baskets

Flour (maida)	100 gms
Baking powder	1/2 tsp
Salt	to taste

For filling

Red cabbage	100 gms (finely shredded)
Green peas	50 gms
Yellow pepper (chopped)	50 gms
Paneer cubes (skimmed milk)	1 tbsp
Lemon juice	1 tsp
Sugar	1/2 tsp
Salt	to taste
Black pepper powder	1/4 tsp
Garam masala	1/4 tsp
Dhania powder	1/2 tsp
Cumin seeds	1/4 tsp

For decoration

Scallions	2
Carrot	1/2
Cherris	12

Method
For basket
1. Make a hard dough of flour, baking powder and salt.

2. Divide into 5 parts.
3. Roll out $1/4$ inch thick rounds and put into tart shells.
4. Preheat the oven to 400^0 F and bake the tarts for 10 minutes or till done. Let them cool.

For filling
5. Heat a karhai and add cumin seeds.
6. Add cabbage and peas (if using fresh add all the spices except garam masala).
7. Cover it and let it cook for 5 minutes on a low flame.
8. Finally add paneer cubes, garam masala, and lemon juice.

To serve
9. Take baskets and put fillings inside.
10. Take a strand of scallion and using a small broken toothpick carefully attach it at one end of the basket.
11. Repeat the same for another end to give it a shape of basket's handle.
12. Scrape the carrots and make a bow with it. Pin it up using a toothpick at the middle of the handle.
13. Cut the cherris into halves. Prick toothpicks in each half and fix it into the baskets.
14. Serve immediately.

Addition of chutneys as per their liking can add more spice and colour to this yummy basket.

Nutritive Information

CALORIES: **356 Cal**   PROTEIN: **2.86 gm**   FAT: **4.8 gm**
CARBOHYDRATE: **73 gm**   FIBRE: **1.10 gm**

218 Meethi Bread

Ingredients

Bread	*4 slices*
Milk (skimmed milk)	*500 gms*
Sugar	*2 tbsp*
Elaichi powder	*a pinch*

Method

1. Dissolve the sugar in milk at room temperature.
2. Add a pinch of elaichi powder.
3. Take a non-stick tawa and heat it.
4. Immerse the slices in milk.
5. Roast the slices lightly from both the sides.
6. Serve hot.

Meethi bread can be used as a dessert also if served with honey or jam.

Nutritive Information

CALORIES: **126.02 Cal**   PROTEIN: **23.06 gm** FAT: **1.10 gm**
CARBOHYDRATE: **76.32 gm**   FIBRE: **0.20 gm**

219 Baked Macaroni with Mixed Vegetable

Ingredients

Macaroni	250 gms (boiled)
Carrot	100 gms (finely chopped)
Beans	100 gms (finely chopped)
Capsicum	100 gms (finely chopped)
Cabbage	100 gms (finely chopped)
Boiled peas	100 gms
Grated paneer	2 tbsp
Tomato sauce	2 tbsp
Chilli sauce	1 tbsp
Salt and white pepper	to taste

For white sauce

Maida	1 tbsp
Cold skimmed milk	300 gms

Method

1. In a pan, sauté beans and carrots first and then add capsicum, cabbage, and peas.
2. Add salt and pepper to taste.
3. Prepare white sauce and add macaroni and half of paneer, salt and pepper to it.
4. In a baking dish, spread half of the macaroni mixture and then the mixture of vegetables. Spread both sauces on it.
5. Now spread remaining mixture of macaroni on it.
6. Dot with the remaining paneer.

7. Bake it in an oven at 350⁰ C for 20 minutes.
8. Serve as an exotic dish at dinner.

This recipe is an erotic, nutritious and multi coloured pasta preparation. Other pastas like noodles, sphagetti may also be used.

Nutritive Information

CALORIES: **674.86 Cal**   PROTEIN: **36.20 gm**   FAT: **2.2 gm**
CARBOHYDRATE: **125.20 gm** FIBRE: **13.12 gm**

220 Oil Free Methi Muthiya

Ingredients

Methi	2 small bunch
Bajre ka atta	3 tsp
Atta	1 ½ tsp
Salt	to taste
Red chilli powder	½ tsp
Dhania powder	½ tsp
Sugar powder	1 tsp
Dahi	1 tsp

Method

1. Clean up methi with water and cut it finely.
2. Then mix all ingredients. If needed add some water.
3. Shape that paste into oval shape. That is muthiya. Boil that muthiya for 20 minutes on slow fire, (like khaman dokhla).
4. After 20 minutes cut it into small and round shape.
5. Serve them with tomato ketchup.

Methi — *It promotes bile and prevents diarrhoea. It is good for the heart and expels gas. It gives benefit in dyspepsia, vomitting, cough, rheumatism, piles, intestinal worms.*

Nutritive Information

CALORIES: **438.32 Cal**   PROTEIN: **26.2 gm**   FAT: **1.32 gm**
CARBOHYDRATE: **186.36 gm**   FIBRE: **1.02 gm**

221 Tikki Chole Bake

Ingredients

For the potato layer

Potatoes	8 (peeled and cubed)
Cumin seeds	½ tsp
Onions	2
Flour	2 tbsp
Coriander leaves	1 tbsp (chopped)
Green chillis	2-3 (chopped)
Garam masala	½ tsp
Salt	to taste

For the chole

Kabuli chana	250 gms
Cumin seeds	1 tsp
Onions	3 (chopped)
Ginger-garlic paste	1 tbsp
Chilli powder	1 tsp
Anardana powder	1 tsp
Tomato purée	500 gms
Salt	to taste
Green chillis	2 (chopped finely)
Mint leaves	2 tbsp (chopped)
Garam masala powder	1 tsp

For garnishing

Bread crumbs	50 gms

Sweet date chutney	50 gms
Coriander mint chutney	2 tbsp
Onion	1 (separated into rings)
Tomato	1 (sliced)
Capsicum	1 (sliced)
Coriander leaves	50 gms (chopped)

Method

For the potato layer

1. Heat a pan. Add cumin seeds and onions and sauté lightly.
2. Add the potatoes and cook for five minutes.
3. Remove from heat. When cool add the remaining ingredients mix well. Keep aside.

For the chole

4. Clean and soak the chana overnight. Pressure-cook till done.
5. Roast cumin seeds. When they splutter add onions and ginger garlic paste and sauté till brown.
6. Add all the masala powders, except garam masala powder and sauté for a few seconds.
7. Add tomato purée and salt and cook it.
8. Add the cooked chana, green chillis, half the coriander leaves and mint leaves.
9. Add half cup water. Cover and cook on low heat till the gravy is thick.
10. Add the remaining coriander leaves and garam masala powder.
11. Stir well and keep aside.
12. Grease a baking dish and sprinkle $1/4$ cup bread crumbs.
13. Divide the potato mixture into three portions.
14. Spread one portion evenly over the bread crumbs.
15. Divide the chana mixture into two portions and spread one portion over the potatoes in the baking dish.

16. Dot with date chutney and coriander mint chutney.
17. Repeat the layers, finishing with the potato layer.
18. Place onion rings, tomato slices, and capsicum slices over it.
19. Bake in a pre-heated oven at 200⁰ C for 15 minutes or till well browned.
20. Serve hot topped with chopped coriander leaves and accompanied by sweet and hot chutneys.

Saunf — *Saunf being a mild expectorant, it is used as an ingredient of beverages and liquors. It is a popular flavouring agent.*

Nutritive Information

CALORIES: **2250.5 Cal**   PROTEIN: **45.2 gm**   FAT: **6.2 gm**
CARBOHYDRATE: **225.2 gm**   FIBRE: **5.2 gm**

222 Ragi Dosa

Ingredients

Ragi	250 gms
Onion	1
Green chilli	2-3 nos.
Coriander leaves	a few
Jeera	½ tsp
Salt	to taste
Water	to taste

Method

1. Mix ragi, chopped onion, chopped coriander, jeera, chilli with water.
2. The consistency should be like that of a regular dosa.
3. Soak for 5 minutes.
4. Prepare dosas in a non-stick pan.

Ragi dosa is one of the good alternatives of normal rice dosas. It can be served with sambhar and any chutney. It is the richest source of calcium.

Nutritive Information

CALORIES: **335.25 Cal**   PROTEIN: **8.2 gm**   FAT: **1.40 gm**
CARBOHYDRATE: **80.1 gm**   FIBRE: **1.40 gm**

223 Rice Rawa Idli

Ingredients

Rice Rawa	250 gms
Water	3 glass
Salt	³/₄ tsp

Method

1. Boil water in a pan. Add salt to it.
2. After water is boiled, add rawa.
3. Cook till it becomes soft like upma.
4. Let it cool down. Make a round ball from the mixture and flatten them like idli.
5. Finally cook them in pressure cooker for 12 minutes without steam cap.
6. Serve hot rice rawa idli with tamarind chutney.

For incorporating more colour and flavour and to increase the fibre content, one can add green leafy vegetables, carrots, beans, sprouts etc.

Nutritive Information

CALORIES: **346 Cal**   PROTEIN: **7.3 gm**   FAT: **1.3 gm**
CARBOHYDRATE: **72 gm**   FIBRE: **30.6 gm**

224 Rice Bullets

Ingredients

Rice powder (coarsely ground)	250 gms
or idli rawa can also be used	
Green chillis	3
Ginger	$1/2$ inch piece (finely cut)
Mustard seeds	$1/2$ tsp
Urad dal	$1/2$ tsp
Hing powder	a pinch
Curry leaves	few
Water	2 cups
Salt	to taste

Method

1. Wash the rice powder well.
2. Heat a karahi and add the mustard seeds.
3. When they splutter, add the urad dal and hing powder.
4. Add the cut green chillis, curry leaves and ginger.
5. Add 2 cups water and salt.
6. When the water comes to a boil slowly add the washed rice powder, stir continuously so as to avoid lumps.
7. Cover and cook for 5-7 minutes.
8. Remove from fire and when it cools slightly make small balls in bullet shape.
9. The above ingredients make 10-12 balls.
10. Steam once again in a pressure cooker or idli cooker for 10 minutes.

Curry leaves: *The leaves of this plant have been used for centuries in South India as flavouring agent in various curries and chutneys. The green tender leaves are eaten raw for the cure of dysentry.*

Nutritive Information

CALORIES: **348 Cal**	PROTEIN: **7.62 gm** FAT: **1.33 gm**
CARBOHYDRATE: **78 gm**	FIBRE: **30.8 gm**

225 Ajwain Chai

Ingredients

Water	2 1/2 cups
Skimmed milk	300 gm
Sugar	4 tsp
Ajwain seeds	3 tsp
Ginger juice	1/2 tsp
Chai masala (tea masala)	1/2 tsp
Cardamom powder (elaichi)	1/4 tsp (optional)

Method

1. Mix water, milk, sugar, ginger juice, elaichi powder and chai masala and heat on a low flame till the mixture starts boiling. Let it boil for 2 minutes.
2. Then add ajwain seeds and simmer for 5 minutes, while stirring at times.
3. Finally bring one more boil and shut the gas.
4. Cover and keep the chai for 5 minutes.
5. Serve it as it is for better results or strain it and serve it.

Cardamom : Large cardamoms are mostly used as a flavouring agent in curries and masalas. The seeds are also used in sweet dishes, cakes and pastries.

Nutritive Information

CALORIES: **108.8 Cal**   PROTEIN: **2.51 gm**   FAT: **0.1 gm**
CARBOHYDRATE: **24.48 gm** FIBRE: **0.05 gm**

226 Makai Da Vermicelli

Ingredients

Vermicelli	1 packet (200 gms)
Water	3 cups
Corn (makai / bhutta)	1
Onion (big)	1
Potato (big)	1
Tomato	1
Curry leaves	few
Mustard seeds	1 tsp
Haldi	1 tsp
Garam masala	1/2 tsp
Ajinomoto	1/2 tsp
Green chilli	1
Ginger & garlic	to taste (shredded)
Salt	to taste

Method

1. Boil the corn seeds separately (adding little salt and turmeric — for good colour)
2. Heat the pan. Add curry patta and mustard seeds.
3. When they splutter add finely shredded ginger and garlic and finely cut green chillis.
4. Now add finely cut onion. Sauté them till they turn golden brown.
5. Now add the pre boiled corn seeds.
6. Sauté a little and then add 3 cups of water.
7. Add turmeric, salt and ajinomoto.

8. Bring it to boil. When boiled, add vermicelli and cook till vermicelli and vegetables are fully done.
9. Now add finely cut potatoes and tomatoes.

Corn dish is not only rich in vitamin A but also high in calories.

Nutritive Information

CALORIES: **356 Cal**   PROTEIN: **2.86 gm**   FAT: **4.8 gm**
CARBOHYDRATE: **73 gm**   FIBRE: **1.10 gm**

227 Soya and Poha

Ingredients

Beaten rice (poha)	250 gms
Soya granules	75 gms
Mustard seeds	1 tsp
Curry leaves	few
Green chilli	1 (chopped)
Coriander leaves	1 tbsp (chopped)
Asafoetida	a pinch
Salt	to taste
Juice of half lemon	1 tsp
Sugar	$1/2$ tsp

Method

1. Wash poha and drain well, soak soya granules for 2 minutes.
2. Heat a pan and add asafoetida, mustard seeds, green chilli, curry leaves, salt, poha and the soya granules.
3. Cover and cook till done for approx 10 minutes.
4. Add sugar and lemon juice.
5. Mix well. Add coriander leaves and serve hot with ketchup or chutney.

Presence of soya in the poha gives it added colour, flavour and above all increases its protein content remarkably.

Nutritive Information

CALORIES: **356 Cal**   PROTEIN: **2.86 gm**   FAT: **4.8 gm**
CARBOHYDRATE: **73 gm**   FIBRE: **1.10 gm**

228 Capsicups

Ingredients

Capsicum (firm)	4
Corn kernels	100 gms
Peas	50 gms
Paneer grated (skimmed milk)	100 gms
Garlic	$1/2$ tsp (crushed)
Green chilli	1 (crushed)
A day old bread	1 slice
Salt	to taste

Method

1. Cut the tops of capsicums like small lids. Keep stalks intact.
2. Make bread crumbs out of bread slice.
3. Put capsicums and tops in salty boiling water for 3 to 4 minutes, drain and keep aside.
4. Remove and add washed corn kernels, peas and sprinkle some water.
5. Cover with a loose lid so that steam can pass.
6. Microwave for 4 minutes on medium.
7. Remove. Add green chilli, garlic, 50 gms paneer, bread crumbs and salt.
8. Return to oven and cook on high for 2 minutes.
9. Stuff this mixture in capsicums, sprinkle paneer on stuffing and place the lids back.
10. Microwave for 2 minutes on high. Stand covered for 3-4 minutes.
11. Serve hot with dinner rolls and ketchup.

Capsicums are available in a wide variety of colours like yellow, red and green and are good source of coloured pigments.

Nutritive Information

CALORIES: **356 Cal**   PROTEIN: **2.86 gm**   FAT: **4.8 gm**
CARBOHYDRATE: **73 gm**   FIBRE: **1.10 gm**

229 Baked Veg Patties

Ingredients

Raw banana	3 pieces (chopped)
Green peas	250 gms
Capsicums	100 gms (chopped fine)
French beans	50 gms (chopped)
Coriander leaves	50 gms (chopped fine)
Corn	250 gms (grated)
Semolina (rawa)	1 tsp
Salt	to taste

Method

1. Boil each vegetable except capsicums.
2. Mash vegetables and mix properly including rawa.
3. Make into small balls and press a little.
4. Put in an oven for 10 minutes.
5. Serve with green chutney or sauce.

Note: This is a Jain recipe, so raw banana is used instead of potato. It is a low calorie dish.

These baked vegetable patties if taken sandwitched between two buns, could then be eaten as baked vegetable burger with potato chips, sauce and shredded cabbage.

Nutritive Information

CALORIES: **356 Cal** PROTEIN: **2.86 gm** FAT: **4.8 gm**
CARBOHYDRATE: **73 gm** FIBRE: **1.10 gm**

230 Mix Vegetable Bhel

Ingredients

Garlic	3 flakes (chopped finely)
Green chillis	2 (chopped finely)
Spring onions with greens	2 (finely chopped)
Green capsicums	2 (chopped finely)
Carrots	2 (chopped finely)
Cabbage	100 gms (shredded finely)
French beans	50 gms (chopped finely)
Cottage cheese (paneer)	100 gms (chopped into tiny squares)
Puffed rice (murmura)	250 gms
Maggi vegetable cube	1
Soya sauce	1 tbsp
Black pepper	$1/_2$ tsp
Cornflour mixed with water to make a paste (about 1 tbsp paste)	$1/_2$ tsp
Potato sev/bhujiya (zero oil)	to taste
Sugar	a pinch
Salt	to taste

Method

1. Steam carrots, capsicums and French beans for 3-5 minutes, drain and keep aside.
2. In a non-stick frying pan add garlic and sauté, add green chillis, then add onions and their greens. Cook for a minute or till onions are transparent, stirring continuously.

3. Add cabbage. Stir and add the steamed vegetables and paneer. Stir continuously.
4. Crumble and sprinkle the Maggi cube, add paneer and pepper and stir.
5. Add soya sauce, salt, sugar and cornflour paste, stir, cover and cook on low flame for 1 minute.
6. Dip the murmuras in water and immediately remove. Squeeze out all the water and add to the vegetable mixture. Stir lightly.
7. Put in a serving plate and top with potato sev/bhujiya.

It comes out to be a colourful, crispy and munchy bhel. To add more crispness to it one need not dip the murmuras in water or one can also add cornflakes to it.

Nutritive Information

CALORIES: **356 Cal**   PROTEIN: **2.86 gm**   FAT: **4.8 gm**
CARBOHYDRATE: **73 gm**   FIBRE: **1.10 gm**

231 Puffed Rice Chatpati

Ingredients

Murmuras (puffed rice)	250 gms
Mustard seeds	1 tsp
Cumin seeds	$1/2$ tsp
Asafoetida (hing)	a pinch
Curry leaves	to taste
Coriander leaves	1 tbsp (chopped fine)
Salt, turmeric and red chilli powders and sugar	to taste
Water to soak the murmuras	1 tbsp

Method

1. First of all soak the murmuras in water for 5 minutes.
2. Then heat a karahi and add mustard and cumin seeds, curry leaves and hing.
3. Then add the murmuras, salt, red chilli and turmeric powders and sugar according to taste.
4. Stir for 4-5 minutes and then garnish with coriander leaves.

To make this recipe more spicy and chatpata, one can always add chutneys (sweet or sour) or lemon juice to it.

Nutritive Information

CALORIES: **812 Cal**   PROTEIN: **18.75 gm**   FAT: **0.25 gm**
CARBOHYDRATE: **184 gm**   FIBRE: **0.75 gm**

232 Tangy Bread Idli

Ingredients

Bread cut into rounds	4
Onions	100 gms (chopped)
Tomatoes	100 gms (chopped)
Coriander leaves	5 tbsp (chopped)
Potatoes	2
Skimmed milk	300 gms
Tomato ketchup	4 tbsp
Salt and pepper	to taste
Bhujia	100 gms

Mix masala

Black salt	1 tsp
Salt	1 tsp
Pepper	1 tsp
Red chilli powder	1 tsp
Roasted cumin powder	1 tsp

Method

1. Mash potatoes, add salt and pepper. Make 4 round tikias.
2. Heat a non-stick pan or tawa. Roast tikias till red.
3. Dip bread in milk and place on the tikias.
4. Cover and keep on low fire for a minute.
5. Smear ketchup on the bread, put onions and tomatoes.
6. Sprinkle masala and bhujia.
7. Garnish with coriander.

This recipe comes out very crispy and consumes very little time to prepare. If high fibre diet is recommended then white bread can be substituted by brown bread (whole wheat bread).

Nutritive Information

CALORIES: **356 Cal** PROTEIN: **2.86 gm** FAT: **4.8 gm**
CARBOHYDRATE: **73 gm** FIBRE: **1.10 gm**

233 Nutritious Bhel

Ingredients

For Topping

Boiled potatoes	2 (finely chopped)
Ginger	1 cm (finely chopped)
Chilli paste	1 tsp
Turmeric powder (haldi)	$1/2$ tsp
Coriander leaves	a few (chopped)
Salt	to taste

For the bhel

Moong	100 gms
Makki	100 gms
Kidney beans (rajma)	100 gms
Kabuli chana	100 gms
Onions	300 gms (grated)
Tomatoes	300 gms (puréed)
Turmeric powder (haldi)	$1/2$ tsp
Chilli powder	½ tsp
Ginger-garlic-green chilli paste	½ tsp
Coriander powder	½ tsp
Salt	to taste
Coriander leaves	for garnishing (chopped)

For garnish

Amchur powder	to taste
Chilli powder	to taste

Beaten curd (skimmed milk)   if desired
Coriander leaves   a few

Method
For topping
1. Soak pulses overnight.
2. Heat a karahi. Add haldi, ginger, and chilli paste. Sauté for 1 minute.
3. Toss the potatoes and add salt. Sauté for 2 minutes. Cover and cook for 5 minutes.
4. Add the coriander leaves.

For the bhel
1. Heat a karahi and add the onions and cook till light pink in colour.
2. Add the chilli, garlic and ginger paste, then add haldi and cook for further 5 minutes.
3. Add the tomatoes, coriander powder and cook until the masala is well cooked.
4. Add the soaked pulses, sauté well and then put in a pressure cooker for one whistle or till done.
5. After it is cooked add the salt as per taste. Garnish with coriander leaves.

Mango powder (amchur) is used as an acidulant or a souring agent for curries. The main purpose of its addition is to lower the Ph of gravy whereby the destruction of spoilage organisms in the vegetable curry is made much easier at boiling point.

Nutritive Information
CALORIES: **356 Cal**   PROTEIN: **2.86 gm**   FAT: **4.8 gm**
CARBOHYDRATE: **73 gm**   FIBRE: **1.10 gm**

234 Makkai Bhel

Ingredients

Fresh Corn (makkai)	4 (boiled)
Boiled potatoes	3 (chopped finely)
Tomatoes	3 (chopped finely)
Onions	3 (chopped finely)
Green chillis	5 (chopped finely)
Garlic paste	15 to 20 flakes
Sugar	2 tsp
Lime juice	1 $1/2$ tbsp
Cumin powder (roasted)	1 tsp
Salt	to taste

For garnishing

Fresh coriander leaves	a few (chopped)

Method

1. Remove the kernels from the boiled corn.
2. Take a bowl, put in garlic paste, cumin powder, lime juice, sugar, green chillis, and mix well.
3. Add corn, chopped boiled potatoes, tomatoes and onions and mix well.
4. Serve in individual plates, garnished with fresh coriander.

Fresh coriander leaves should always be preferred for garnishing dishes as it provides various nutrients.

Nutritive Information

CALORIES: **722.19 Cal**   PROTEIN: **9.42 gm**   FAT: **3.49 gm**
CARBOHYDRATE: **232.82 gm**   FIBRE: **1.12 gm**

235 Bhelpuri

Ingredients

Coriander leaves	100 gms (chopped)
Juice of a lemon	to taste
Tamarind chutney	to taste
Mint chutney	to taste
Salt	to taste
Sev (roasted)	50 gms
Papri	50 gms (coarsely crushed)
Puffed rice	100 gms
Chilli powder	1 tsp
Chaat masala	1 tsp
Onion	1 (chopped)
Raw mango	2 tbsp (chopped)
Green chillis	2 (minced)

Method

1. Mix all the ingredients together in a bowl.
2. Adjust the chilli powder according to taste.
3. Serve immediately in individual plates.

Bhelpuri is a famous food item available in packets also. Ready to eat and tasty dish.

Nutritive Information

CALORIES: **692.12 Cal**   PROTEIN: **11.08 gm**   FAT: **0.92 gm**
CARBOHYDRATE: **100.18 gm**   FIBRE: **2.12 gm**

236 Rajgirah Thalipeth

Ingredients

Rajgirah flour	250 gms
Potatoes	250 gms (boiled)
Coriander leaves	a few (chopped finely)
Green chillis	to taste (chopped finely)
Curry leaves	a few (chopped finely)
Cumin seeds	1 tsp
Fennel	$1/2$ tbsp
Salt	to taste

Method

1. Make a paste of coriander leaves, cumin seeds, green chillis, curry leaves and fennel.
2. Add potatoes, salt and ground paste to the flour and knead it into a tight dough.
3. Add a little water if required.
4. Roll the dough into 1 cm thick roti (sprinkle a little dry rajgirah flour while rolling if it is sticking to the rolling pin).
5. Put the roti on a preheated tawa.
6. Make holes lightly in the roti and roast till golden brown on the lower side.
7. Turn it and repeat the procedure.
8. Serve it hot with fennel chutney or potato vegetable.

Asafoetida stimulates the intestine, respiratory tracts and the nervous system. It is useful in asthma, whooping cough and chronic bronchitis. It is also administered in hysterical and epileptic attacks and in cholera.

Nutritive Information

CALORIES: **546.0 Cal**   PROTEIN: **4.5 gm**   FAT: **3.6 gm**
CARBOHYDRATE: **230.8 gm**   FIBRE: **1.10 gm**

237 Dal-Dhokli Delight (Health Recipe)

Ingredients

For dal

Toor dal	250 gms (boiled and blended)
	100 gms (finely grated Cauliflower)
Mixed vegetables (green peas, French beans)	100 gms (boiled)
Tomatoes	1-2 (chopped)
Ripe bananas	100 gms (sliced)
Kokam soaked in water	3-4
Jaggery or brown sugar	300 gms
Cilantro	2 tbsp (finely chopped)
Salt	to taste

For tempering

Asafoetida (hing)	a pinch
Mustard seeds, cumin seeds	½ tsp
Dry, red Kashmiri chillis	2
Green chillis	3 (slit)
Small pieces of ginger	1-2 (chopped finely)
Curry leaves	a few

For dhoklis

Whole-wheat flour	500 gms
Fenugreek leaves (optional)	(finely chopped) ½ cup
Turmeric powder (haldi)	1 ½ tsp
Red chilli powder	1 ½ tsp
Coriander-cumin powder	1 tsp

Salt	*to taste*
Water	*as required*

Method

For dhoklis

1. Sieve the flour. Add all the masalas, fenugreek leaves (optional), and water to form a semi-soft dough. Cover and keep it aside for 30 minutes.
2. Knead well and divide the dough into about 7-8 portions.
3. Roll out each portion into a thin chapati with the help of little flour.
4. Cover the chapatis with a piece of paper, don't let them dry or overlap each other, or they would get stuck.

For dal

1. Heat a deep vessel. Add mustard and cumin seeds. As they splutter, add dried red chillis, green chillis, curry leaves and ginger to it.
2. Add the finely grated cauliflower to it. Let it cook well. With a hand-blender, crush the remaining boiled vegetables and add them too.
3. Add tomatoes and toor dal and ½ cup of water or as required. Add salt, jaggery, kokam and ripe bananas.
4. Let the dal cook till it is well blended.
5. Take each rolled chapati and with a knife cut it out into horizontal and vertical small pieces like shakarparas or like a diamond.
6. While you cut, immediately start adding them one by one to the boiling dal. Repeat until all the chapatis are done.
7. Let the dal boil until all the dhoklis are properly cooked, but not overcooked.
8. Garnish with fresh cilantro.
9. Serve hot.

As the name suggests it is a nutritious and complete food recipe.

Nutritive Information

CALORIES: **3324.10 Cal**   PROTEIN: **29.26 gm** FAT: **12.46 gm**
CARBOHYDRATE: **1932.11 gm** FIBRE: **15.11 gm**

238 Masala Macaroni

Ingredients

Shell macaroni	200 gms
Tomato (big)	1
Onion (medium)	1
Garlic	3 pods
Ginger	a small piece
Red chilli powder	1 tsp
Capsicum	1
Maggi sauce seasoning	1 cube
Tomato ketchup	1 tbsp
Salt	to taste
Coriander leaves	for garnishing (chopped)

Method

1. Boil 6 cups of water. Add macaroni and salt. Cook till macaroni is done. Drain and keep aside.
2. Chop ginger, garlic, onion, tomato and capsicum finely.
3. Heat a pan, add ginger and garlic. Cook till a nice aroma comes.
4. Add onion and sauté till they turn pink.
5. Add tomato, chilli powder and sauce seasoning and cook till tomato becomes soft.
6. Add capsicum, tomato ketchup, salt and little water. Cook for a few minutes.
7. Add boiled macaroni and sauté till the masala gets mixed well with the macaroni.
8 Add coriander.

9. Remove from fire.
10. Serve hot.

In place of macaroni various other pasta products can be used. They are available in various shapes and sizes as desired.

Nutritive Information

CALORIES: **195.12 Cal**   PROTEIN: **6.92 gm**   FAT: **1.01 gm**
CARBOHYDRATE: **78.32 gm**   FIBRE: **0.95 gm**

239 Kela Patara

Ingredients

Bananas (big)	6 raw
Ginger-chilli paste	3 tsp
Coriander leaves	2 tbsp (chopped finely)
Lemon juice	1 tbsp
Salt	to taste
Sugar	to taste

For the dough

Wheat flour	750 gms
Salt	1 tsp
Water	as required

Method

1. Boil the bananas with the peel
2. After they cool a bit remove the peel and mash them.
3. To the mashed bananas add ginger-chilli paste, chopped coriander leaves, lemon juice, salt and sugar to taste.
4. Mix well.
5. Divide the mixture into 2 portions.
6. Make dough and divide into 2 equal halves.
7. Roll them into big chapaties and spread 1 part of the mixture on the chapati.
8. Now roll the chapati as you do for Swiss roll or as you do for a normal patara. Seal the sides.
9. Now cut the roll into slices.

10. Repeat the same with the rest of the mixture. Bake them in the oven for 20 minutes.
11. Serve hot with chutney or ketchup.

Kela patara appears like namkeen Swiss roll. To add more colour to it, one can use any green leafy vegetable like spinach and grated carrots and if raw bananas are not available boiled potatoes may be used.

Nutritive Information

CALORIES: **1904.21 Cal** PROTEIN: **9.5 gm** FAT: **0.95 gm**
CARBOHYDRATE: **262.29 gm** FIBRE: **2.0 gm**

240 Microwave Khandvi

Ingredients

For khandvi

Gram flour (besan)	250 gms
Buttermilk	3 cups
Salt	to taste
Turmeric powder (haldi)	a pinch

For garnishing

Mustard seeds (sarson)	1 tsp
Green chillis	2-3 (thinly sliced)
Little bit of water	as required
Coriander leaves	a few (chopped finely)

Method

For khandvi

1. Mix together besan, buttermilk, salt and turmeric powder in a microwave safe bowl. Make sure all the besan is mixed well in the buttermilk.
2. Put the batter in the microwave for 5 minutes.
3. Take out the batter, stir well and put it back in the microwave for 3 more minutes.
4. Take out again and stir well and put it back for 2 more minutes.
5. Spread the cooked batter over aluminium foil (or back of a steel thali) very thinly, while it's still hot.
6. Let it cool a bit. Then cut the strips 7-cms wide and 23-25 cms long. Roll them neatly.

For garnishing
1. Heat a small pan, add mustard seeds.
2. When mustard seeds crackle, add green chillis.
3. Spread them over the khandvi.
4. Garnish with coriander leaves and serve.

An easy-to-prepare and cook oil free khandvi comes out to be a tangy tea time snack and can be served with green chutney.

Nutritive Information

CALORIES: **286.21 Cal**   PROTEIN: **4.26 gm**   FAT: **0.92 gm**
CARBOHYDRATE: **83.11 gm**   FIBRE: **1.21 gm**

241 Microwave Khicchu

Ingredients

Rice flour	500 gms
Paste of green chilli and ginger	2 tsp
Cumin seeds (jeera)	1 tbsp
Water	4 cups
Salt	to taste

Method

1. In a microwave bowl put water and all the ingredients except rice flour for 3 minutes.
2. Take a bowl, put in rice flour and add the boiled water to it. Mix it properly. Now take a microwave dish 15 x 20 cms and spread a thin layer in it.
3. Put the tray in microwave for 3 minutes.
4. Repeat the same procedure with the remaining dough.
5. Serve hot with red chilli powder.

Salt intake should be monitored and should be taken in small quantities by all individuals.

Nutritive Information

CALORIES: **569.23 Cal** PROTEIN: **11.12 gm** FAT: **1.21 gm**
CARBOHYDRATE: **109.16 gm** FIBRE: **0.26 gm**

242 Microwave Dhokla

Ingredients

Semolina (rawa)	500 gms
Curd	250 gms
Water	250 gms
Turmeric powder (haldi)	1 tsp
Salt	to taste
Eno fruit salt	2 tsp

For seasoning

Curry leaves	handful
Green chillis	2-3 (diced)
Black mustard seeds	1 tbsp
Water	2 tbsp
Coriander leaves	$1/2$ bunch (chopped)

Method

1. Soak 2 cups of rawa, 1 cup curd and 1 cup of water for 30 minutes.
2. Take a microwave proof pan, not plastic and add 2 tsp of Eno to the rawa mixture. Pour immediately in the prepared pan. Cook it in the microwave covered for 12 minutes.
3. After the dhoklas are done, heat a pan, add black mustard seeds, curry leaves and green chillis. Once the ingredients start spluttering, add water and immediately pour the tadka over the dhokla.
4. Cut the dhokla into pieces and garnish with dhania leaves.

Turmeric vitalizes the liver by stimulating it. It has the property of purifying the blood and it is a good antiseptic.

Nutritive Information

CALORIES: **354.12 Cal**   PROTEIN: **12.32 gm** FAT: **0.95 gm**
CARBOHYDRATE: **79.8 gm**   FIBRE: **0.89 gm**

243 Open Grilled Sandwich

Ingredients

Potatoes	4 (boiled and mashed)
Onion	1 (chopped)
Ginger	2-cm piece (minced)
Coriander leaves	1 tbsp (finely chopped)
Green chilli	1 (chopped)
Garam masala	$1/2$ tsp
Bread slices	4
Cottage cheese (paneer) (skimmed milk)	30 gms
Salt	to taste

Method

1. Heat a pan and sauté onions till golden brown. Add ginger, coriander leaves, green chilli and garam masala and cook for a while.
2. Add mashed potatoes and cook well. Keep it aside to cool.
3. Take a bread slice, spread the potato mixture over it and place a slice of cottage cheese on it.
4. Similarly make more and grill them in the oven.
5. Serve hot with ketchup.

It is an oil free breakfast preparation which is liked by all the age groups. One can add sprouts to it when cheese is not available.

Nutritive Information

CALORIES: **194.95 Cal**   PROTEIN: **4.36 gm**   FAT: **0.32 gm**
CARBOHYDRATE: **39.02 gm**   FIBRE: **1.68 gm**

244 Palak and Paneer Tikki

Ingredients

Spinach (palak)	500 gms (finely chopped)
Cottage cheese (paneer) (skimmed milk)	250 gms
Mixed vegetables	250 gms (finely chopped)
Green chillis	2 (finely chopped)
Bread slices	2 to 3
Salt and pepper	to taste

Method

1. Mash paneer. Add palak and other boiled vegetables, add green chillis and mashed bread. Then add salt and pepper to taste. Mix well and make tikkis.
2. Take tikkis and roast them in the oven.
3. Serve hot with green chutney.

Combination of palak, paneer and mixed vegetable not only adds different flavours and colour to this tikki but also incorporates nutrients like protein, iron and B-vitamins, B-carotene.

Nutritive Information

CALORIES: **189.42 Cal** PROTEIN: **12.14 gm** FAT: **1.36 gm**
CARBOHYDRATE: **64.32 gm** FIBRE: **2.52 gm**

245 Kala Chana Kebab

Ingredients

Kala chana	250 gms
Potatoes	250 gms (mashed)
Coriander leaves	250 gms (chopped)
Green chillis	5-6 (chopped)
Salt	to taste
Garam masala	1 tsp
Chilli flakes	2 tsp
Cornflour	2 tbsp

Method

1. Soak chana overnight in water.
2. Pressure-cook chana and potatoes separately.
3. Mash them well.
4. Mix them with the remaining ingredients.
5. Make rolls and roast in the oven.
6. Serve hot with mint chutney.

Fresh coriander is finely chopped and mixed with vegetables and other food items. This gives a special flavour to the food and makes it easily digestible. We usually prefer the paste like chutney of coriander but drinking its juice has special advantages.

Nutritive Information

CALORIES: **351.02 Cal**   PROTEIN: **25.11 gm**   FAT: **5.7 gm**
CARBOHYDRATE: **101.17 gm**   FIBRE: **0.46 gm**

246 Capsicum Rings

Ingredients

Capsicums	2
Flour (maida)	4 tbsp
Salt and pepper	to taste
Eno fruit salt	1 pinch
Water	as required
Mustard paste	3 tbsp
Chaat masala	1 tsp

Method

1. Cut the capsicum in rings, cutting them across the diameter.
2. Soak maida in water; add salt and pepper and Eno fruit salt.
3. Soak it for 15 minutes and then add more water for batter consistency.
4. Apply the mustard paste to capsicum rings.
5. Dip the rings in the maida batter and roast them in the oven.
6. Sprinkle chaat masala on top and serve hot.

Water is one nutrient that is most often neglected. It should be consumed as much as possible — at least 6-8 glasses per day is necessary.

Nutritive Information

CALORIES: **164.26 Cal** PROTEIN: **4.36 gm** FAT: **0.36 gm**
CARBOHYDRATE: **23.62 gm** FIBRE: **0.61 gm**

247 Maharashtrian Fatka

Ingredients

Green chillis	5
Garlic flakes	15
Coriander leaves	1 small bunch (chopped)
Asafoetida (hing)	$1/4$ tsp
Mustard seeds	$1/2$ tsp
Salt	as per taste
Curd (skimmed milk)	250 gms

Method

1. Roast chillis, coriander and garlic.
2. Cool and grind fine.
3. Mix with curd.
4. Add salt, mustard seeds and hing.
5. After cooling add it to the mixture. Now the fatka is ready to serve with rotis or jowar roti.

Green chillis should be preferred in comparision to red chilli powder to make the food spicy and tasty.

Nutritive Information

CALORIES: **45.36 Cal** PROTEIN: **2.67 gm** FAT: **0.25 gm**
CARBOHYDRATE: **7.9 gm** FIBRE: **0.56 gm**

248 Onion Rings

Ingredients

Onions (big)	2
Flour (maida)	250 gms
Chaat masala	1 tsp
Salt	to taste
Water	as required

Method

1. Mix maida, salt and enough water to make a thick batter like the cake batter.
2. Cut onions into rounds and separate each ring.
3. Dip each ring in the batter and roast.
4. Sprinkle chaat masala on the rings and serve hot.

Onions: *From medical point of view white onions are more useful. They are stimulant, vitalizing, promoters of virility, refreshing and induce sleep.*

Nutritive Information

CALORIES: **349.36 Cal**   PROTEIN: **12.10 gm**   FAT: **1.79 gm**
CARBOHYDRATE: **79.9 gm**   FIBRE: **0.51 gm**

249 Palak Tikki

Ingredients

Potatoes	6
Palak	1 bunch
Stale bread pieces, 1 day old	6
Ginger, garlic and green chilli paste	2 tsp
Coriander leaves	3 tbsp (finely cut)
Salt	to taste
Cumin seeds (jeera)	1 tsp
Lemon juice	1 tsp

Method

1. Boil potatoes and mash them well while still hot. Boil spinach and make purée.
2. In a dish place the mashed potatoes. Add palak purée. Dip bread in water, press it and squeeze dry and add.
3. Add all the other masalas to it and mix well.
3. Make a dough and form into small balls and flatten them.
5. Roast them in the oven.
6. Serve with mint chutney.

It stimulates peristalsis and is a mild laxative. It is easy to digest and assimilate. It is heavy and palatable.

Nutritive Information

CALORIES: **358 Cal** PROTEIN: **10.7 gm** FAT: **1.75 gm**
CARBOHYDRATE: **82.8 gm** FIBRE: **4.85 gm**

250 Tandoori Chunks

Ingredients

Soya chunks	*100 gms*
Tandoori masala	*2 tbsp*
Curd (skimmed milk)	*2 tbsp*
Ginger-garlic paste	*1 tsp*
Green chilli paste	*1 tsp*
Salt	*to taste*

Method

1. Soak soya chunks in warm water.
2. Mix together curd, tandoori masala, salt, green chilli paste, and ginger-garlic paste.
3. Squeeze the water from the chunks and add them to the mixture.
4. Let it stand for 30 minutes.
5. Arrange chunks on skewers and put them in the oven.
6. Serve hot.

A protein rich dish, as good as non-veg tikkas.

Nutritive Information

CALORIES: **435 Cal**   PROTEIN: **43.5 gm**   FAT: **9.2 gm**
CARBOHYDRATE: **21.9 gm** FIBRE: **3.7 gm**

251 Corn Boat

Ingredients

Corn	15 gms
Raw banana	25 gms
Whole red chana	5 gms
Green chana	5 gms
Tomatoes	10 gms
Tomato sauce	1 tsp (without onion garlic)
Ginger	$1/2$ tsp
Green chilli	$1/2$ tsp
Zeera	$1/2$ tsp
Hot dog bread	1 no
Carrots	20 gms
Paneer	5 gms

Method

1. Make a filling by boiling corn, banana and grams.
2. Then add the above mixture.
3. Fill it in the bread vertically.
4. Decorate by making flags of curry leaves.
5. Serve with grated carrots and paneer.

Banana is an energy dense fruit and a boon for malnourished individuals.

Nutritive Information

CALORIES: **105.2 Cal** PROTEIN: **2.5 gm** FAT: **2.52 gm**
CARBOHYDRATE: **54.86 gm** FIBRE: **2.1 gm**

252 Paneer Pudina Kebab

Ingredients

Paneer (skimmed milk)	200 gms
Hung curd (skimmed milk)	250 gms
Garlic-ginger paste	1 tbsp
Green chilli paste	2
Mint leaves	250 gms
Coriander leaves	100 gms
Besan	1 tbsp
Ajwain powder	$1/2$ tsp
Jeera powder	$1/2$ tsp
Black salt	$1/4$ tsp
Chaat masala	$1/4$ tsp
Kasoori methi powder	$1/2$ tsp
Salt	to taste

Method

1. Cut paneer into 1-$1/2$" cubes.
2. Make paste of mint and coriander leaves in a mixer without adding water.
3. Heat a pan and add 1 tbsp of besan and roast continuously for $1/2$ a minute. Keep aside.
4. Take a bowl. Put curd, mint paste and mix very well.
5. Now add all other ingredients except paneer and mix well.
6. Coat paneer cubes one by one in mint-curd paste in a bowl and keep in the fridge for 30 minutes.
7. Now take a square glass bowl (micro proof) and put 10-12 coated

paneer pieces in it and micro high for 4 minutes.
8. Serve hot.

Kasooa methi powder is prepared by drying methi leaves in the shade and it gives very good flavour even if other spices are not used.

Nutritive Information

CALORIES: **486.20 Cal**   PROTEIN: **82.10 gm** FAT: **4.8 gm**
CARBOHYDRATE: **136.02 gm** FIBRE: **0.86 gm**

253 Soya Tikkas

Ingredients

Soya beans (soaked and blended)	250 gms
Cauliflower	1/2 cup (grated)
Garlic	5-6 cloves (crushed)
Ginger	1 tbsp chopped
Salt	to taste
Mango & Red chilli powder	1-1 tbsp
Cornflour	2 tbsp
Potatoes	1 cup (grated)
Raisins (kishmish)	1 tbsp
Red chilli paste	accompaniment
Lemon juice and chaat masala	for garnishing

Method

1. Blend the soaked and blended soya beans with cauliflower, garlic, ginger, salt, mango and, red chilli powders, corn-flour and grated potato.
2. Add raisins. Blend once again.
3. Take out the mixture in your hands.
4. Make small balls of this mixture.
5. Put these balls on skewers and cook.
6. Serve hot with lemon juice and chaat masala sprinkled over them with the red chilli paste.

As the potato is alkaline, it is very helpful in maintaining the alkali reserve of the body and preventing acidosis. It is useful for patients suffering from gout as the mineral elements of potato help in the elimination of uric acid from the body.

Nutritive Information
CALORIES: **659.02 Cal**   PROTEIN: **53.6 gm**   FAT: **10.10 gm**
CARBOHYDRATE: **362.10 gm**   FIBRE: **4.5 gm**

254 Chinese Jain Cutlets

Ingredients

Raw bananas	2
Green peas	250 gms
Cabbage	250 gms (thinly sliced)
French beans	100 gms (cut and boiled)
Capsicum	2 tbsp (diced)
Coriander leaves	2 tbsp (chopped)
Vinegar	1 tsp
Salt	to taste
Green chillis	2-3 (chopped)

Method

1. Boil raw bananas and green peas and mash them well.
2. Add the remaining ingredients and roll into a cutlet shape.
3. Cook them in a non-stick pan and then roast them in the oven.

The outer green leaves of the cabbage are an excellent source of vitamin A. The inner white leaves are devoid of it. Hence the outer leaves should not be thrown away. The percentage of iron is also higher in the outer greens.

Nutritive Information

CALORIES: **592.01 Cal**   PROTEIN: **20.26 gm**   FAT: **3.2 gm**
CARBOHYDRATE: **232.10 gm** FIBRE: **4.8 gm**

255 Enchilada

Ingredients
Cornflour roti

Yellow cornflour	250 gms
Salt	to taste

For filling

Baked beans	1 tin
Onion	1
Tomatoes	2
Oregano	$1/_2$ tsp
Salt and red chilli powder	to taste

For purée

Tomatoes	1 kg
Onions	2 (cut into small pieces)
Capsicum	1 (cut into small pieces)
Oregano	$1/_2$ tsp
Salt and red chilli powder	to taste

Method

For cornflour roti

Take cornflour with a pinch of salt and make a soft dough with required amount of water. Roll this into chapatis.

For baked beans

Cut and sautè the onion. Add cut tomatoes and when they get soft add the baked beans. Put $1/_2$ tsp oregano, salt and red chilli powder to taste.

For tomato purée

1. Grate tomatoes. Sautè small cut onions; add tomatoes, capsicum,

salt, oregano and red chilli powder.

2. Prepare all the rolls with the chapati as the cover and beans as the filling. Place the rolls evenly in a baking tray and pour the tomato purée till the rolls get submerged. Bake for 10 minutes. Serve hot.

Tomato *contains some vitamin B1 and B2. It is rich in vitamin A. It is remarkable that vitamin C in tomato is not destroyed quickly because it is protected by the acid it contains.*

Nutritive Information

CALORIES: **987.32 Cal**   PROTEIN: **32.17 gm**   FAT: **8.9 gm**
CARBOHYDRATE: **369.25 gm**   FIBRE: **6.1 gm**

256 Vegetable Sizzlers

Ingredients

For the vegetable cutlets

Potatoes	3
Carrots	3
French beans	250 gms
Cabbage	500 gms
Onions	2-3 (chopped)
Turmeric powder	$1/4$ tsp
Chilli powder	1 tsp
Plain flour	3 tsp
Coriander	2 tsp (chopped finely)
Green chillis	2-3 (minced)
Salt	to taste
Bread crumbs	

For the stuffed capsicums

Capsicums	5-6

Ingredients same as for vegetable cutlets excluding bread crumbs

For stuffed tomatoes

Medium sized tomatoes	5-6
Boiled rice	1 tsp
Tomato ketchup	4-5 tsp
Plain flour	2-3 tsp
Chilli powder	$1/4$ tsp
Salt	to taste

Other ingredients

Boiled green peas	100 gms
Boiled carrots	100 gms
Potato chips baked in the oven	100 gms
Boiled spaghetti	100 gms
Garlic (optional)	10 gms (crushed)
Tomato ketchup	to taste
Salt and pepper	to taste

Method

Advanced preparation

1. Chop all the vegetables finely.
2. Sautè onions for one minute. Add all the vegetables, turmeric and chilli powder and salt and continue cooking until the vegetables are cooked.
3. Sprinkle plain flour on the vegetables, mix and cook again for a few minutes.
4. Mash the vegetables. Add coriander and green chillis and mix well.
5. Shape into cutlets.
6. Roll in bread crumbs and roast in a non-stick pan.

For the stuffed capsicums

1. Remove the top part of the capsicums and scoop out the centres.
2. Proceed to make the stuffing as per steps 1 to 4 for vegetable cutlets.
3. Fill the capsicums with this mixture. Put the tops back and cook them till done.

For the stuffed tomatoes

1. Remove the top portion of the tomatoes and scoop out the centres.
2. Mix rice, tomato ketchup, flour, chilli powder and salt.
3. Fill the tomatoes with this mixture.
4. Pour a little tomato ketchup in the centre. Add potato chips, sprinkle

salt and pepper on top and cook for 1 minute. When cooked, push to the sides to make yet another border.

5. Put the crushed garlic in the centre. Add spaghetti. Sprinkle salt on top and cook for a few minutes.
6. Put the cutlets in between the tomatoes and capsicums.
7. Serve hot with warm crisp bread.

Nutritive Information

CALORIES: **2632.10 Cal** PROTEIN: **43.92 gm** FAT: **15.1 gm**
CARBOHYDRATE: **892.10 gm** FIBRE: **10.1 gm**

257 Falafel

Ingredients

For dhokla

Whole green gram (moong dal)	250 gms
Salt	to taste
Chilli, ginger	to taste
Eno fruit salt	$1/4$ spoon

For tahini

Chana dalia	100 gms
Sesame seeds	100 gms
Cumin seeds (jeera)	½ tsp
Mustard seeds	½ tsp
Salt	to taste
Curd (skimmed milk)	to make paste

For Salsa

Tomato	1
Garlic cloves	2
Spring onion	1
Salt, lime, and red chilli	to taste

Salad

Cucumber	100 gms
Tomatoes	100 gms
Carrots	100 gms
Cabbage	100 gms
Spring onions	3

Salt, lime and pepper   to taste

Method

Falafel bread: oval or round pita bread

For the dhokla

Soak moong dal for four hours. Remove the skin and grind coarsely. Add green chilli, salt, ginger and Eno fruit salt. Pour in the thali and steam the dhokla. Make small pieces out of the dhokla.

For tahini

Grind chana dalia and sesame seeds dry. Add salt, jeera and mustard seeds and grind again. Add curd to this and make a thick paste.

For salsa

Grind tomato, onion, garlic, salt and red chilli powder. Add lime juice also.

Salad

Cut the cucumber, tomatoes, spring onion, and cabbage into small pieces. Grate carrots. Add salt and pepper and lime juice.

Table preparation

Take pita bread and cut into two pieces. Make a pocket and stuff dhokla, tahini, salsa and salads.

It is nutritious as well as filling dish which provides all the nutrients present in vegetarian diet.

Nutritive Information

CALORIES: **2994.62 Cal**   PROTEIN: **69.23 gm** FAT: **16.26 gm**
CARBOHYDRATE: **982.10 gm** FIBRE: **20.21 gm**

258 Sherbet

Ingredients

Orange (medium)	1
Tomatoes	20 gms
Lemon juice	1 tsp
Salt	a pinch
Artificial sweetener	to taste
Water	1 cup

Method

1. Peel the orange and remove seeds.
2. Cut tomatoes into cubes.
3. Blend ingredients with half cup of water and strain.
4. Add lemon juice, salt, artificial sweetener.
5. Serve chilled.

Tomato is an excellent food for diabetics and for those who desire to reduce their weight. Tomato juice cleanses the stomach and intestines.

Nutritive Information

CALORIES: **30.85 Cal** PROTEIN: **0.58 gm** FAT: **0.59 gm**
CARBOHYDRATE: **6.72 gm** FIBRE: **0.31 gm**

259 Curd Delight

Ingredients

Soda	1 bottle
Lemon juice	2 drops
Ginger juice	2 drops
Curd (skimmed milk)	2 tsp
Artificial sweetener	to taste
Mint leaves	for garnishing
Crushed ice	as required

Method

1. Blend curd, lemon and ginger juices, sweetener, soda and crushed ice.
2. Serve immediately with mint leaves.

This is a refreshing dessert with the aroma of mint leaves as well as nutritious.

Nutritive Information

CALORIES: **6 Cal**   PROTEIN: **0.31 gm**   FAT: **0.4 gm**
CARBOHYDRATE: **0.3 gm**   FIBRE: **0 gm**

260 Peach Drink

Ingredients

Fresh peaches	500 gms
Banana	1
Vanilla essence	1 drop

Method

1. Peel and store peaches. Peel banana
2. Purèe all the ingredients together.
3. Sieve and serve cold.

Peach is a sub-acid fruit. It is one of the juiciest of fruits and contains on an average about 80 per cent water. Peaches like most fruit are a valuable diet for neutralizing blood acidity and as regulating material for their mineral, vitamin and cellulose content.

Nutritive Information

CALORIES: **308 Cal** PROTEIN: **6.6 gm** FAT: **1.65 gm**
CARBOHYDRATE: **66.1 gm** FIBRE: **6.2 gm**

261 Banapple Sauce

Ingredients

Apples	2
Banana	1

Method

1. Peel and core apples. Peel banana.
2. Purèe them until smooth.
3. Pour in a tall glass, top it up with soda and serve.

It contains an abundance of minerals and vitamins.

Nutritive Information

CALORIES: **117 Cal**   PROTEIN: **0.8 gm**   FAT: **0.65 gm**
CARBOHYDRATE: **27 gm**   FIBRE: **1.2 gm**

262 Minty Syrup

Ingredients

Apple juice	½ cup
Mint leaves	50 gms (finely chopped)
Honey	1 tbsp
Lemon juice	1 tbsp
Orange juice	1 cup

Method

1. Boil apple juice, honey and mint leaves in a saucepan for 5 minutes.
2. Bring it to room temperature and stir in lemon and orange juice.
3. Serve decorated with orange peel and mint leaves.

Honey is the most concentrated sweet found in nature. Besides two types of sugar, honey contains wax, volatile oils, proteins, carbohydrates, mucilaginous matter. In short, honey is a complete food which requires practically no digestion but is quickly absorbed and utilized by the body.

Nutritive Information

CALORIES: **143.9 Cal**   PROTEIN: **2.85 gm**   FAT: **0.485 gm**
CARBOHYDRATE: **30.83 gm**   FIBRE: **1.0 gm**

263 Smoothie Shaky

Ingredients

Curd (skimmed milk)	250 gms (plain or flavoured)
Any seasonal fruit	100 gms
Any fruit juice	$2/3$ cup
Low fat soya flour	2 tsp

Method

1. Blend all the ingredients.

Any seasonal fruit which is readily available can be used in this recipe.

Nutritive Information

CALORIES: **261.2 Cal** PROTEIN: **14.02 gm** FAT: **12.53 gm**
CARBOHYDRATE: **24.89 gm** FIBRE: **1.37 gm**

264 Refreshing Fruit Shake

Ingredients

Apple or orange juice	½ cup
Frozen strawberries or raspberries or peaches	100 gms (deseeded)
Flavoured curd (skimmed milk)	250 gms
Soya flour	2 tbsp

Method

1. Mix all the ingredients vigorously in a blender till well mixed and smooth.

Fresh strawberries are considered a delicacy. The fruit is distinctive because of its unusual flavour.

Nutritive Information

CALORIES: **88.6 Cal** PROTEIN: **22.11 gm** FAT: **16.65 gm**
CARBOHYDRATE: **37.67 gm** FIBRE: **3.31 gm**

265 Nutmeg Divine

Ingredients

Banana	1 (peeled and cut)
Honey	1 tbsp
Nutmeg (freshly grated)	¼ tsp
Skimmed milk	250 gms

Method

1. Combine all the ingredients in a blender and process until smooth.

Skimmed milk *is milk from which fat is removed. It contains protein and calcium as does the whole milk but less of vitamins because most of the vitamin A being soluble in fat, is removed with the cream.*

Nutritive Information

CALORIES: **178.35 Cal**   PROTEIN: **6.85 gm**   FAT: **0.40 gm**
CARBOHYDRATE: **37.02 gm**   FIBRE: **0.4 gm**

266 Banana-Ginger Fizz

Ingredients

Skimmed milk	250 gms
Banana	1 (peeled and cut)
Lime sherbet	as required
Ginger ale	as required

Method

1. Put milk, banana and lime sherbet in a blender.
2. Cover and blend slowly until smooth.
3. Pour into 9 glasses and fill up by adding ginger ale.

Bananas are high in food value, containing vitamins B and C and as well as minerals. Not only is the fruit utilised, banana leaves serve as an all purpose wrapping for steamed or baked food and as a disposable plate.

Nutritive Information

CALORIES: **130.5 Cal** PROTEIN: **6.85 gm** FAT: **0.40 gm**
CARBOHYDRATE: **25.1 gm** FIBRE: **0.4 gm**

267 Makhmali Khazoori

Ingredients

Apples	2
Oranges	2
Bananas	2
Dates	6 (deseeded)
Soda	1 bottle

Method

1. Wash the apples thoroughly and cut into sections. Remove the core and put into high-powered blender.
2. Peel the oranges, separate the segments and put into blender. Add peeled bananas and dates.
3. Blend thoroughly into a smooth paste. Add soda.
4. Serve in tall glasses with thin shreds of dates and straw.

Dates *contain a very high percentage of sugar in natural form which is immediately absorbed. They are rich in protein, lime, iron, vitamins and other essential food constituents.*

Nutritive Information

CALORIES: **559 Cal**   PROTEIN: **5.2 gm**   FAT: **2.0 gm**
CARBOHYDRATE: **130 gm**   FIBRE: **9.4 gm**

268 Hot Pineapple Sip

Ingredients

Pineapple juice	1 cup
Cranberry juice	1 cup
Honey	3 tbsp
Ground cloves	1/3 tsp
Lime peel	1 tsp (grated)

Method

1. Combine pineapple juice, cranberry juice, honey and cloves in a large saucepan.
2. Heat to boil for one minute. Remove from heat.
3. Serve sprinkled with grated lime peel, if desired.

Cranberry juice cocktail: It is a refreshing drink that's good any time. A bright red fruit juice made from cranberry sugar.

Nutritive Information

CALORIES: **347.55 Cal** PROTEIN: **2.8 gm** FAT: **1.4 gm**
CARBOHYDRATE: **80.77 gm** FIBRE: **1.3 gm**

269 Mango Paradise

Ingredients

Ripe mango	*1*
Strawberries	*250 gms*
Ice cubes	*to taste*

Method

1. Peel and cut mango. Combine strawberries, mango and ice in a blender. Blend until thick and smooth.
2. Pour in a tall glass. Decorate with strawberry and serve.

***Mango** is not only the most delicious fruit but also the greatest nourisher of the body. The ripe mango is rich in sugar. It is laxative, diuretic and rich in vitamins A and C.*

Nutritive Information

CALORIES: **118 Cal**   PROTEIN: **1.3 gm**   FAT: **.6 gm**
CARBOHYDRATE: **25.7 gm**   FIBRE: **1.8 gm**

270 Flavoured Hot Sip

Ingredients

Pineapple juice	5 cups
Apple juice	1 lt
Cinnamon sticks	3
Whole cloves	1 tsp
Apple	1 (cored and sliced)
Spiral peel of	1 orange
Brown sugar	50 gms

Method

1. Combine pineapple and apple juices, cinnamon, cloves, apple, orange peel and brown sugar in a saucepan.
2. Boil and then cover and cook for 5 minutes on low flame.
3. Serve decorated with apple and orange peels.

It is nourishing and easily digestible. It helps to quench thirst. It appeases bile and windiness, cures dysentery and strengthen the intestines. Its pectin content relieves cough and helps in eliminating toxic elements from the body.

Nutritive Information

CALORIES: **1078 Cal**   PROTEIN: **4.2 gm**   FAT: **6 gm**
CARBOHYDRATE: **207.4 gm**   FIBRE: **1 gm**

271 Cholesterol Lowering Tonic

Ingredients

Ginger	1 cm slice
Garlic clove	1
Parsley	handful
Carrots	4 (peeled and cut)
Apple	1 (cut into wedges)
Tabasco sauce	a splash (optional)

Method

1. Fill the hands with parsley. Now place the ginger and garlic in the centre of a handful of parsley and squeeze.
2. Now feed them into the juicer followed by carrots and the apple.
3. Grind them to a fine purèe.
4. Strain and pour into a glass. Decorate with carrots and serve.

Garlic is the poor man's musk and an indigenous medicine. It is a tonic for the hair. It helps the process of calcification in fractures and is also useful in dyspepsia, cough, heart disease, asthma, piles, odema, constipation.

Nutritive Information

CALORIES: **112.9 Cal**   PROTEIN: **2.1 gm**   FAT: **0.8 gm**
CARBOHYDRATE: **24.26 gm**   FIBRE: **2.1 gm**

272 Avocado Blend

Ingredients

Pear	1 (chopped)
Green grapes	100 gms
Avocado	100 gms
Honey	2 tsp
Lemon juice	1 tsp

Method

1. Blend all the ingredients together.
2. Pour in a tall glass over crushed ice and serve.

Avocado is rich in fat, potassium and sodium with a small amount of fluorine and iodine. It is a good body builder for a weak stomach and convalescents. It is also indicated in cases of malnutrition, stomach ulcers, enteritis, insomnia and impotency.

Nutritive Information

CALORIES: **147.15 Cal**   PROTEIN: **0.975 gm** FAT: **5.95 gm**
CARBOHYDRATE: **75.9 gm**   FIBRE: **1.95 gm**

273 Soudate Milk

Ingredients

Soya milk	*250 gms*
Dates	*10 (deseeded and chopped)*
Curd (skimmed milk)	*250 gms*
Ice cubes	*4*

Method

1. Blend the first three things together in a blender till smooth.
2. Put crushed ice in a glass, and top it with the mixture.

Soya milk *is a smart choice for anyone seeking to limit their cholesterol, fat or sodium intake. It is a good source of protein, thiamine, iron, phosphorus copper, potassium and magnessium.*

Nutritive Information

CALORIES: **1374.0 Cal**   PROTEIN: **116.7 gm** FAT: **59.15 gm**
CARBOHYDRATE: **93.55 gm**   FIBRE: **3.7 gm**

274 Peachy Cherry Juice

Ingredients

Apple juice	*1 cup*
Peach juice	*1 cup*
Frozen cherries	*50 gms (deseeded)*
Ice	*1 cup*

Method

1. In a blender combine the juices with cherries and ice.
2. Blend for 2 minutes.
3. Serve immediately.

Cherries *like most fruits, are palatable and wholesome either raw or cooked. Cherries are highly alkaline, stimulate the flow of bile and act beneficially upon the kidneys and bowels.*

Nutritive Information

CALORIES: **234 Cal**   PROTEIN: **3.075 gm**   FAT: **1.325 gm**
CARBOHYDRATE: **51.25 gm**   FIBRE: **2.10 gm**

275 Pineapple Lade

Ingredients

Pineapple	200 gms
Hot water	to taste
Lemon juice	to taste
Sugar and salt	to taste
Ice cubes	as required
Pepper	optional

Method

1. Peel and chop the pineapple.
2. Add hot water, lemon juice, sugar and salt to it. Keep aside for 2 hours.
3. Mix it in a blender, strain and chill it.
4. Serve chilled with ice cubes.
5. Add pepper if you like.

Pepper constitutes an important component of culinary seasonings of universal use and an essential ingredient of numerous commercial foodstuffs.

Nutritive Information

CALORIES: **131.8 Cal**   PROTEIN: **0.8 gm**   FAT: **0.2 gm**
CARBOHYDRATE: **31.54 gm**   FIBRE: **1 gm**

276 Jeera Sip

Ingredients

Water	1 １/₂ cups
Roasted cumin powder	1 tsp
Sugar	1 tsp
Black salt (sendha namak)	1/₂ tsp
Pepper	1/₄ tsp
Lemon juice	1 tbsp
Mint leaves	to garnish and to give flavour

Method

1. Take 1½ cups of water and put in all the ingredients except lemon juice and allow it to boil properly till it is reduced to 1 cup.
2. Sieve it in a cup and put lemon juice and some mint leaves.
3. Serve it hot and enjoy the flavour. It is good for the stomach and sore throat.

Mint rich in vitamin E prevents the wear and tear of the body and energizes the blood vessels. Application of mint juice on ringworm has beneficial effects.

Nutritive Information

CALORIES: **46.25 Cal**   PROTEIN: **1.085 gm**   FAT: **0.88 gm**
CARBOHYDRATE: **8.465 gm** FIBRE: **0.60 gm**

277 Cool Blast

Ingredients

Spinach leaves	*a handful*
Sugar	*1 tbsp*
Lemon juice	*2 tbsp*
Salt	*1 tsp*
Soda	*1 bottle*

Method

1. Take a handful of prewashed spinach leaves.
2. Grind them well in a mixer with some water and strain.
3. In the sieved juice, put sugar, salt, lemon juice and ice. Mix it well.
4. Then add plain soda and serve.

A refreshing summer cool beverage having a sweet and salty flavour. Presence of spinach not only adds colour and flavour but also the beta-carotene.

Nutritive Information

CALORIES: **102.8 Cal** PROTEIN: **2.30 gm** FAT: **0.97 gm**
CARBOHYDRATE: **21.13 gm** FIBRE: **0.6 gm**

278 Water Melon Punch

Ingredients

Watermelon	500 gms
Ginger	50 gms
Lemon juice	2 lemons
Rose syrup	1 cup
Salt	to taste
Pepper	to taste

Method

1. Peel and grate the ginger and take out the juice.
2. Cut the watermelon into small pieces, removing the seeds.
3. Put it in a mixer and strain out the juice.
4. To the strained watermelon juice, add lemon and ginger juices, rose syrup, salt and pepper and mix well.
5. Serve topped with crushed ice.

Watermelon is an excellant summer food and in hot weather it not only quenches thirst but it is also a cooling and refreshing drink containing valuable salts and vitamins. Watermelon is a good diuretic in cases of fever.

Nutritive Information

CALORIES: **142 Cal** PROTEIN: **2.65 gm** FAT: **1.9 gm**
CARBOHYDRATE: **28.2 gm** FIBRE: **2.2 gm**

279 Kashmiri Soda

Ingredients

Lemon juice	1
Black salt	to taste
Salt	to taste
Chilled soda	1 bottle

Method

1. In a glass add lemon juice, black salt and salt and top with soda.

Lemon juice rich in vitamin C is very effective because it is combined with bioflavenoids. It also contains niacin and thiamine in small amounts.

Nutritive Information

CALORIES: **28.5 Cal**   PROTEIN: **0.5 gm**   FAT: **0 gm**
CARBOHYDRATE: **5.5 gm**   FIBRE: **0 gm**

280 Ginger Surprise

Ingredients

Sweet lime sherbet	4 glasses
Orange pieces	4 tbsp
Pineapple pieces	4 tbsp
Ginger	1 small piece

Method

1. Crush the ginger and put it in $1/4$ cup of water for sometime. Then sieve it.
2. Add the sieved liquid to the lime sherbet.
3. In a glass add orange and pineapple pieces and top with lime sherbet.
4. Serve garnished with mint leaves.

Ginger juice's perennial use before meals prevents malignancy of tongue and throat. It stimulates the secretion of digestive juices. Also helps digestion and prevents gas troubles. It dislodges cough and exterminates catarrh and cold.

Nutritive Information

CALORIES: **118.01 Cal**   PROTEIN: **10.36 gm**   FAT: **2.3 gm**
CARBOHYDRATE: **52.10 gm**   FIBRE: **1.2 gm**

281 Cool Mint Magic

Ingredients

Mint leaves	1 small bunch
Lemon juice	2
Honey	2 tbsp
Soda	2 bottles
Ice cubes	a few
Water	½ glass
Black salt	1 tsp

Method

1. Blend mint leaves, lemon juice, water, ice cubes, honey and salt in a blender.
2. Strain to extract the juice.
3. Finally, before serving, add chilled soda.

Honey is full of powerful anti bacterial properties. Ulcers heal rapidly when honey is applied to them. Honey is a mild laxative. It cures constipation and gives relief in cold, cough and sore throat. It is helpful in disturbed urination.

Nutritive Information

CALORIES: **102.36 Cal**   PROTEIN: **5.9 gm**   FAT: **1.2 gm**
CARBOHYDRATE: **62.36 gm**   FIBRE: **0 gm**

282 Cucumber Mint Soup

Ingredients

Cucumber	1 (small cubes)
Curd (skimmed milk)	250 gms
Mint leaves	50 gms
Salt	to taste
Chilled water	1 tall glass

Method

1. Put cucumber cubes and mint leaves with little water in the blender. Blend it for a minute.
2. Add 1 cup of curd and blend it again. Add 1 glass of chilled water and salt as per taste. People suffering from poor digestion can strain and sip it and instantly feel the cooling effect in the stomach. Alternatively you can drink it without straining.

A heat relieving, summer cold soup. Both cucumber and mint leaves add colour and flavour to the beverage whereas the curd invites sweetness, proteins and calories.

Nutritive Information

CALORIES: **112.18 Cal**   PROTEIN: **1.26 gm**   FAT: **1.36 gm**
CARBOHYDRATE: **36.20 gm**   FIBRE: **1.59 gm**

283 Tulsi Pudina Drink

Ingredients

Mint leaves (pudina)	$^1/_2$ bunch
Fresh basil leaves (tulsi)	10 to 15
Honey	$^1/_2$ tsp
Water	2 glasses

Method

1. Wash the greens and boil together in water for 5 minutes.
2. Cool for 5 minutes.
3. Add honey and mix well.
4. Drink it while it is warm.
5. Best results if you drink it every day early in the morning.
6. It is very good for gastric problems.

Basil leaves are considered to be very good for people having blood pressure problem and mint is good for the stomach disorders.

Nutritive Information

CALORIES: **9.57 Cal**   PROTEIN: **0 gm**   FAT: **0 gm**
CARBOHYDRATE: **2.385 gm**   FIBRE: **0 gm**

284 Saunf Ka Sherbet

Ingredients

Cold water	2 glasses
Fennel (saunf)	2 tbsp (powdered)
Sugar	2 tsp

Method

1. Mix water, powdered fennel and sugar well and serve with ice cubes.

Fennel is a good blood cleanser and if possible should always be taken after meals.

Nutritive Information

CALORIES: **39.8 Cal** PROTEIN: **0 gm** FAT: **0 gm**
CARBOHYDRATE: **9.94 gm** FIBRE: **0 gm**

285 Blue Nile

Ingredients

Lime cordial	1 tbsp
Lemon juice	$1/4$ tbsp
Sugar syrup	2 tbsp
Soda	$1/2$ bottle
Ice	crushed
Blue colour	2 drops

Method

1. Mix all the above and while serving add soda.

Sweet lemon: *The juice of sweet lemon increases vitality and resistance against diseases. Chewing sweet lemon cleanses and strengthens the teeth. Its fibrous elements are useful in removing constipation.*

Nutritive Information

CALORIES: **68.20 Cal**   PROTEIN: **3.20 gm**   FAT: **0.45 gm**
CARBOHYDRATE: **20.19 gm**   FIBRE: **0 gm**

286 Dudhi Ka Ras (Bottle gourd juice)

Ingredients

Bottle gourd (dudhi)	1
Basil leaves	8-9
Mint leaves	5-6
Salt	to taste
Black pepper	$1/2$ tsp

Method

1. Peel and cut bottle gourd in small cubes.
2. Add all the other ingredients to it.
3. Take out the juice in a juicer.
4. Get a clear juice from a muslin cloth.

The fresh juice of the white gourd is as nourishing as mother's milk. A tuberculosis patient if given the juice of white gourd, experiences relief in coughing. It provides good nourishment to a pregnant woman.

Nutritive Information

CALORIES: **56.36 Cal** PROTEIN: **0.456 gm** FAT: **0.36 gm**
CARBOHYDRATE: **12.92 gm** FIBRE: **0 gm**

287 Ginger-Apple Fruit Punch

Ingredients

Ginger	50 gms
Orange juice	2 cups
Apple juice	2 cups
Pineapple juice	1 cup
Strawberry pulp (optional)	1/4 cup
Salt	a pinch
Water	1/2 bottle

Method

1. Grind ginger.
2. Boil water, and when it starts bubbling add ginger to it.
3. Add sugar and boil on high flame for 2 minutes and switch off.
4. Strain through a filter.
5. Combine ginger water with all the juices.
6. Refrigerate this concentrate and blend it with ice cubes or soda. Add salt to taste.

Pineapple contains sufficient chlorine which stimulates the activity of the kidneys and helps to remove waste products from the body.

Nutritive Information

CALORIES: **152.19 Cal** PROTEIN: **12.1 gm** FAT: **1.36 gm**
CARBOHYDRATE: **43.62 gm** FIBRE: **0 gm**

288 Angoor Ka Sherbet

Ingredients

Seedless grapes (angoor)	225 gms
Castor sugar	3 tbsp
Pepper	$1/_2$ tsp
Roasted cumin powder	1 tsp
Salt	$1/_2$ tsp
Lemon juice	2 tsp
Chilled water	3 cups

Method

1. Wash grapes and crush them thoroughly. Pour in water. Mix well. Strain through a sieve.
2. Add all the seasonings. Mix well. Chill. Serve garnished with mint leaves.

Grapes have justifiably been called the 'queen of fruits'. They contain proteins, carbohydrates, vitamins A and B and minerals in varying amounts. Due to the presence of acid, grapes are laxative and the liver and kidneys are stimulated, assisting in the elimination of toxins.

Nutritive Information

CALORIES: **136.20 Cal**   PROTEIN: **5.36 gm**   FAT: **1.92 gm**
CARBOHYDRATE: **24.86 gm**   FIBRE: **0 gm**

289 Ash Gourd Chiller

Ingredients

Ash gourd	1/2 kg
Salt / pepper	to taste
Jaggery (for sweetness)	to taste
Roasted cumin powder	to taste
Black salt	a pinch
Dash of lime juice	to taste
Few mint leaves	for decoration

Method

1. Peel and cut ash gourd into small pieces.
2. Put into a mixer and with the help of minimum water make into a paste, adding jaggery according to taste.
3. Remove from mixer and strain with the help of a juice strainer.
4. Add salt, black salt, cumin powder and chill in the fridge for approx. 1/2 an hour.
5. Serve in a tall glass with a dash of lime. Add few mint leaves for decoration.

Jaggery is rich in iron. It is made from either sugarcane or dates.

Nutritive Information

CALORIES: **113.32 Cal** PROTEIN: **6.9 gm** FAT: **0.92 gm**
CARBOHYDRATE: **36.20 gm** FIBRE: **0 gm**

290 Real Cooler

Ingredients

Lime juice	2 tbsp
Pineapple juice	2 tbsp
Orange juice	2 tbsp
Honey	1 tbsp
Mint juice	1 tbsp
Salt	a pinch
Soda	a bottle
Lots of ice	as required

Method

1. Combine all the ingredients except ice and soda in a bowl.
2. Pour equally into 2 tall glasses.
3. Put lots of ice and fill up with soda.
4. Decorate with mint leaves and lime wedges.

Honey imparts a rich taste to this drink as well as provides nutritional benefit.

Nutritive Information

CALORIES: **352 Cal**   PROTEIN: **2.85 gm**   FAT: **0.95 gm**
CARBOHYDRATE: **82.95 gm**   FIBRE: **0 gm**

291 Citri Carrotti

Ingredients

Carrot juice	1 cup
Sugar syrup	4 tbsp
Lemon juice	2 tbsp
Orange juice	$1/4$ cup
Lemon rind	for garnish

Method

1. Mix all the ingredients.
2. Pour in a tall glass and garnish with lemon rind.

This is another drink that is colourful as well as refreshing.

Nutritive Information

CALORIES: **136.20 Cal** PROTEIN: **10.39 gm** FAT: **1.01 gm**
CARBOHYDRATE: **40.26 gm** FIBRE: **0 gm**

292 Peppy Papaya

Ingredients

Fresh ripe papaya	250 gms (chopped)
Sugar	1 tbsp
Ice cubes crushed	5
Water	1 cup

Method

1. Chill the papaya and water.
2. Just before serving, blend well in a mixie.
3. Pour in chilled glasses and serve immediately.

Ripe papaya contains an enzyme papain that helps to soften and to digest food easily.

Nutritive Information

CALORIES: **91.7 Cal**   PROTEIN: **0.6 gm**   FAT: **0.1 gm**
CARBOHYDRATE: **12.11 gm**   FIBRE: **0.8 gm**

293 Soda-Orange Punch Cocktail

Ingredients

Orange juice	3-4
Lemon juice	2
Pineapple pieces	4
Castor sugar	2-3 tbsp
Sugar syrup or any sweet fruit	2-3 tbsp
Ice cubes	4-5
Soda water	300 ml
Orange or lemon rind	as required
Mint leaves	to garnish

Method

1. Put all the ingredients in the mixer/mixie except the soda water and blend it into a purèe.
2. Strain the blended fruit purèe.
3. Pour the soda water in a jug and mix it with fruit purèe. This cocktail is vitamin C dense and a good appetizer as it contains various juices of citrus fruits.

Serve cold in a glass garnished with orange or lemon rind and mint leaves.

Nutritive Information

CALORIES: **300.1 Cal**   PROTEIN: **1.8 gm**   FAT: **1.2 gm**
CARBOHYDRATE: **70.43 gm**   FIBRE: **0 gm**

294 Jholia

Ingredients

Mangoes (keri)	500 gms
Sugar	200 gms
Salt	1 tsp
Black salt	1/2 tsp
Coriander leaves	500 gms
Mint leaves	500 gms
Green chillis	4-5
Jholia masala	2 tsp
Water	2 glasses

Method

1. Boil mango in a pressure cooker with a little water.
2. When it is cooked take out from the cooker and make juice.
3. Add water and sugar and mix well.
4. Make paste of green chillis, coriander and mint leaves.
5. Mix salt, black salt, jholia masala and paste of green chilli etc.
6. Mix all the ingredients well.
7. Strain through a muslin cloth.
8. Chill and serve.

This drink is the most refreshing drink specially in summer.

Nutritive Information

CALORIES: **37.9 Cal**   PROTEIN: **1.55 gm**   FAT: **0.3 gm**
CARBOHYDRATE: **82.6 gm**   FIBRE: **0.22 gm**

295 Mango Curd

Ingredients

Mangoes (large, ripe)	5
Lime juice	2 tsp
Sugar	500 gms
Curd (skimmed milk)	250 gms

Method

1. Peel the mangoes and slice them in about $1/2$ cm slices.
2. Put them in a shallow dish and sprinkle lime juice. Pour 2 cups of sugar and curd over the mangoes. Cover, and refrigerate for 2 to 3 hours.
3. Remove from the refrigerator 1 hour before serving and taste for lime juice.
4. There should be a hint of lime flavor; add more juice if necessary.

Nutritive Information

CALORIES: **249 Cal** PROTEIN: **4.1 gm** FAT: **0.8 gm**
CARBOHYDRATE: **133.91 gm** FIBRE: **1.4 gm**

296 Poached Pears

Ingredients

Sweet white wine	1 cup
Apple juice concentrate	$1/4$ cup
Vanilla extract	1 tsp
Pears	2 (peeled and cored)
Water	$3/4$ cup

Method

1. Heat wine, water, apple juice concentrate and vanilla to near boiling point. Lower the flame before adding the pears.
2. Cover and simmer for 5 to 7 minutes in the hot liquid or until the pears are soft. Take care not to overcook the pears, or they well turn mushy and fall apart. Cool and serve.

The key to this simple, elegant dessert is cooking the pears until they have softened but are still firm.

Nutritive Information

CALORIES: **112 Cal**   PROTEIN: **1.25 gm**   FAT: **0.4 gm**
CARBOHYDRATE: **107.35 gm**   FIBRE: **2.25 gm**

297 Lemon Semolina Pudding

Ingredients

Water	2 1/4 cups
Semolina	100 gms
Fresh lemon juice	1/4 cup
Honey	2 tsp
Sugar	2 tsp
Apple juice concentrate	3 tsp
Fresh mint leaves	for garnish

Method

1. Bring the water to a boil and gradually whisk in the semolina, stirring to prevent lumps from forming.
2. Let cook for about 2 minutes. Turn off the heat. Whisk in the lemon juice, honey, sugar, apple juice concentrate.
3. Cool. Serve garnished with mint leaves.

Even though it uses semolina, this dessert is very light and has the delightful tartness of lemon.

Nutritive Information

CALORIES: **71 Cal**   PROTEIN: **5.2 gm**   FAT: **0.3 gm**
CARBOHYDRATE: **47.34 gm**   FIBRE: **0.1 gm**

298 Rice Pudding

Ingredients

Short-grain white rice	500 gms
Milk (skimmed milk)	750 gms
Cinnamon sticks	2
Vanilla extract	1/2 tsp
Apple juice concentrate	1/4 cup
Honey	2 tbsp
Pineapple	8 -10 (diced and drained)
Raisins	100 gms
Cinnamon powder	for garnish

Method

1. Put rice into a large pan and add the skimmed milk. Cover and bring to a boil.
2. Reduce the heat and simmer for 20 to 25 minutes. Stir frequently throughout the cooking until the rice grains plump up.
3. Then add the cinnamon sticks, vanilla, and apple juice concentrate or honey, if using. Continue stirring to prevent the rice from sticking and burning.
4. When the mixture is thick, stir in the sugar substitute, if using, the pineapple and raisins.
5. Remove the cinnamon sticks and pour the rice pudding into a serving dish. Dust with cinnamon.

Rice pudding is commonly known as kheer and it is a nutritious wholesome recipe.

Nutritive Information

CALORIES: **223 Cal**   PROTEIN: **14.33 gm**   FAT: **0.5 gm**
CARBOHYDRATE: **99.95 gm**   FIBRE: **0.2 gm**

299 Peach Bread Pudding

Ingredients

Peaches (medium)	6
Skimmed milk	500 gms
Salt	1/2 tsp
Loaf of stale sour dough bread	500 gms
Freshly grated nutmeg	1/4 tsp
Apple juice concentrate	1/2 cup
Lemon juice	1/2 tbsp
Egg whites	6 (beaten)

Method

1. Blanch, peel, pit, and then dice the peaches. Set aside. In a large bowl mix together the skimmed milk and salt.
2. Tear the bread into 1 cm cubes. Mash the bread into the milk and let it soak for 15 minutes.
3. In another bowl combine the Amaretto, nutmeg, apple juice concentrate, lemon juice, and peaches.
4. Add the beaten egg whites. Mix with the bread mixture and toss gently. Pour into a non-stick 20-23 cm square pan.
5. Bake in a pre-heated oven at 177°C. for 45 minutes, or until set and browned on top. Serve warm.

The peaches and Amaretto give a decidedly non-traditional twist to this wonderfully old-fashioned dessert.

Nutritive Information

CALORIES: **122 Cal**   PROTEIN: **8.8 gm**   FAT: **1.3 gm**
CARBOHYDRATE: **114.1 gm**   FIBRE: **3.6 gm**

300 Moong Missal

Ingredients

Bean sprouts (moong)	250 gms
Fresh curd	250 gms
Sweet and sour chutney	4 tsps
Tomatoes	200 gms (chopped)
Onions	100 gms (chopped)
Roasted cumin seed powder	a pinch
Salt	to taste
Chilli powder	to taste

Method

1. Take a pan, add the bean sprouts, half cup of water and salt. Cover and cook on a low flame until it is soft.
2. Beat the curd with a pinch of salt.
3. Spread the hot bean sprout on a serving plate. Top with the beaten curd, chutney, tomatoes, onions, cumin seed and chilli powders and salt.

This is a healthy and nutritious chaat and can be consumed as much as desired.

Nutritive Information

CALORIES: **87 Cal**   PROTEIN: **5 gms**   FAT: **2.5 gm**
CARBOHYDRATE: **12.5 gms**   FIBRE: **4.8 gm**

SECTION V

ADDRESSES OF SAAOL CENTERS

HEAD OFFICE
Ms. Meera
SAAOL Heart Center
14/84-85, Vikram Vihar, Lajpat Nagar-IV, New Delhi-110024
Tel: 26235168, 26283098, 26211908 • Fax: 26212016
e-mail : info@saaol.com

MUMBAI OFFICE
Mr. Deepak Dalal
B-301, Gold Mist, Thakur Complex,
Kandivili (E), Mumbai-400101
Ph: 56995378, 28543088 • Fax : 28544217

CHENNAI OFFICE
Kamal Chhajer
C/o Jeans Park India Pvt. Ltd.
566, Anna Salai, Chennai-600018
Ph: 24337236, 55360450

CULCUTTA OFFICE
Mr. Praveen
65/4A, Flat No.: 1A,
Sarat Bose Road, Kolkata-25
Ph: 30930329, 24545981 • Mob .: 9330870713.

BANGALORE OFFICE
Mr. S.S. Prasad/Ramani
3/1, 4th Temple Street 13th Cross
Malleswaram, Bangalore-560003
Ph: 23310856, 23344626 • Mobile : 9343736554
E-mail: ssprasaa@yahoo.com

HYDERABAD OFFICE
S.L. Chhajer
Sarda Adeifice, Flat No. 203,
H.No. 3-5-590, Himayat Nagar
Hyderabad-500029 Ph: 23224084

HOW TO REGISTER FOR SAAOL HEART PROGRAM

The **Residential SAAOL Heart Program**-3 and a half days training course costs Rs. 18,000/- (Eighteen thousand) in Delhi and Rs.20,000/- (Twenty thousand only) in Mumbai. This include fees for training, stay food, SAAOL kit and the course materials. As the participation of spouse or one close relative is compulsory-this fees also includes the stay, food training of the accompanying person. The whole amount is payable in advance.

In case the Patient is allowed to join alone the total cost would be Rs. 4,000/- less (i.e. 14,000/- in Delhi & 16,000/- in Mumbai).

For **Non Residential three day course** the cost will be Rs.12,000/- (Twenty thousand). This include patient and spouse. These courses are available in Culcutta, Bangalore and Chennai and the future destinations. In Mumbai these non-residential course will cost Rs. 14,000/- (Fourteen thousand only).

REGISTRATION PROCEDURE

For registration for a course the initial booking amount is Rs. 5,000/- (for Residential) and Rs.3,000/- (for Non Residential) course. This money is to be paid either in cash or Demand Draft (payable to **SAAOL Heart Pvt. Ltd.,** New Delhi) and is **Non refundable and non transferable.**

SAAOL HEART CLUB

SAAOL runs follow-up meetings, short courses, medical check ups and follow-ups in the form of Heart Club. The Delhi **SAAOL Heart Club** meets once every month and new topics are discussed everytime during these meeting. In other cities SAAOL arranges together from time to time.

SAAOL HEART HEALING CORRESPONDENCE COURSE

For those heart patients who not come to Delhi or other major cities to join SAAOL Heart Program we are starting a correspondence course-as a soft substitute of Heart Reversal Program. This correspondence program will need the help of local general physician, who has to fill up the forms, informing us about your exact state of health and the on-going medications. You also need to fill up an extensive form about your disease, food, past habits, weight etc. alongwith your blood reports. SAAOL will give you through correspondence appropriate guidance about the food habits, Yoga, meditation, Education and specific advice, after going through your physicians form and your details. The course will be approximately three months duration with a lifetime follow-up. A personal meeting can also be organized with our SAAOL doctors.

The course is expected ton be launched in January, 2000 and the cost of the treatment is going to be about Rs. 3500/- (for three months) and a maintenance or follow-up cost of Rs. 100/- per month. You can write to the course coordination in our Delhi office for more details and prospectus.

SAAOL Health Research Foundation (SHARF) runs a unique magazine for heart disease and prevention called "Heart Talk" from 16th October 1998 released by Shri. L.K. Advani Honorable Union Home Minister at FICCI Auditorium, New Delhi. This magazine will give you all the possible news and views on heart disease, risk factors, latest research results and all the news about SAAOL Heart Program. The magazine will be of eight pages to begin. For a person who is not a doctor, this magazine is one of the best way to keep yourself informed. It is going to be a monthly magazine. Those who re interested to subscribe for the magazine please fill up the form and send your subscription to us by Cheque/Cash/DD. This subscription would also give you a free membership of **Heart Care Club of India,** run by SHARF.

Those who re interested to subscribe for the magazine please fill up the form and send your subscription to us by Cheque/Cash/DD. This subscription would also give you a free membership of **Heart Care Club of India,** run by **SHARF.**

FOR HEART CLUB MEMBERSHIP APPLICATION

ENROLLMENT FEES : RS. 100/-

SUBSCRIPTION FOR HEART TALK : Rs.240/- (for 1 year)

Note: if you are a SAAOL participant, please mention your place and date of joining.

MEMBERSHIP FORM

I am applying for the membership of the **Heart Care Club of India (HCCI)***. On being accepted as a member, I shall abide by all the aims and objectives of the club and shall; endeavour to make them a success with all my will and capacity.

Personal Information   A Draft/Cash for Rupees

*..............................No.......................

Surname & First Name

Dated................Drawn on......................In favour

Mr./Mrs.. of SAAOL Health And Research Foundation payable in Home Address...

....Delhi is enclosed, towards Enrollment fees &/or Subscription for one Year..

.... (Add Rs. 20/- for the outstation cheque).

Phone (O).........................Phone (R)...................... **To Mail to**

Occupation...

Date............................

Signature of the Applicant

*To obtain this magazine being launched in October, 1998 you have to

1. Enroll as a member of HCCI by filling up the above form and send to our address below. Those who already have.

2. Send a subscription of Rs.240/-.

Product Stock List

S. No.		BOOKS
1.	201 Diet Tips (English)	150
2.	201 Diet Tips (Hindi)	95
3.	A complete guide management stress (Hindi)	95
4.	A complete guide management Stress (English)	195
5.	201 Tips for Diabetes Patient (Hindi)	95
6.	201 Tips for Diabetes Patient (English)	150
7.	Food for Reversing Heart Disease (FFRHD) (English)	450
8.	Heart Talk (English)	30
9.	Heart Talk (Hindi)	30
10.	Reversing Heart Disease (RHD) (English)	195
11.	Hriday Rog Se Mukti (HRSM) (Hindi)	150
12.	Understanding Heart Disease (UHD) (English)	100
13.	Understanding Heart Disease (UHD) (Hindi)	100
14.	Zero Oil Cook Book (ZOCB) (English)	150
15.	Zero Oil Cook Book (ZOCB) (Hindi)	95
16.	Zero Oil Snacks Book (ZOSB) (English)	150
17.	Zero Oil Snacks Book (ZOSB) (Hindi)	95
18.	Zero Oil South Indian Cook Book (English)	150
19.	Zero Oil South Indian Cook Book (Hindi)	95
20.	Zero Oil Sweet Book (English)	150
21.	Zero Oil Sweet Book (Hindi)	95
22.	Zero Oil Thali (English)	150
23.	Zero Oil Thali (Hindi)	95
24.	Saaol Heart Program Manual (English)	350
25.	Saaol Heart Program Manual (Hindi)	350
26.	201 Tips for loosing weight (English)	150

27.	201 Tips for Loosing weight (Hindi)	95
28.	Health in Your Hand: (Single Copy @ 50) (A set of 12 books)	600

Cassette & VCDs

S. No.		Cassette & VCDs
1.	Meditation Cassette (English)	75
2.	Meditation Cassette (Hindi)	75
3.	RHD in 5 easy Steps (Lecture) 2 CDs (English)	199
4.	RHD in 5 easy Steps (Lecture) 2 CDs (Hindi)	199
5.	Yoga for Heart Patient (English)	125
6.	Zero Oil Cooking (English)	125
7.	Diet for Your Heart (English)	125
8.	Diet for Your Heart (English)	125
9.	Stress Management & Your Heart (English)	125
10.	Stress Management & Your Heart (Hindi)	125
11.	Saaol Tea	100
12.	C.D. Meditation (English)	125
13.	C.D. Meditation (Hindi)	125
14.	C.D. Diabetes (English)	125
15.	C.D. Diabetes (Hindi)	125
16.	C.D. Obesity (English)	125
17.	C.D. Obesity (Hindi)	125
18.	Notepads	
19.	Folders	

•••

FULL CIRCLE

FULL CIRCLE publishes books on inspirational subjects, religion, philosophy, and natural health. The objective is to help make an attitudinal shift towards a more peaceful, loving, non-combative, non-threatening, compassionate and healing world.

FULL CIRCLE continues its commitment towards creating a peaceful and harmonious world and towards rekindling the joyous, divine nature of the human spirit.

Our fine books are available at all leading bookstores across the country.

FULL CIRCLE PUBLISHING

Editorial Office

J-40, Jorbagh Lane, New Delhi-110003
Tel: 24620063, 24641011 • Fax: 24645795
E-mail: fullcircle@vsnl.com
website: www.atfullcircle.com

Bookstores

5B, Khan Market, New Delhi-110003
Tel: 24655641/2/3

N-8, Greater Kailash Part I Market, New Delhi-110048
Tel: 29245641/3/4

Join the WORLD WISDOM BOOK CLUB

Get the best of world literature in the comfort of your home at fabulous discounts!

Benefits of the Book Club

Wherever in the world you are, you can receive the best of books at your doorstep.

- Receive FABULOUS DISCOUNTS by mail or at the **FULL CIRCLE** Bookstore in Delhi.
- Receive Exclusive Invitations to attend events being organized by **FULL CIRCLE**.
- Receive a FREE copy of the club newsletter — The World Wisdom Review — every month.
- Get UP TO 25% OFF.

Join Now!

It's simple. Just fill in the coupon overleaf and mail it to us at the address below:

FULL CIRCLE
J-40, Jorbagh Lane, New Delhi 110003
Tel: 24620063, 24641011 • Fax: 24645795 • www.atfullcircle.com

Yes, I would like to be a member of the
World Wisdom Book Club

Name ☐ Mr ☐ Mrs ☐ Ms _____

_____

Mailing Address _____

_____

_____

_____

City _____ Pin _____

Phone _____ Fax _____

E-mail _____

Profession _____ D.O.B. _____

Areas of Interest _____

_____

Mail this form to:
The World Wisdom Book Club
J-40, Jorbagh Lane, New Delhi-110003
Tel: 24620063, 24641011 •Fax: 24645795 •E-mail: fullcircle@vsnl.com

MEDITATIONS

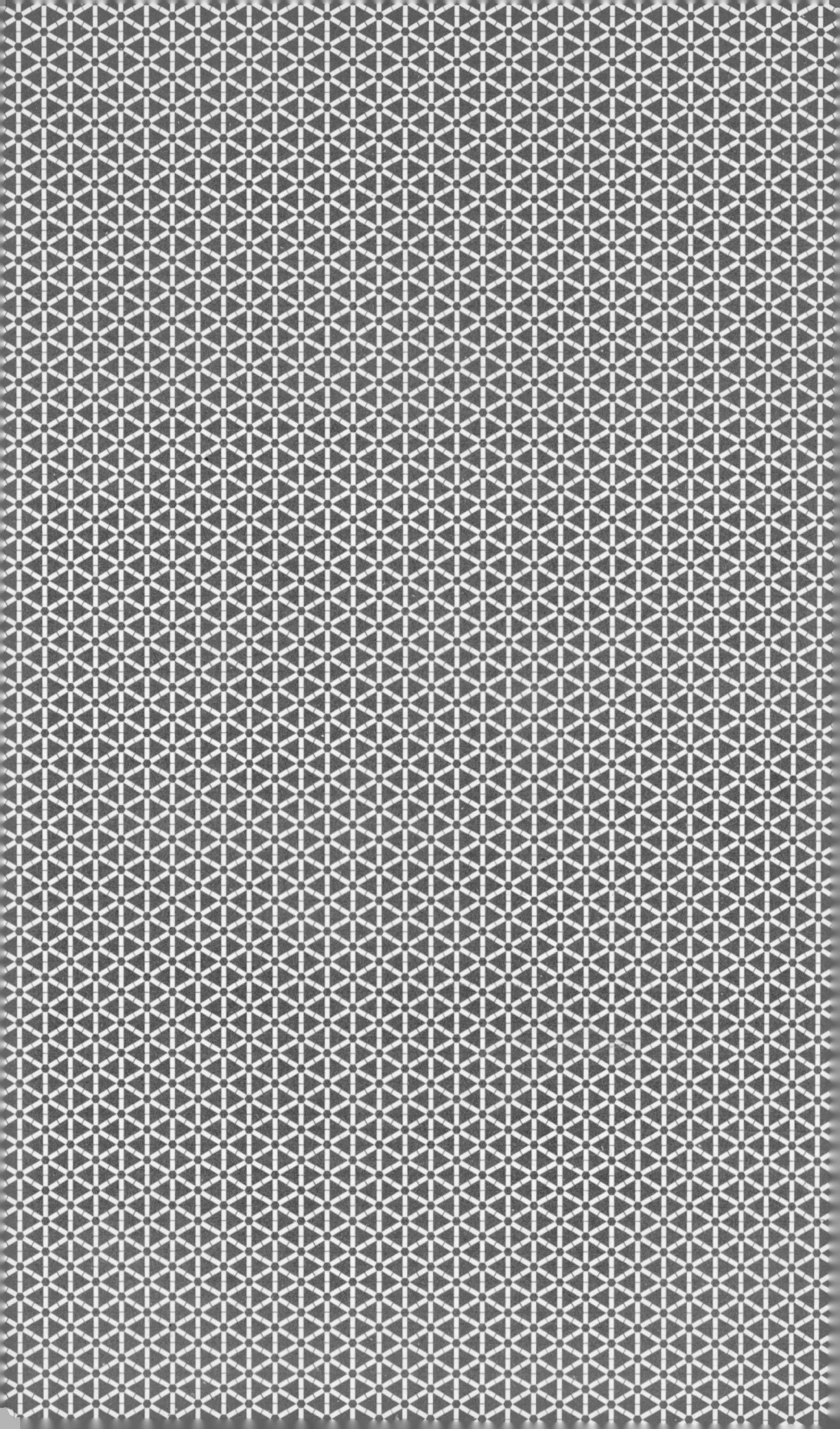